Unearth the Wit, Wisdo
and Ways of our Ancest

In our era, much insightful, earth-centered knowledge-often disguised as old wives' tales or village customs-has been left by the wayside. Yet there is something powerful beneath folkways which science is only now beginning to understand. Take, for example, the country quote which says that when the swallows fly low, rain is soon to follow. Meteorologists now know that various insects move to lower levels of the atmosphere when rain comes because of barometric changes-thus the swallows move to follow their lunch! With Folkways, you win be able to gather up this lost wisdom, blend it with a modem sensibility and create a new system of myths to enrich your magic.

Within each subject category of this book are practical suggestions for applying these folkways in your magical workings. When you're looking for an idea for creating an effective spell, simply page to the corresponding subject and browse the relevant entries-you will find hundreds of ideas for personalizing and enriching your practice.

◆ ◆ ◆

"Why wasn't this book written twenty years ago?! All that time I could have spent as I've spent the last several weeks, sampling its pages for inspiration, knowledge and pure enjoyment. Telesco has compiled an exhaustive and charming compendium of folk wisdom that is like a table full of all the ingredients and tools you need to make a fabulous meal. I encourage all readers to use this book for practical advice and background for their magickal practice, but I invite them to let it work its magick on them, teasing each one's imaginative flame into a festive bonfire!"

— Nan Hawthorne
author, *Loving the Goddess Within*

About the Author

Patricia Telesco is an ordained minister and a professional member of the Wiccan-Pagan Press Alliance. Her hobbies include antique restoration, folk music, historical costume design, herbalism, and the Society for Creative Anachronism (a historical recreation group). Many of these activities have extended themselves into a small, eco-friendly business, called Hourglass Creations. Her articles and poems have appeared in journal such as *Circle*, *Silver Chalice*, and Llewellyn's *New World's of Mind and Spirit* (formerly *New Times*), and she is also the author of a children's book *Brother Wind, Sister Rain* (Altar Publications), has two short stories in the fictional collection *Folklore, Fable and Fantasy* (Galde press),She welcomes the opportunity to do workshops and lectures. Patricia lives in Buffalo, New York with her husband, son, dog, and five cats.

To Write the Author

If you wish to contact the author or would like more information about this book, please write to the author in care of Llewellyn Worldwide, and we will forward your request. Both the author and publisher appreciate hearing from you and learning of your enjoyment of this book and how it has helped you. Llewellyn Worldwide cannot guarantee that every letter written to the author can be answered, but all will be forwarded. Please write to:

Patricia Telesco
c/o Llewellyn Worldwide
P.O. Box 64383-787, St. Paul, MN 55164-0383, U.S.A.
Please enclose a self-addressed, stamped envelope for reply or $1.00 to cover costs.
If outside U.S.A., enclose international postal reply coupon.

Free Catalog from Llewellyn

For more than 90 years Llewellyn has brought its readers knowledge in he fields of metaphysics and human potential. Learn about the newest books in spiritual guidance, natural healing astrology, occult philosophy and more. Enjoy book reviews, new age articles, a calendar of events, plus current advertised products and services. To get get your free copy of Llewellyn's *New Worlds of Mind and Spirit,* send your name and address to:

Llewellyn's *New Worlds of Mind and Spirit*
P.O. Box 64383-787, St. Paul, MN 55164-0383, U.S.A.

Llewellyn's World Religion and Magic Series

FOLKWAYS

Reclaiming the Magic and Wisdom

Patricia Telesco

1995
Llewellyn Publications
St. Paul, Minnesota 55164-0383

FIRST EDITION
First Printing, 1995

Cover design by Llewellyn Art Department
Cover photograph by Russell Lane

Library of Congress Cataloging-in-Publication Data
    Telesco, Patricia, 1960-
        Folkways: reclaiming the magic & wisdom / by Paricia Telesco.
           p. cm.-- (Llewellyn's world religion & magic series)
        Includes bibliographical references (p.) and index.
        ISBN 0-87542-787-1
        1. Magic 2. Folklore. I. Title. II. Series
    GN475.3.T45 199   94-37093
    133.4'3--dc20   CIP

Llewellyn Publications
A Division of Llewellyn Worldwide, Ltd.
P.O. Box 64383 St. Paul, MN 55164-0383

Llewellyn's World Religion and Magic Series

At the core of every religion, at the foundation of every culture, there is MAGIC.

Magic sees the worlds as alive, as the home which humanity shares with beings and powers both visible and invisible with whom and which we can interface to either our advantage or disadvantage—depending upon our awareness and intention.

Religious worship and communion is one kind of magic, and just as there are many religions in the world, so are there many magical systems.

Religion, and magic, are ways of seeing and relating to the creative powers, the living energies, the all-pervading spirit, the underlying intelligence that is the universe within which we and all else exist.

Neither religion nor magic conflict with science. All share the same goals and the same limitations: always seeking truth, forever haunted by human limitations in perceiving that truth. Magic is "technology" based upon experience and extrasensory insight, providing it practitioners with methods of greater influence and control over the world of the invisible before it impinges on the world of the visible.

The study of magic not only enhances your understanding of the world in which you live, and hence your ability to live better, but brings you into touch with the inner essence of your long evolutionary heritage and most particularly—as in the case of the magical system identified most closely with your genetic inheritance—with the archetypal images and forces most alive in your whole consciousness.

Also by Patricia Telesco

A Victorian Grimoire
The Urban Pagan
The Kitchen Witch's Cookbook
A Witch's Brew
Victorian Flower Oracle

Dedication

This book is dedicated to the Bards of all ages who cherished oral tradition and guarded the Sacred stories, the Gods of old and the folk-ways they inspired and the sincere prayer that this legacy will continue to be honored by future generations.

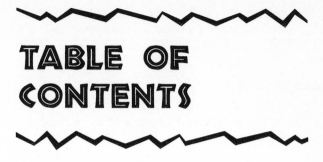

TABLE OF CONTENTS

Acknowledgements

I sit at my typewriter and think, who have I forgotten to thank? I haven't applauded my computer, fondly named Sarek II, my dining room table for the abuse it's seen or the cats for keeping my lap warm!

When I first started writing I never really expected to get this far. Now, three books later, I look at my world and how it has changed and know what a tremendous growing experience this has been for me, but it hasn't been without a lot of help and encouragement.

First, for my children Karl and Samantha who have tolerated countless hours of me pouring over books while they colored patiently. While I am not always the perfect "mommy," I love you more than the world. Thank you for all those hugs which make my day a little brighter.

To Leonard Nimoy, whose beautiful poetry so deeply moved me when I was younger that I was no longer afraid to dip down into my heart and find the words to fill a page.

To Kim and Dave for their friendship and constant caring across the miles. I miss you guys.

To friends for acting as relief babysitters so I could periodically catch a nap, clean the house, or run an errand.

And to anyone else who I have forgotten, who has kindly lent a book for research, found a neat quote, or just called to say hello when I needed it most, thank you for caring.

INTRODUCTION

Each day foretells the next, if one could but read the signs.
♦ John Burroughs ♦

SUPERSTITION. THIS is one of the great strands that connects all humanity: the belief that the law of cause and effect goes slightly beyond the construct of science. Webster's *New World Dictionary* defines superstition as coming from a French term meaning "to stand over," with implications of superseding reason. It also states that such beliefs derive from reliance on chance and fear of the unknown. They shape our notions about our world—our folklore.

Superstition and folkways continue to influence our lives, more from habit than actual belief in them. In our scientifically centered society, we must ask why? Why do these practices still influence us so strongly?

Part of this answer must be left to conjecture, because the roots of folkways are ancient. We can hypothesize that something happened at one time to bring a particular occurrence to public attention. If it happened more than once, our ancestors considered it an important sign. So, when a red sun appeared in the morning several times before a storm, that emblem became equated with a series of events. This information was then handed down through oral tradition.

With many folk practices, people later forgot the reason for the con-
vention, but its enactment continued out of habit. As a case in point, it
is still common to say, "God bless you" when someone sneezes to be
polite. To our ancestors, this phrase carried a completely different
meaning. They believed the spirit could leave the body when one
sneezed. By saying, "God bless you" they invoked Divine favor to keep
the spirit tied to the flesh. When the fear of losing one's soul waned, the
extension of a thoughtful courtesy, that of blessing, remained.

Studying folklore and superstitions helps us understand ourselves.
They offer one piece of the puzzle of understanding our thoughts. Further, tracing lore helps us discern the roots of our Craft. The most predominant exhibition of this is magical herbalism.

The correspondences and associations we use for plants today are, for
the most part, based on herb lore. Garlic protected the bearer from ghosts
and sickness because of its pungent smell. Science now tells us that garlic
is good to safeguard one's health because of its purgative qualities.

We respond to superstition on both a conscious and subconscious
level until certain actions become habitual. Do you walk around ladders,
or periodically toss salt over your shoulder? Most people aren't doing
so for luck or to keep evil spirits away. Yet, somewhere in our behav-
ioral codes we have accepted the merit of these folkways or they
wouldn't be observed!

Consider a belief repeated regularly for a hundred years. If only one
person followed that assumption consistently for their entire life, it
would endow that thought-form with tremendous energy. If hundreds of
individuals held that same belief as true and followed it consistently, the
energy endowed that thought-form would increase exponentially.

Folk magicians tap this well of accumulated energy and direct it
toward positive goals. Since these beliefs and practices already have elements of ritual integrated within them, and are familiar to us, they are a
perfect vehicle to enhance magic. To illustrate, when you find a penny
the phrase, "see a penny, pick it up and all the day you'll have good
luck" comes to mind. You can continue to recite this rhyme as it stands,
thereby encouraging a little serendipity. Additionally, retain the penny
and use it later as an amulet for good fortune.

There is an old rural quote that tells us when the swallows fly low,
rain is soon to follow. Meteorologists know that some insects move to

lower levels of the atmosphere when rain comes because of barometric changes. Thus, the swallows move to follow their lunch!

This folk saying again shows how science and superstition can have common ground, once we gather the facts. Even without this confirmation, superstition was vitally important to our predecessors. It provided a means to take greater control over what they perceived as the whims of fate.

Ultimately, there is a unique, powerful magic in any attempt at mastery and deeper comprehension. It is born from the abiding conviction that we have the responsibility to make our lives, and those of our children, better. *Folkways* examines this element of superstition as well as considering how it can be used for modern practices.

These pages offer you a "slice of life" peek at histories not normally presented. Progress has granted us many wonderful things, but it has not done so without a cost. Much of the insightful, earth-centered knowledge, delicately disguised by tribal custom, village observances and country sayings have been left by the wayside. It is this rich legacy that we should make time to rediscover. Otherwise we will lose thousands of years of oral and written tradition on some library shelf.

The chronicles of humanity are not just those of war and pestilence. They are also filled with the individual struggle to survive, grow and understand this world, filled with love and permeated with the quest to comprehend the divine nature of things. Our ancestors were not so different from us. They searched to discern the grand stage of the universe and the tiniest grain of sand, looking for God and discovering themselves. This undertaking is not just one for our forefathers; it is our search as well.

I encourage you, therefore, to think about old wives' tales, family traditions, customs or charms you have heard or used yourself. As you ponder them, consider how these have changed the way you react or relate to specific situations. Meditate on how you can apply the power of this personal tradition to your Path.

With each section of this book, and the superstitions presented therein, I have given some examples of how to apply folkways practically and effectively in modern rites. In the process, some must change slightly to fit the brave, new world we live in. We cannot use feathers of an endangered bird to cure sickness and maintain reciprocity with nature, nor does King James English come trippingly off the tongue, but we can be creative.

For example, if you believe that the leaves on the trees bend differently when it rains, and happen to be performing an incantation to ease drought, add a leaf to your spell components. Or, if you knock on wood for luck, wood is a fitting ingredient for incense and charms designed to aid fortuity. This redesign and personalization results in some truly remarkable magic being born from your own inventive insight.

Even when superstitions are too unconventional or improper for adaptation, they still hold import. I can't quite see the modern magician tossing dead snakes to foretell the weather, for example (see Chapter 2: Animals and Insects). Nevertheless, this type of action is a direct reflection of a special human exploration that touches the essence of the individual soul. Studying them will teach us about the nature of human thought and our own ways of perceiving the universe. Then, as spiritual seekers, we have the chance to gather up these lost arts and ideals, blend them with modern awareness, and create a new system of myths to enrich our future.

Because of the abundance of the assortment, I will attempt to focus on the most interesting beliefs herein, their origins, and a means to combine them into a harmonic magical practice. Just for fun, and to appease trivia buffs, some of the really unusual ones will be explored as well. Part of the enjoyment of superstition and folklore comes from simply savoring its amazing variety and charm.

This collection represents only a small portion of available folk knowledge, and the examples I share are illustrations only. They furnish a spark for your imagination so you can begin producing folk magic appropriate to your Path and learn a little history in the process.

In other words, nothing in this book is carved in stone, other than the wit and wisdom our ancestors have left us to ponder.

USING THIS BOOK

*Thoughts give birth to a creative force... thoughts
create a new heaven, a new firmament, a new source
of energy from which new arts flow.*
♦ Zolar ♦

WILLIAM JOHN Thoms examined the definitions of folkways while writing for *California Folklore Quarterly* during the 1940s. He and other folklorists determined that folklore is a framework of ideas about the supernatural, wisdom, beauty, and ethics. This framework springs from an oral tradition developed among a group of people sharing common factors. Over time, repeated expression through local myth, superstition, and ritual sustains some of these ideas.

As folk magicians, we can gather this preserved knowledge and use it as a substructure for our work. Since many of our ancestors' adages are familiar to us, we react to them more positively than to more obscure stimuli. Additionally, some of our superstitions become ingrained behavior. Add a little creativity, and habits became helpful to metaphysical efforts.

Let's use tossing spilled salt as an illustration. The old superstition says to toss a pinch of the salt that was spilled over the left should to ward off bad luck and scare away the devil. It is highly unlikely that someone today would repeat this action to scare away the devil. Yet we follow the ritual precisely because something within us believes in the gesture's importance. Extending this idea into a magical setting, salt can be tossed around the perimeter of a circle for protection, sprinkled over items to keep them clean and safe, and added to charms to guard against negativity.

In the above example, we have taken the positive emotional response a superstition brings and allowed it to empower our magic through symbolic application.

Folkways is a resource designed to aid every aspect of your magic. It is filled with time honored symbols, sayings, items, and ideas that can be adapted to your magical practices. Where possible, I have included examples of ways to use the folk belief in modern magic. The purpose of this specific chapter is to provide additional information and examples that will make *Folkways* more adaptable to your personal needs.

Where to Find It

Table of Contents: This book is a compilation of folk beliefs and practices from around the world. It is organized into broad, often over-lapping subject areas that best represent the major theme or subject matter of the folklore.

Every effort has been made to cross-reference ideas throughout these pages. When such information doesn't satisfy your needs, turn to the index or other associated topics for assistance. For example, the folklore of herbs can be augmented (or further delineated) by exploring kitchen and gardening lore.

Index: Certain topics, such as divination and protection, are examined in many sections because they are common elements of nearly all folkways. The index will help you locate specific terms and concepts that fall under a variety of subjects and categories. For example, looking under safety, oracles, prophesy, and psychic ability in the index as well as the table of contents helps locate folkways with which these topics are associated. Here are other examples of how to cross -reference information in the index:

♦ Crystals: Look for the name of the specific stone in question. If these aren't given, check under the stone's color instead.

♦ Elements: Review items that have the appropriate elemental correspondence desired, such as feathers and leaves for

Air magic, soil for Earth magic, dried woods and herbs for fire magic, and seashells or sand for Water magic.

♦ Sea: Study the elemental section, any water listings, and items specifically associated with the beach, such as boats, seaweed, holy stones, etc.

Glossary: There are some terms in this text with which you may be unfamiliar. To help with this, a complete glossary of terms is furnished at the back of the book. If the word you're seeking isn't there, check the index, or turn to a good dictionary for assistance.

Who's Who: Historical, divine, and mythical characters appear on many of the following pages. Not all of these names will be well known to you. To provide context and elaborate on each individual's identity, a who's-who directory is supplied.

Reviewing this information can have an extra bonus; in the process, you may discover names of gods and goddesses to bless and sanctify your endeavors in specific areas. For example, when adding lore surrounding love to your magic, you could call on Freyja (Scandinavia) or Isis (Egypt) for aid. Which you choose depends solely on personal preference. (Invoking God/dess is not an essential step in folk practices, but it can be helpful, especially in circumstances that seem hopeless. Tapping divine energy to guide your magic reaps the greatest good possible from your effort.)

Visualization/Meditation Aids

Most people find that meditation and visualization help their magical attempts tremendously. These two techniques bring the body and mind into a more receptive state where energy flows freely. The use of specific focus for attention can aid both methods.

In meditation, candles are commonly used. Here, the individual sits and watches the flame while breathing slowly. As relaxation comes, the eyes usually flutter closed and the focus is no longer needed. To add folkways to this procedure, look up candles in the index and review the entries to see if any suit your goals. You could, for example, anoint the candle with a special oil to accentuate your meditative state (nutmeg, jasmine, or myrrh).

For visualization, choose your candle's color so that it is compatible with your intentions, such as yellow for divination. When you close your eyes return the image of the taper in your imagination to continue augmenting your visualization. Please note that in both meditation and visualization a congruity of meaning is the most important factor. If the focus of your attention is symbolically appropriate and personally meaningful, its use improves overall results.

Ritual and Spell Components

When using this book, consider what items you have available for rituals and spells. If you have plenty of culinary herbs, for example, check the herbal section for those appropriate to your needs. Also bear in mind your spatial constraints or special circumstances. Heavy incense can be difficult to handle in small rooms. Breakables should not be used around children, and anything poisonous needs to be kept well out of reach of both young ones and pets.

This bit of caution aside, finding suitable ritual embellishments and spell components within this book should be easy. For rituals that are seasonal in nature, check to see if there is a listing for that holiday. Review the themes of your ritual and any major items you plan to use in the sacred space. Detail all the potential bits of lore surrounding these items (or the date), then decide the best ones to inspire yourself or the members of your gathering.

To show you how this can take shape, let's use Yule as an example. In Bulgaria, it is customary to make a wish for luck as the first spark jumps from the Yule log. Additionally, we know that in Europe the ashes of the Yule log are either kept safe or given to the fields to bring bountiful harvest. As part of the Yule celebration, we might light the Yule log with a silent wish. In closing, we can share the ashes among all those gathered so they carry blessings home with them.

Summer Solstice provides another illustration. English folklore says this is a good day to conceive a child. We also know ancient Druids gathered at dawn to hold their ceremonies. If you want to have a baby, you might combine these two ideas and hold a special conception ritual at sunrise on this date.

Applying this information to spells is not much different. Find the topic of your spell or a synonym for it in the index. Review the methods traditionally used to achieve that goal, and decide which emblems are most meaningful to you. These are the ones to mix in with your spell's procedure. For psychic awareness, for example, steep a moonstone in hot water with bay, cinnamon, and peppermint. Stir the mixture clockwise and add an incantation for psychic awareness. All these ingredients are in sympathy with that goal. The hot water helps "heat up" the energy; stirring clockwise draws the power to you, and drinking the mixture internalizes the magic.

Meeting Specific Needs

Needs make themselves known in our lives regularly. Knowing that we can magically do something about them gives us peace of mind. To these ends, use *Folkways* as a handy reference any time you're contemplating magic.

If you're sick, look under "Health and Medicine." If you need extra cash, check "prosperity." When going on a vacation, review protection and travel customs, especially those associated with your destination. There is no goal so unique that these pages leave it completely wanting. However, unusual situations may require unusual adaptations of the material to make it functional in your setting.

Allergies are a good example. Some folk remedials call for ingredients that a few individuals find bothersome, such as honey. These people may have to look a little deeper for emblems to empower their magic. In this instance, if a tea called for honey, I might suggest using a clean, wooden honey spoon to mix the tea instead, allowing the symbol to substitute for the aggravating ingredient. Another option is a cup bearing the depiction of a bee. Both the cup and the spoon maintain consistent representation for your magic.

Another instance is the use of feathers in divination. We would not want to gather feathers from a living creature to aid our magic, and finding high quality feathers is difficult. In this case, we could choose to buy imitation feathers at a craft shop instead. These can then be cleansed, blessed, placed in a bag, and drawn out for interpretation like runes.

Some people might feel integrity is lost by using facsimiles. Yet, facsimiles honor the Earth while maintaining relevance. Keeping in mind that symbols are just as powerful as what they represent in your sacred space, you will rarely be disappointed by your choices.

Celebration Planning

One of the beauties of folkways is the special ambiance they add to holiday observances throughout the year. Much holiday lore can be found in the section entitled "Holidays." More ideas still can be discovered under the listings for the foods you plan to prepare (or their ingredients), and all the activities you regard as traditional.

In planning a special observance, folkways can be applied in two fashions. First, you can adapt customs from other cultures relating to your holiday. This will enrich your celebration and give it a universal flavor. Returning to Yule for a moment, this might mean putting out wooden shoes in place of stockings for Santa to fill. This gives you an opportunity to share the rich history of Father Christmas with the children in your life. For magic, wooden shoes then become an emblem of gathering joy and sweetness!

Second, you can use folkways to accent your celebration, whether or not they were initially connected to that observance. Many people who practice folk magic blend culinary spices into their incense to encourage specific results at a gathering where it will be used. It does not matter if these spices were originally burned for that occasion. What's really important is the incense's meaning to the participants, and its correlation with the theme of the festival. On Samhain, for example, one might add bits of clove to the brazier for protection, or dried carrot peel to encourage psychic awareness. Both items are steeped in folklore, suit the mood of the occasion, and add an extra dimension to the magic being performed.

Interpreting Dreams, Omens, and Signs

As a guide to discerning the meaning of your visions and unusual occurrences in life, this book is a valuable tool. Say you have a disturbing dream and wish to understand it better. Begin by looking under dreams in the index, or under any specific items in the dream that stood out in your memory. If you envisioned a huge cat prowling the woods, you would review the entries for both cats and trees. If your dream sequence was seen taking place during a specific time frame, you would check the listing specific it to it, such as "dusk," "dawn," "noon," etc. Write these references down together and see if the additional information doesn't help sort out the meanings.

I usually recommend that people keep a special diary to record their dreams and other unique happenings. This diary serves many functions. First, it sometimes takes days, weeks, and even years before the meaning of certain omens become clear. By keeping a written record, you affirm your ability to receive messages from the Higher Self, and can return to that information for perspective.

Second, your diary allows you to chronicle the specific details of your experience. As you write, you may find that other parts of an incident become clearer, thus defining its central connotation even further. Once you have this information written down, you can take your time reviewing and researching it for symbolic importance.

The only caution here is not to overspiritualize the mundane. Leaves can fall at your feet and birds sing without any deep significance to your life. Similarly, hot sausage and cold beer can make for interesting dreams that have nothing to do with divine messages. We simply need to be attuned and aware enough to recognize the difference between a natural occurrence and a universal nudge. If you feel uncertain in this regard, write down your impressions anyway, and then share them with a friend experienced in magic for feedback.

Finding Uses for Personal Items

If you have special items you would like to use in magic but don't know how to adapt them, check the listings in this book. Nearly everything we own can function in a spell, visualization, or ritual once we reconsider it with an inventive eye.

For example, if you have a favorite silk scarf, review the folkways surrounding fabric and knots for possible applications. If nothing in those sections strikes a harmonic cord for you, consider the color and shape of the scarf as alternatives, and study those listings. From these four sections of text you can assemble the following uses (and many more):

- ♦ Bind a specific type of magic within the scarf by tying it in a knot. The color or pattern of the scarf may help determine the best spells to fasten there. If it has strong golden hues, house magic for your conscious mind within the knots. If it's blue, use it for rain magic, untying one knot to bring precipitation. Remember to check the meaning of numbers to ascertain how many knots are best to tie.

- ♦ Tie the scarf in one specific symbolic knot, like the Herculean for strength.

- If the scarf is red, wear it around your neck in the winter to keep from catching colds.

- Wrap magical tools in the scarf to keep them safe from unwanted energy. This is especially potent if the scarf is white, the color of protection.

- Fold the scarf into a triangle and sit on it during meditations to center and balance your spirit. The triangle is the emblem of the body, mind, and soul in perfect symmetry.

Historical Considerations

In assembling *Folkways*, I have relied heavily on the research of historians, anthropologists, philosophers and folklorists for insight. Sources were compared to determine the most consistent, reliable interpretations and derivations of superstitions. Nonetheless, folklorists themselves admit that some beliefs are so ancient as to defy tracing to a specific time and place.

We were not alive to see the geneses of these beliefs. Therefore, certain assumptions must be made about their beginnings, changes that have occurred over time and distance, cultural influences, etc. Wherever drawn, such hypotheses are noted and left to your ponderings to determine their validity.

Additionally, folklore is a subjective study, sometimes limited by its cultural and historical setting. Where an obvious connection to modern magic is not readily available, I have provided functional adaptations of the information. These modifications are only suggestions, to be applied according to your vision and path.

On a final note, I think it's important to realize that the creation of folklore is an ongoing process. Some of our present notions about magic will become tomorrow's myths. Bearing that in mind, the personalization of this material is very important. You are a unique person living among other unique individuals. Together, your interpretation of symbols and signs today can lay a foundation that can empower magic for many years to come. Therefore, keep the past as a friend and stay aware of the superstitions we're building here and now. By so doing, you provide a valuable gift to the future: an abundance of tradition to inspire spiritual revival.

1 AMULETS AND TALISMANS

Can wisdom be put in a silver rod, or love in a golden bowl?
♦ William Blake, *The Book of Thel* ♦

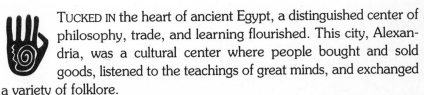 TUCKED IN the heart of ancient Egypt, a distinguished center of philosophy, trade, and learning flourished. This city, Alexandria, was a cultural center where people bought and sold goods, listened to the teachings of great minds, and exchanged a variety of folklore.

Around 2 A.D., Gnostic sects, which blended ancient Pagan and Christian ideology, cultivated these local bits of lore into a functional religious system that included the use of amulets. The Gnostic *Abrasax* appeared on talismans along with an acrostic word, *IAO*. The latter inscription was most likely associated with Greek letters corresponding to the great names of God in the Gnostic tradition. Likewise, amulets containing designs of Isis and Horus crossed over to Christianity as representations of Mary and Jesus.

Throughout the ancient world, amulets served as a way to transport protective magic. How well a particular amulet or talisman functioned, according to historical treatise, depended greatly on when it originated, what materials and symbols were used, and if the intended function of the piece matched its base materials. This is why ancient alchemists and magicians were often consulted for assistance in their production.

Amulets and talismans are still used in modern magic. Simple items such as a lucky penny or worry stone might easily fall into this category. Not all of the amuletic devices discussed in this book will be useful to you; however, their symbolism or manner of devising can inspire ideas of your own.

Abracadabra

Known more popularly in stage magic for pulling a rabbit out of a hat, this particular charm has been used since the second century A.D. to guard against disease and disaster. A poem written in 1864 in *Gnostics and Their Remains*, by C.W. King, is one of the most recent references to the proper use of this charm:

> *Each under each in even order place,*
> *but the last letter in each line efface*
> *As by degrees the elements grow few*
> *still take away, but fix the residue*
> *Till at last, one letter stands alone*
> *and the whole dwindles to a tapering cone*
> *Tie about the neck with a flaxen string*
> *might the good 'twill to the patient bring*
> *Its wondrous potency shall guard his head*
> *and drive disease and death far from his bed.*

Modern researchers theorize that a more ancient source, the Cabbalah, may have originated this particular amulet. If such was the case, the word would have been a derivative of a Chaldee phrase *Abbada Ke Dabra* which roughly translates to "perish like the word." The shape of its phrasing creates a funnel to symbolically drain sickness away.

```
ABRACADABRA
ABRACADABR
ABRACADAB
ABRACADA
ABRACAD
ABRACA
ABRAC
ABRA
ABR
AB
A
```

The inverted triangle was one of the most popular shapes for healing amulets. For example, when creating an amulet to improve health you

might write abracadabra on paper and place it
in a poppet, or cloth image of yourself, along
with herbs associated with health (allspice,
chamomile, black tea, etc.). Or, you might
burn the paper, thereby releasing your wish to
the God/dess as it rises with the smoke.

Words from any language with which you
are familiar can also be substituted. Think of a
term or short phrase that strongly portrays
your objective. Write that term in descending
form, eliminating one letter with each line
while focusing strongly on your goal. An
example for someone who bites their nails might be to inscribe "nail biting" backward on the paper (to turn the negative habit), then in descending form. Finally, the paper can be burned, buried, or tossed in water
moving away from you to likewise carry the bad tendency away (see
Chapter 13: Health).

Abrasax

The words *Sator* and *Arepo* in the
form of a square reading correctly
in all four directions create one of
the more famous Gnostic magical
talismans. This design appears in
many cultures around the world.

Scholars hypothesize that the
words *Sator* and *Arepo* may have
been an anagram for the Latin
Lord's Prayer, where the *A* and *O*
stand for *Alpha* and *Omega*. It
originally appeared in the House of Pompeii in the first century A.D.
and was attributed with wondrous properties, not the least of which
was safe childbirth. For this function it had to be inscribed on cloth and
laid across the womb. This example shows how magical and religious
symbols were sometimes mingled here to create metaphorical, and
often potent, charms.

Akhtaba

The *akhtaba*, a Samaritan phylactery similar to a prayer scroll, was worn as an amulet of protection. The text inscribed was usually Biblical in nature, written from top to bottom, in the belief that God's *logos* (power of divine words) could be carried with the bearer.

A contemporary version of this is to carry sections of your personal Book of Shadows, or favorite quotes from literature in a small container to transport their magical energy with you everywhere you go. Simply choose the segments or quotes according to your needs and spiritual goals at the time.

Amulet Cases

The owners of amulets often grew quite fond of them, treasuring not only their inherent power but also their sentimental value. Many amulets and talismans became family heirlooms. In an effort to protect the cherished token, special boxes of precious metal, or bags of silk or linen or other fine cloth were created to carry the amulet and protect it from contamination or injury when not in use. Sometimes another charm would be placed in this case, such as a god/dess figure, to strengthen the atmosphere of safety by invoking that deity's favor.

This special treatment of magical tools continues. Reference to proper housing for items such as the athame, tarot deck, wand, or any other personal tool for ritual is usually found in current magical texts. I sincerely believe this treatment is quite proper and respectful. It also helps keep unwanted energy and/or hands away from your personal tools.

The container you choose is a matter of preference, but it should be reflective of the item it holds, its magical function, and your personal Path. If possible, make a special receptacle so that your tools will be continually surrounded with personal energy.

Arabic Amulets

For hundreds of years, the most popular type of amulet in the Arab world was a simple piece of paper with a prayer from the Koran inscribed on it by a holy man. The ink was most frequently made of charcoal and water. The amulet was then wrapped in leather and tied to the left arm or around the neck. Those who could afford it had the supplication inscribed on gazelle skin, then preserved in a silver tube.

Another well-known amulet of the Arab region was a rectangle divided into forty-nine squares. Each line had seven signs, and one usually contained the names of gods. Other lines listed the names of guardian spirits, planets, days of the week, and other devices to help the owner call on the protection of all creation.

An appropriate modern application of this amulet is to inscribe a piece of paper with a specific attribute you want to bring to your life, or the name of an appropriate deity to invoke for this blessing. Consecrate this paper at your altar. Carry it with you so that each time you see it you are reminded of that desire and positive energy.

Babylonian Amulets

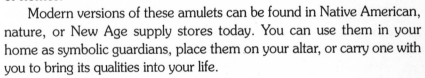

Clay figures were the most popular form of charms in Babylonia. The frog was a symbol of fertility, as were two fish (Pisces). The bull stood for strength and virility. A bear holding a club granted protection. Archaeologists have also found clay sculptures of dogs (which were used to repel evil spirits) planted under the doorways of homes.

Modern versions of these amulets can be found in Native American, nature, or New Age supply stores today. You can use them in your home as symbolic guardians, place them on your altar, or carry one with you to bring its qualities into your life.

Bulla Beads

This type of amulet was known to both the Romans and Christians during the first centuries of this millennia. It was usually used as a bead, rounded in an oblong shape like a door bolt, with a small loop on one end to hang from the body. It was inscribed with an appropriate charge or prayer, and/or filled with materials which corresponded to the wearer's need. It was also hung near or planted in fields to ensure good harvests.

Bullas can be made fairly easily from good modeling clay, and inscribed or painted with any personal symbol you prefer. Runes make excellent tokens for the bulla as do astrological signs, and the emblems of your patron gods or goddesses. The best part about this type of bead is that you can adjust its size, emblems, and base materials for a variety of gift-giving occasions. (If stringing them on a belt for a robe, or wearing as a necklace on a leather thong, remember to make sure you leave a large enough hole in the clay when forming to put your rope or thong through.)

If you have a magical garden, you can make a few extra to plant along its boundaries as a way of sharing your energy with the land, to hang nearby. To hang, set up a small branch or bit of wood from which the bulla can dangle freely (like a wind chime). Again, you can alter the size, shape and thickness so that they may lightly tinkle when the breeze takes them, thereby doubling as a deterrent to hungry birds! An appropriate rune symbol for this illustration would be *gera,* or the harvest.

Charms

Charm bracelets, with depictions of various symbols for luck, became popular during the late 1800s. The symbols themselves are based on far older traditions. Some of the more popular charms and their meanings were:

All of these symbols can function as components of spells which you create for yourself. For example, if you are trying to bring harmony into your home, use a piece of knotted rope during your rite and untie it to

- ♦ Acorn—youth and love.
- ♦ Arrowhead—protection from the "evil eye."
- ♦ Bee—energy and success in business.
- ♦ Cat—safe travel.
- ♦ Coin—luck and wishes
- ♦ Corn—prosperity.
- ♦ Coral beads—children's safety and good health.
- ♦ Egg—protection from misfortune, health.
- ♦ Fish—affluence, plenty.
- ♦ Four-leaf clover—love, wealth, good fortune.
- ♦ Glass beads—averting danger.

- Hearts—fidelity, devotion.
- Horseshoe—gathering luck, protection.
- Penny—luck.
- Key—opening doors, good judgement.

- Knot—unity and harmony.
- Lyre—accentuation of good qualities.
- Ring—timelessness.
- Shoe—fortuity.

ease the tensions. Similarly, if your family is in need of sustenance, give a small bit of fish back to the earth during a ritual to ensure revitalization.

Bracelets with many of the listed items can be found at a variety of shops, if you would like to use an actual charm as a decoration or component. However, I do suggest that any such jewelry be cleansed and blessed for its intended use before actually performing the spell. This will eliminate any residue energy that might hamper your efforts.

Cylinder Seal

The cylinder seal was made of semiprecious stones and filled with a substance appropriate to its design. The cylinder seal served a dual purpose. It was a good way for its owner to sign contracts because it could leave an imprint in wax or clay. Its contents, however, were usually combined for magical purposes according to prevalent superstition. Some of these recipes were guarded as family confidences passed down from generation to generation.

I have not seen a contemporary version of a cylinder seal which allows for filling, but one alternative might be metal tubing capped at both ends. This tubing is readily available at hardware stores. For a more decorative seal, use fitted cork that is glued in place with ribbons, feathers, etc. as accents. Fill the tube with herbs, flowers, and crystals that reflect your metaphysical intentions.

Wax letter seals can be purchased in gift shops and could easily act as a modern replacement. Here, you would choose a symbol appropriate to your Path or desired magical goal and use it with scented wax on any papers relating to your enchantments, and even to protectively seal parts of your Book of Shadows. If you cannot find scented sealing wax, you may add a drop of essential oil to the hot mixture before it dries for a long lasting, personally significant aroma.

Death Amulets

Many ancient cultures, most notably the ancient Egyptians, took great care preserving the physical body after death, believing its connection to the individual's spirit was still very strong. Egyptian tombs show an array of symbols to assist the soul in a safe passage through the afterlife and to protect the corpse. These include various forms of crosses, a dove of peace, bone figures of gods or goddesses, fish symbols, and prayers on papyrus. This practice may have evolved into the special clothing and items often placed in coffins today.

In Wiccan Summerland rituals, similar tokens made by the family of the deceased would be appropriate. The effort provides comfort to the living, and the spirits of those passed over will not disapprove of the thoughtfulness. This particular amuletic rite also offers us clues as to one of the best ways to handle magical items after death. Unless otherwise requested by the owner, it might be best to leave them with the body so that their intense personal energy can be released with the spirit into its next incarnation.

Egyptian Amulets

Made out of just about every material available, some of the most popular Egyptian amulets were of bone, silver, gold, wax, ivory, and wood. Those blessed by a mage were considered doubly potent. Although perhaps best known for their part in the embalming process, amulets were used to protect the living and their homes too.

The oldest regional Egyptian amulets date to the Neolithic period where mostly flint figurines of animals, women, or arrowheads are evidenced. Later devices were usually carved with hieroglyphics and other symbols with specific meaning. For example, the *ankh*, which means "life which cannot die," was predominant among warriors. The scarab, associated with the God of creation and the sun's power, was an amulet of strength. Both these emblems are popular today.

Another widely-used image was that of the *Ab* or heart, which was left in placed of a mummy's heart. The heart was then embalmed separately. The Egyptians considered this the center of all life and thought, guarded it carefully.

Other predominant emblems include:

♦ Papyrus scepter in mother of emerald; to give youth and vitality.

♦ Eye, or *Udjat,* for health, soundness, safety; known today as the Eye of Horus.

♦ Frog for rebirth and fertility.

♦ The Egyptian God Ba for the vital strength.

♦ The symbol Shen (in the form of a full sun just over the horizon) for eternity and the power of the Sun God.

♦ A ladder or stairs as a means of ascension or rising.

♦ God and Goddess images to invoke their approval and blessing.

Archaeologists have uncovered giant representations of common amulets. One of the largest discoveries to date is a five-feet-by-three-feet green granite scarab (beetle) weighing two tons uncovered at Constantinople. Two obelisks, symbols of the God Amen, found along the Nile at Karnack and Tanis are two other similar illustrations. These instances of territorial amulets give us pause to wonder about the possible protective purposes of many other megaliths around the world.

Finally, another interesting Egyptian amulet was that of the open hand. It meant liberality (in legal matters) or generosity and is believed to have eventually developed into what we now know as the hand of Fatma.

If you happen to be drawn to modern Egyptian magical traditions, it would be well worth your time to study more of the ancient works on this subject. These people had a wealth of mystical ideas which can be creatively adapted to your own working. An illustration might be to place a depiction of the Eye of Horus on your suitcases for safe travel, or wear an image of Ba during times when you feel weak or weary.

Ethiopian Amulets

The most popular form of amulet in ancient Ethiopian culture was a parchment strip of sheepskin varying in size from five inches to six feet. Positioned inside a cover and stitched into clothing, or worn around the neck and left arm, the parchment contained inscriptions of the names of God, words of power, and various spells in the Geez language (old Ethiopic). It served to protect the bearer from sickness, improve his or her vitality, and ensure fertility.

In the fourth century A.D., Ezana ruled Ethiopia. During his reign he renounced Paganism and adopted Christianity. The use of amulets and talismans remained, however. For example, crosses were laid on the bodies of sick people to keep evil influences away. There are also tracings of the cross and cross groupings in the *Lefafa Sedek (Book of the Dead)*, each of which has specific powers. When inscribed on the sheepskin and carried, certain sections of this book promised merchants prosperity in business. Other sections written on sheets and wrapped around the dead insured safety in the afterlife and peaceful rest.

Another amulet was a little book filled with spells, prayers or collections of words. Usually carried by a person, this object bore instructions to the bearer to repeat the directions seven times to affect the results needed (see Chapter 21: Numbers). An example of this is an amulet known as the *Walatta Kidan*. It had three words inscribed in descending form seven times. Supposedly this protective device was discovered through divine inspiration and could cure all manner of stomach disorders. The *Walatta Kidan*:

shar	shar	shar	shar	shar	shar	shar
djar	djar	djar	djar	djar	djar	djar
tje	tje	tje	tje	tje	tje	tje

For modern practitioners, similar pieces of paper with wishes or prayers can be placed within containers for magical tools, or on the inside ritual robes during rites to increase their potency. For the latter, I suggest sewing a little pocket as a permanent part of your robe which can be refilled any time. Here you can house a number of treasures, from a stone or measures to a satchel of powdered incense for use later in the ritual.

Engraved Stones

Perhaps the most famous talismanic carved stones are the Scarabs of Egypt. The representation of the beetle, which was the male principle, also symbolized immortality. Frequently carved in jasper, amethyst, lapis, or carnelian, the name of the patron God along with other hieroglyphs would be added to increase the scarab's power. The most frequently engraved figures are those of the *ankh* for life, *ha* for power, and *tet* for stability.

Other stone amulets from ancient times were engraved in the form of personal seals to convey magical energy. In Rome, signet rings included figures of Isis or zodiacal signs carved into onyx or carnelian. The etched image of Alexander the Great was also believed to bring health and good fortune. Other, more offensive likenesses designed to crudely show the owner's disdain for evil intentions.

This tradition continued through the thirteenth century. At this time an entire book was printed dedicated to discerning what different symbols engraved on various gemstones meant. Entitled *The Book of Wings,* by Ragiel, the title had come from an earlier source, the Hebrew *Book of Raziel.* This version bore little resemblance to its namesake, however. Here are some of the interpretations provided:

- ♦ A dragon on red stone is a charm for joy and health.

- ♦ A falcon on topaz insures the goodwill of leaders and judges, especially in legal matters.

- ♦ An astrolabe on sapphire will improve foreknowledge.

- ♦ A lion on garnet is an icon of honor and protection.

- ♦ A ram on sapphire will cure all manner of illness.

- ♦ A frog carved into beryl will bring reconciliation.

- ♦ A bat on bloodstone will improve incantations and all types of magical efforts.

- A man with a sword featured on carnelian will guard against lightning.

- A swallow on celonite is the bearer of peace.

- The draped figure of a virgin with laurel is good luck. This is sometimes considered a goddess figure.

- A stag on jasper helps cure madness.

- A triangular stone looking much like an eye will protect its owner from the "evil eye."

- Andromeda with flowing hair will bring peace to husband and wife.

- A Sard is lucky for a woman, especially if engraved with grape vines and ivy (associated with Bacchus and fertility).

- A donkey on chrysolite imparts to the wearer visions of the future.

- A vulture on chrysolite confers the power to control winds.

- An armored man with bow and arrow on iris keeps both the owner and his or her residence safe from evil.

- A bull on prase (a rare greenish metal) brings favor in the courtroom.

- A bear on amethyst prevents drunkenness.

In the fourteenth century another anonymous, untitled treatise on talismanic gems appeared. This manuscript added the following correlations:

- A gem that bears the image of a man with a goat's head brings the love of men and creatures to the owner.

- The image of a man with a scythe provides strength and courage.

- The sun and moon engraved together preserves chastity.

- The carving of a man with a palm branch in his right hand brings favor from powerful people.

- Jasper with the image of a dog or stag will allow the owner to heal the insane.

The love of stones certainly has not diminished among spiritual seekers today. Any one of these symbols can be employed in a carving, painting, etc. for the same type of purpose. If the stone desired is not available, try a similar color of wax or cloth.

Also, don't be afraid to substitute symbols which more closely reflect your magical tradition and vision. This will serve to create items empowering the best vibrations along the path of beauty you walk.

Fetish

Of Portuguese origin, the word *fetish* refers to an object that is believed to have magical powers. The fetish was often regarded as a type of medicine containing a god or spirit. The simplest was a natural object believed to have inherent power. More complex fetishes were combinations of objects placed in a container (such as the medicine bag of many Native American tribes).

The type of object carried as a fetish varied greatly according to culture, availability, and its owner's desires. A tiger's tooth might be included for strength, a feather for rapid movement or improved eyesight, the skin of a snake for shrewdness, and even dust from the tomb of a saint or venerated individual for protection.

Most magical and New Age stores stock small pouches which can be used to carry your own personal fetishes. Better yet, make one of your own. The enclosed items can be objects which have symbolic value or special memories for you.

To make a fetish pouch, you will need white cotton thread (for protection and purity), some sturdy cloth of a personally favorite color, and, if you like, a few feathers or beads to add as a finishing touch. Fold over the top of the pouch, leaving a space for the drawstring and hand stitch this in place (see illustration A). Next, sew up the side to the opening

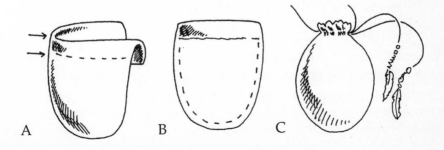

A   B   C

(illustration B). Now, draw through one piece of thong which is long enough for your neck, and another thinner cord which will draw the pouch together (illustration C). Place your cache of fetishes inside and tug on the draw string. Finally, add a few decorations and wear as desired.

Gnostic Amulets

Besides the well-known *Abracadabra,* the Gnostics used many other forms of amulets, frequently carved from semiprecious stones for wisdom, strength, and increased spiritual insight. Usually, they were shaped into squares, circles, or ovals and were a half-inch to three inches long.

Any words written on the amulet were usually in Greek, yet many of the depictions of gods and goddesses were Egyptian, such as Anubis, whom the Gnostics identified with Christ. Besides the images, names of God such as *IAW, IAO* (the Greek, O in *Omega* appears as a W to an untrained eye) and *Adonay* were also carved to invoke divine blessing. Other engravings on the stone included names of archangels or prophets, animal representations, astrological signs and a certain amount of numerological associations (see Chapter 21: Numbers).

One of the most popular Gnostic amulets was made from iron ore or hematite. It was engraved with a crescent moon, star, and figure holding a scorpion's tail. This charm was believed to be effective against scorpion stings. While most people today are not worried about being bitten by a scorpion, this symbolism as protection against gossip or backbiting could prove quite powerful, with a little creativity!

Gossip

Heliotrope harvested under the sign of Virgo, wrapped in laurel leaves, and bound together with a wolf's tooth is said to stop gossip.

Blessed lamb, fashioned from wax and given by the pope was believed to avert slander and even protect the carrier from sudden death. This was also true of saintly relics.

Both of these approaches, with minor variation, are still quite useful today. Instead of a wolf's tooth, toss the heliotrope in a stream rushing away from you (or down a toilet, if fresh water is not available) and allow it to carry away the negative energy. Or carve the image of a lamb in your altar candles before lighting them when you seek protective energy. Focus on the gentle spirit of this creature to help keep your life calm and undisturbed.

Hare's Foot

A hare's foot bound to the left arm protects travelers from danger. This superstition has two distinct sources. First, rabbits are quick, clever creatures able to keep perfectly still to protect themselves from predators. Thus, the foot was thought to endow its owner with that protection when carried or worn. Second, I believe the reason for attaching it to the left arm has to do with superstitions pertaining to that side. In the Middle Ages it was referred to as "sinister" in heraldry, pointing to a general belief that left is the side of evil (i.e. the "left hand path"). Placing the hare's foot on that arm was partly to protect one from the evil nature of the left side (see Chapter 4: Body Divination).

It is probable that our modern notion of carrying a hare's foot for luck originated in these types of customs (see Chapter 2: Animals and Insects).

Healing Amulet

Peeled cloves of garlic, cinnamon, sage, and saffron, combined and sewn into a piece of blue or green cloth, should be carried by a sick patient until the illness is gone. An alternative version of this amulet is to combine rosemary and carnation petals. This creation also smells wonderful, and since all the ingredients are edible, you could create a healing tea from the same recipe (go light on the saffron to avoid indigestion).

Hebrew Amulets

The Old Testament provides many clues to the amulets used by the ancient Hebrews (Isaiah 3:18, Judges 8:21, 26). The *saharan*, a figure of a waxing crescent moon, was worn by women, kings, and even camels for protection from the evil eye. The *teraphim* was a small figure of a god in human form made out of clay or stone and that remained in the home for protection (Judges 18:24). Teraphims also had some connection with an ambiguous divinatory practice the technique of which is lost to history. All we know of this method is that the prophets condemned it as idol worship (2 Kings 23:24).

Certain inscribed amulets were acceptable in the Cabbalah, namely those which used Biblical extracts in various forms. The most popular pattern for these verses to take was that of an inverted triangle to diminish the power of sickness (see Abracadabra). Other prevalent symbols employed were the Tree of Life and Shield of Solomon, known today as the Star of David. This shield was thought to be the bearer of deliverance and protection, much as the "armor of God" is spoken of metaphorically in the Old Testament as a type of spiritual haven.

The *lehashim* was an ornament which was activated by prayer, spell, or incantation. These included items such as finger rings, ear rings, arm chains, scent tubes and small mirrors of polished metal. In studying the Lehashim, it appears that the ornament was not considered functional without a specific triggering word, similar to an incantation, usually known only to the owner and maker.

A *mezuzah* was a strip of leather inscribed with Deuteronomy 6:4-5:

Hear, O Israel: The Lord our God, the Lord is one. Love the Lord your God with all your heart and with all your soul and with all your strength.

It was then placed on doorposts for protection. Finally, the *sisith* was a tassel of fabric or lock of hair tied with gems and blessed by a priest to avert the *evil eye*.

Those who practice cabbalistic traditions today could incorporate any of these into their personal rites. The symbols are fairly simple, and most of the items used are not distasteful to modern minds. Even outside of this realm, the meaning inherent in much of the Hebrew tradition is rich and enduring. Visualize the Tree of Life when you need to connect to Gaia and reaffirm your foundations, or draw a shield of white light with your athame in the air when you need refuge.

Kedada

The *kedada* is a silver amulet of Ethiopian origin, frequently carried in a gold box (*hekat*). It is used in the belief that the item, usually a cross or crescent moon and star, will give the bearer power over their enemies.

If you happen to be going into a difficult situation where there is animosity toward you, carry a small Celtic cross (emblematic of the four directions) and/or a crescent moon and star to help avert the anger.

Magical Bowls

Ancient Babylonians buried a terra cotta bowl inscribed with magical words near the base or under the foundation of a home to protect the lands of the occupants.

Similar bowls, known as devil traps, were found at Niffar. These handcrafted wares are etched with a spiral or circular pattern with magical Hebrew letters for safety.

With this in mind, a hand crafted bowl could be part of the magical regalia on your altar, for use in any spell or ritual where you are working with protective energy. Or, if you own your home, create a specially painted bowl with runes of protection on it and bury it as an alternative version of a Witch Bottle.

Mascot

Another type of amulet, which could be an object, animal, or person, is a mascot. This tradition was adopted by military groups and sports teams and grew such that to be without the mascot was thought to deprive a group of good fortune. It is not surprising, then, that certain college fraternities still steal each other's team mascot before a game!

For contemporary groups, this could have an interesting application. If your coven has a totem or spirit animal, keep an image of that creature as a mascot. The responsibility for its care could fall to a guardian (any dependable individual, even perhaps a child). This image would be present at all coven functions, with proper adornment (such as flowers or robes), and offerings could be left before it in thanks to your mascot for its wisdom and care.

Pehlevi Gems

Found in Iran and Persia, dating from A.D. 200-600, these gems were inscribed either with their owner's name or that of a god for protection. The characters were generally derived from the Semitic alphabet, and the stones had a small hole so they could be worn on string. The smallest of the stones was attached to ring bezel and could have doubled as a signet.

Ring Amulets

Probably first associated with the solar sphere, ring amulets were made of wood, metal, or stone. The ring amulet was created to grant or show sovereignty, strength, and power (note the prevalent use of signet rings in the Middle Ages), and was worn predominantly by people of authority.

The giving of a ring sometimes symbolized a grant of power to the recipient, such as with the Pharaoh and Joseph as told in the Old Testament. Depending on the final proposed function of the amulet, its bezel, shape, and materials would be chosen accordingly.

Two popular ring amulets were the posy ring and the fede ring. The posy ring is a love amulet used frequently in the Victorian era. This ring was inscribed with a motto or verse. The fede ring depicts two hands clasped in truth, thus serving as an icon of friendship and trust. Other ring amulets include memorial rings to insure the safety of the spirit, dial rings for astronomical observation and interpretation, perfume rings whose scent determined their use (similar to aromatherapy), and holy rings thought to have been owned by saints.

One ring which has been translated recently into a necklace is the mitzpah. In this case, one word is separated in half carried with the lovers or close friends each carrying a half. It is meant as an invocation of God to watch over them whenever they are apart.

For modern magic there are a myriad of uses for ring amulets. When a coven changes leadership, a ring could be transferred to the next Priest/ess as a symbol of his or her position and responsibility. Rings can be exchanged in handfasting rites, given as gifts to special friends, and/or worn personally to help carry that metal or stone's aspects with you.

Subhah

The Muhammadan rosary, or *subhah*, has a hundred beads, each of which correlates with one of the names of Allah. The last bead (number one hundred), elongated in shape, bears the ineffable name of God. From it hangs a tassel that protects the owner from the evil eye. This rosary is also used in divination.

The dividing marks at the thirty-third and sixty-sixth beads of the *subhah* are routinely made of ivory, wood, or bone, and the beads frequently are of carnelian, agate, or mother of pearl. Since it is required to be blessed by a holy man, its carrier is likewise considered to be endowed by grace.

Pilgrims who have made their *hajj*, or journey to Mecca, carry large numbers of subhah beads with them. Before returning to their homeland, they carefully dip the beads in the Zemzem well where Ishmael drank. The beads can then be dyed at home and put to use.

A version of this for modern witches might be a circle of polished, blessed stones to wear for ritual, each one of which represents the name of a God or Goddess by color, texture, etc. An alternative would be to make rose beads yourself from the recipe given below.

To prepare your rose beads, begin with about two cups rose petals well packed and a half cup of water. Chop the petals finely and simmer over low flame, adding water as necessary until the petals are a reddish-black color. You will note at this point that most of the water has dissipated and the petal mixture has taken on a pasty texture. Form this into whatever size beads you prefer. If they do not hold together well, add a bit of orris root and rose oil, which will give better texture and longer-lasting scent. Allow them to dry for a little while on a wooden board, but make sure to poke a hole with a pin before they are totally dry. String as desired.

If you would rather use a different type of flower because of its relevance to you, I have also had some success making these beads with lavender, carnation, and even certain vegetable flowers. Just watch the temperature and realize it may take you a couple of tries to get the proportions just right.

Syriac Book of Protection

A small text of instructions for canting various charms of blessing, spiritual growth, protection, fishing luck, peace in the home, business success, riches, and other types of magic needed on a daily basis, this book was apparently made small enough to carry readily and was thought to bring good luck to the bearer. However, it was considered most efficacious if the enclosed charms were actually used as directed.

An alternative for contemporary practice might be to translate important parts of your Book of Shadows into something readily transportable so that you have that information available in times of need.

2 ANIMALS AND INSECTS

I am a swallow, I am that scorpion, the daughter of Ra.
♦ *Papyrus of Ani, Book of the Dead* ♦

ANIMALS WERE deeply respected and even worshiped in ancient Egyptian, African and Native American cultures.Believed to possess all manner of virtues, animals were frequently eaten or sacrificed to release their positive attributes. For example, a lion's heart would be eaten to impart courage, while earthworms rubbed on the skin provided athletes with flexibility.The likenesses of creatures also appeared on amulets to confer similar power (see also Chapter 1: Amulets and Talismans).

The Egyptians describe in the *Book of the Dead* many images, including those of bull, ram, crocodile, hippo, lynx, hawk, heron, turtles and even grasshoppers (see Chapter 1: Amulets and Talismans) that were used as amulets. People honored each animal for its most positive attribute. For example, a ram represented strong will, a lynx grace and cunning, and turtles, protection.

In modern metaphysical studies, there has been a rebirth of interest in animal symbolism, widely evidenced by discussions about familiars, totems, and power animals. The latter is most often associated with Native

American shamanism, whereas the concept of familiars is more strongly rooted in Europe. Animal totems have been used in both settings.

Today we esteem the familiar as a magical partner who protects, watches, assists, and provides companionship. These creatures come to us quite unwittingly (like a stray cat or dog, or through spontaneous purchase at a pet store). With time, the animal becomes an important figure in the home, making its intentions known by wandering into the sacred space, sitting nearby during magical discussions, etc. These creatures become our friends to be treated with tremendous respect and love.

Totems and power animals are different from familiars. They are primarily spiritual entities (although they sometimes take a physical form), brought to our attention for lessons or aid. In native civilizations, the animal guide for a group was sacred and regarded as a protector. The group might even name itself after that creature. For example, in Japan a household bearing the name Tetsutaka (Iron Hawk) portrayed its strength, vision, and reverence for the hawk. The family emblem was then a black hawk on a field of red (blood).

In addition to family insignias, totem depictions surface in carving, painting, costume, dance, and numerous other arts. This veneration eventually developed into what we now call totems—animal guides that stay with you for a season or a lifetime. It also should be noted that nearly any natural objects, such as trees, rivers, and stones, can be totems.

Power animals can, but don't have to be totems. The power animal is most often a temporary visitor. It may come in a dream, in the woods, or as a gift in statue form from a friend. When such instances happen, the creature may be trying to teach or share its central attribute with you. For example, if you have found yourself feeling exposed to criticism lately, a fox might appear in a vision to teach you the art of spiritual camouflage.

These spiritual teachers and friends can, and do, change to suit the situation at hand. If, for example, you are in circumstances requiring great personal strength and a lion appears in your dreams, you could take comfort in knowing this animal's energy is being carried with you. Once the need for the power animal has passed, its presence usually will fade as well. Its lesson, however, remains firmly planted in your heart.

Since our ancestors found so much symbolism in the animal kingdom, it is not surprising our language reflects that symbology. People of all backgrounds still talk of being brave as lions, strong as bears, busy as bees, playing 'possum, eating like a bird, or singing our swan song!

Animal symbols can be applied to visualization, meditation, and magical decoration for the home and ritual space. For example, when you need strength, envision the image of a huge bear near your navel (your center of gravity). To provide elemental correspondences for your sacred space, place tropical fish in the West (water), a bird feeder outside in the East (air), a statue of a yellow lion in the South (fire), and perhaps a poster of a mole in the North (earth). Exercise creativity and keep your eyes open for adaptable trinkets when you're browsing garage sales and gift shops!

Ants

Being bitten by an ant was sign of a quarrel soon to come. Since the time of Aesop's fables, ants have symbolized not only diligence, but also community and social structure, since they rarely live alone. So to be bitten by one did not bode well for social activities.

Since ants are noted for their industriousness, they are good creatures to focus on in spells for stamina and fortitude. Worker ants are especially potent in this regard, being expert craftsmen. They can empower the foundations from which to build your dreams.

Ape/Monkey

In ancient Egypt, the ape was sacred to Thoth (God of Wisdom) who periodically took on this form. In the Judgement Hall of Osiris, four apes sit by the lake of fire to hear the appeals of those passing over before entering the sacred realms. Bes was an Egyptian monkey-faced god sometimes used as an amulet of protection (see Chapter 1: Amulets and Talismans). Hindus regard the monkey as an emblem of benevolence.

When you are being misjudged or unjustly accused, envision four apes standing guard by your side (one each at the four compass points). Carry a carving of a monkey to engender the attributes of shrewdness or charity in your life.

Bats

Thanks to the poet Virgil's portrayal of bats as blood-sucking creatures, the bat is often considered an ill omen and often a sign of death. However, early healers decided that because of this animal's ability to see in the dark, its blood applied to the eyes would grant keen sight.

Bat blood was popular in flying ointments, love potions and other charms. Gypsy lore says to mix it with meal, a bit of hair, and salt to cure a bewitched horse. In Germany, the heart of a bat worn on the left arm was considered the best amulet to help bring luck at cards. Asian cultures viewed the bat as an excellent symbol of joy and longevity because it suckles its young, and is therefore the most perfect bird (see Chapter 3: Birds).

The bat was an emblem of the soul in Babylonia. Meso-american tribes consider bats to be spiritual guides because of their uncanny ability to navigate the darkness. Many Native American cultures look to the bat as a token of rebirth because it predominantly dwells in caves, the Earth's womb. Some African cultures believe bats carry the souls of the dead.

Some people have even have likened them to miniature dragons, giving tremendous potency to a very small form!

For magic, the bat best personifies keen vision and the ability to navigate through difficult circumstances. Use the bat in meditations where you are trying to enhance your spiritual insight.

Bear

An emblem of power and protection, two things about the bear stand out in folklore: its fur and its ability to hibernate. Bear meat was considered a cure for baldness and insomnia. The long resting period of the bears was regarded almost as a kind of death by many early cultures, and as such, the bear was believed to be the reborn messenger of spring. As tribute to its authority over death, bear fur or meat was also often employed as a last-resort effort in healing.

The Samoyed shamans (Ural-Altaic inhabitants of the northeastern Soviet Union and northwestern Siberia) travel the world of the dead on the back of a bear. Frequently bear claws and fur dangle from the Shaman's drum to increase his magic. Other cultures, such as the Swiss and Lapp, so revere the bear that it is impolite to call him by his proper name. In these regions they call the bear Old One or Old Forest Apples, respectively.

Native Americans regard the black bear as the guardian of the West. In this form the bear is an excellent token for the western point of your altar. This creature is also identified with supernatural power and fortitude because of its ability to sleep (die) for a season and reemerge from the Earth whole.

In Teutonic traditions, the bear is dedicated to Thor because of its strength. In Greece, Artemis sometimes appears with the head of a she-bear.

The modern use of the phrase *to go berserk* may derive from a specific group of Norse warriors dedicated to the cult of Odin. These warriors, called *berserkers*, worked themselves into a frenzy before battle. However, the term *berserker* originated in the fact that they went into battle wearing bear shirts (*sarks*). These sarks were basically cloak or vest-like coverings cut from bear fur to make the wearer look frightening and fearsome.

The honey bear is symbolic of sweetness and truth.

If a bear has recently appeared in a nearby woods or visited your dreams, it can signal many things, not the least of which is a period of rest before the birth of power comes. Consider if you have need of a personal retreat, or perhaps have been solitary too long and should emerge from the caves of solitude. The bear is a strong, swift animal that can carry you toward spiritual sustenance.

Bees

Bees are messengers of the Gods. Like birds, their wings allow them to move between this world and the next, bearing important news. I cannot help but wonder if we get stung when we don't listen to their tales!

In Hinduism, Krishna, Vishnu, and Indra are called "nectar born" and have the bee listed as one of their aspects in the *Rig Veda*.

Both Pliny and Aristotle regarded the bee as having divine attributes and believed that good souls could be reincarnated in these insects.

Beekeeping was an important occupation until well into the 1900s as honey was the primary sweetening agent for food. These busy little creatures take an active interest in the affairs of their owners, too. Rural Victorian custom, for example, instructed beekeepers to tell their swarms about all the important events of the house. Additionally, the swarm should always be properly purchased. To disregard either of these rules was considered very bad luck; that careless owner might die by bee sting.

In ancient mythology, the bee was sacred to Venus and represented wisdom and productivity because of the queen bee's many followers. Most cultures considered a bee in the house to be quite lucky. However, Romans considered a swarm of bees to be terrible trouble. (This particular superstition probably found its roots in the story of Caesar at Pharsalus, who was defeated in 48 B.C after a swarm of bees settled on the sacred altar.)

Bison/Buffalo

Among the Plains Indians of North America, the buffalo is the most important totem. As their major source of food, clothing, and shelter, it embodied abundance and answered prayers. Zulus believe that souls can pass into buffalo and find new life, and the Pawnee regard it as the Father of the Universe.

In the stories of the Lakota tribe, a white buffalo calf-woman taught the Lakota how to pray. With this in mind, use the image of a buffalo to improve your meditative focus, or in times of great need.

Boar

In the *Veda*, the storm god Ruda is "boar of the skies." Vishnu's third incarnation was as a boar who saved the earth from the waters of chaos by tilling the soil. Greco-Roman mythology associated the boar with Ares/Mars as the personification of victorious battle. This was such a strong connection that Homer said warriors affixed boars' teeth to their helmets.

Celtic mythology regards the boar as a commemorative food for heroes. In Teutonic tradition, both Odin and Freyja have this creature in their domains. Finally, in China the boar symbolizes the wealth of the forest.

Magically speaking the boar works well in matters of success and protection in trying circumstances and personal honor.

Bones and Shells

Bones and shells of various animals, especially turtles, were used as a divinatory tool in China as early as 3500 B.C. Most prevalently used in the palace of the Shang Kings (1400 B.C.) the use of both materials extended into the Christian era by two hundred years.

In its earliest form, the Chinese king or priest offered an animal upon the altar. If accepted by the gods, then any markings on the bones or shells were interpreted as omens. Once deciphered, these divine messages were conveyed to ritual participants. Upward cracks, straight lines, and movement to the right in an oracle portended favor. For more details about this specific form of divination, read *Sources of Shang History* by Professor N. Keightley (University of California Press, 1978).

The Chinese were not alone in their use of bones and shells. In the Bazaar at Cairo, and in Persia, shell amulets to avert the evil eye were commonly worn. In Africa and Egypt, bones added to fetishes or medicinal mixtures assured the lucky owner of immortality. This is an example of sympathetic magic: bones in this setting equate with maintaining dominion over death.

Today the use of bones is not advisable, as they can carry disease. Shells found at the beach should be washed thoroughly before magical application. To use shells for divination, first determine what the cracks will stand for. Then crack the shell while focusing on your question. Look to the general image produced first to see if an obvious form is there. If not, move to each line following the guide you have created to discover the message.

Bull

Sumero-Semitic tribes believed that a great bull cultivated the furrows of the sky. Their Sun God rides on the back of a bull, and Sin, the lunar god, takes the shape of a bull.

In ancient Sumeria, when a bull roared and stomped its feet it was a sign of fertile rains. In this largely agrarian region, the bull was important as a work animal.

Zoroastrian doctrine states that the bull was the first-generated creature. When slain, its soul provided the spark for all creation.

In Minoa there was an unusual custom known as bull-leaping. This rite honored the Minoan goddesses of the hearth, home, fields, animals and crops during the years 3000-1100 B.C, and was strongly connected with magic for fertility and vitality. Bull leaping began with participants lined up to do hand-springs over a bull's back. In the process, the acrobats grabbed the bull's horns to propel themselves. Our contemporary phrase, "seize the bull by its horns," has its origins in this activity.

Adapting the symbology here is not difficult. Visualize bull horns in meditation to inspire motivation. Another option is using carvings of bulls near your garden, threshold, and other openings to bless your pets, plants, and home.

Butterfly

The butterfly's body has three distinct parts—head, abdomen, and thorax—which the ancients believed represented the threefold nature of God and humankind. Its amazing metamorphosis from larva to butterfly likens this gentle insect to the spirit in transformation, and the soul looking for a home.

In China the butterfly is an emblem of a happy union. Newlyweds often receive them carved from jade (see Chapter 7: Crystals, Gems and Metals). Native Americans also regard the butterfly with honor, its presence for many being an omen of positive change and joy. The Hopi, specifically, revere and honor the butterfly as they believe they carry the souls of the dead.

Greco-Roman stories relate the butterfly to Horae, the spirit of the seasons, aptly depicted with butterfly wings as the wheel of the year is always in motion.

For drastic change in your own life, see yourself as a larva in a cocoon. Within this warm, safe shell, make the changes you desire in yourself. When you feel as if the transfiguration has begun (sometimes evidenced by a tingling sensation), tear free of the cocoon and see yourself emerge as a beautiful being of light. If it helps, allow yourself to have wings so you can soar above your present circumstances and achieve the newness you desire.

Cats

The cat was an object of worship in Egypt, Rome, and Persia. In Greek legend, Artemis sometimes took the form of a cat. Scandinavians portray Freyja with cats drawing her cart. Similarly, in Egyptian myth, cats attend Bast, who herself has the face of this creature. The Egyptians also sometimes depicted Ra in the form of a cat striking a serpent to symbolize the power of good over evil.

With its tenacity, agility and strong associations to the divine, it is not surprising that people though the cat had nine lives. Nine is the number of universal truth (see Chapter 21: Numbers).

So why did black cats get such a negative reputation in the Middle Ages? Because their eyes glow brightly in the dark when the body cannot be seen! To poorly educated, unsophisticated people this was an ill omen. Making matters worse was the cat's knack for hiding. This made it seem as if they could disappear at will (see Chapter 18: Magic and the Supernatural).

American folklore took a more favorable view of cats, probably because they caught disease carrying mice. If a stray cat comes to your home, money should follow, and if a black cat crosses a road, the next person passing gets a wish. Cats also influence the weather. This last idea grew out of the nervous behavior and vocal tendencies cats exhibit before electrical storms.

A unique form of Victorian divination involving cats was to concentrate on a question, and then watch a feline. If it entered the room right paw first, the answer to the question was yes.

The cat was adopted as a popular amuletic symbol to protect travelers on dangerous journeys. Lastly, cats became potent amulets for sailors and travelers because they always land on their feet unscathed!

Chameleon

Pliny said that chameleons live on air, and change to every color but red or white. This changing color was a symbol of inconsistency and the ever-changing future.

In African myth, the chameleon gave the divine message of immortality to humankind by teaching them of resurrection. Bushmen in Australia believe it to be a rain-bringer. The chameleon's ability to blend into its surroundings gives it a strong association with concealment and may prove magically useful at times when you feel too noticeable.

Chickens

In rural England, an old tradition held that chicks hatched on the New Moon grew more quickly than others. They believed that as the moon grew to full, so the chicks would grow. If they hatch during a fruitful sign (see Chapter 12: Gardening and Farming), they were said to mature faster. Those born during the sign of Gemini were not thought to be good egg-layers.

Eggs laid on Good Friday assure fertility to those who eat them. (Since Good Friday comes near the beginning of spring the natural productive symbolism carried over.)

For modern magic, the chicken (or alternatively, an egg) is an emblem of fertility and health.

Cow

The cow was sacred in ancient Assyria, Egypt and India. Egyptians regarded it as a representation of the great horned Mother, Hathor. The rarity of meat and the creature's cost made it highly valued in these regions and many others. In India, specifically, it is a terrible offense to harm this animal. Here the life-giving milk of cows nourished Kings and priests.

Common rural traditions both in Europe and the U.S. claim that red cows bring hope to the owner. Because they give milk and nourish their young, cows are an emblem of the Mother aspect of the Goddess and are lunar in nature. Use a cow as an emblem in any magic pertaining to abundance, nurturing, or hope.

Cricket

It is an old Chinese belief that crickets bring good cheer and abundance. They believe that some crickets are actually the spirits of departed family members who have returned to bless the home. In Japan, the *sami* (tree cricket) is popular because its singing resembles the chanting of Buddhist priests. The Japanese sometimes keep crickets as special pets to bring blessings on the home. This has carried into the American tradition that a cricket living in your chimney is a very good sign for the entire household, and that if one should leave, trouble or sickness is on the way. If you happen to find one in your home, greet it as a small representative of the natural world, leaving a small gift of grass where it most likes to hide. Each time you hear it singing, give thanks for the joyful fortune it brings to your dwelling.

Deer

Deerskin was once thought to be a cure for epilepsy. In several Native American cultures, such as Seneca, Cherokee and Lakota, the deer is considered a teacher in the ways of the Gods. While the exact characteristics change slightly depending on the tribe, one theme comes through: the deer's ability as a gentle, sure-footed pathfinder.

Deer also have a substantial presence in mythic cycles, as evidenced by the White Hart of Celtic legend. Here and in Anglo-Saxon stories, the deer appears to a hero and leads him on a great journey into the deepest forest to learn valuable lessons. Most often, these lessons pertain to the inner self or our connection to nature.

In the Bible, a loving wife is personified as a doe (Proverbs 5:19) and the spirit of a true seeker after divine knowledge is called a deer (Psalms 42). Greeks portrayed the deer as blessed by Artemis, Aphrodite, and Diana. In the *Veda*, deer provide Vayu, the Wind God, with transportation. Similarly, in Irish and Gaelic stories, deer transport souls to the next life.

If a deer has suddenly appeared to you, this is good news. The mentor you have long awaited, especially in the realms of psychic healing arts, may soon make himself or herself known. Alternatively, you may experience a revitalized interest in spiritual learning.

Divine Pets

In folklore, myth, and legend, almost every god or goddess is associated with a specific animal. Sometimes the animals are companions, sometimes they are part of an important series of events, and periodically the divine being shape-changes him/herself or another individual into an animal for a particular purpose. The purpose is later reflected in many of the interpretations of animal symbolism.

Here is a brief list of some of the gods and goddesses of the world and animals they are thought to protect. This list is especially useful when you are doing magic for your pets or creatures of the earth so that you can call on the appropriate form of the divine to aid you:

- ◆ Akupera: Hindu—tortoise whose back supports the world.
- ◆ Amaterasu: Japanese Sun Goddess—she-crow.
- ◆ Amun: Egyptian—any hatched creature, cow.
- ◆ Anubis: Egyptian guide of souls—dolphin, jackal.
- ◆ Aphrodite: Greek Goddess of Love—dolphin, goat, swan.
- ◆ Apollo: Roman God of Light—magpie, horses, pure breeds.
- ◆ Arachne: Greek Spider Goddess, weaver of fate.
- ◆ Aristaeus: Greek protector of flocks and beekeeper.
- ◆ Artemis: Greek Moon Goddess—bears, fowl, wild beasts.
- ◆ Athena: Greek Goddess of Arts/War—snow owl, peacock, eagle.
- ◆ Atergatis: Syrian Fertility Goddess—fish, snakes.
- ◆ Avilayoq: Inuit—seals, whales, and all sea creatures.
- ◆ Bast: Egyptian—cats (both domestic and wild).

- Benten: Japanese Love Goddess—snakes, the dragon.
- Blodeuwedd: Welsh—owl.
- Bullai-Bullai: Australian aborigine—parrot.
- Chingchinich: Native American—coyote, birds.
- Diana: Roman goddess of nature—dog, elephant.
- Ganymede: Greek cup bearer—eagle, peacock.
- Hecate: Greek crone and keeper of mysteries, often pictured as having the head of a dog, horse, or boar.
- Hermes: Greek Messenger of Gods—goat, ape, swallow; any winged, swift or sure-footed creature.
- Isis: Egyptian—owl, lion, ram, snake.
- Jana: Roman Goddess of the Year—woodland creatures.
- Loki: Scandinavian trickster—any animal considered "crafty," such as fox or cat.
- Luonnotar: Finnish Goddess of Creation—eagle, duck, and any egg-laying animal.
- Manabozho: Native American inventor of arts and crafts—raven, otter, muskrat, hares.
- Mari: Celtic Goddess of Sea and Poets—ram, raven, crow, animals of the water, horse.
- Nuit: Egyptian Sky Goddess—winged creatures, specifically the peacock and eagle; all "air" creatures.
- Odin: Scandinavian God of Cunning—raven, horse.
- Pan: Greek God of the Woods—forest creatures, flocks; all "earth" creatures.
- Poseidon: Greek God of the Sea—dolphins, snake, scorpion, fish, eagle; all water creatures.
- Sadhbh: Irish Deer Goddess.
- Sigu: Guyanese lord of beasts and of the forest.
- Vesta: Roman Fire Goddess—goat, donkey, and all fire creatures (see elemental correspondences).
- Zeus: Greek God of Gods—eagles, elephants, bulls, and swans.

Dog

Dogs have long been considered as possessing a kind of second sight that makes them wise about ghosts and strangers. Canines are believed to be able to sniff out trouble; thus when they howl at the moon it is a bad sign. If they hide under the table for no reason, folklore has it there will be a thunderstorm. Should you have a dog for a pet, it may be well worth your while to observe these types of actions and see how accurate your canine friend is, especially if you are planning an outdoor gathering.

Some coastal cultures claim that a coral necklace for a dog will protect it from various diseases. In Scotland, tradition holds that a strange dog coming to your house portends a new friendship. Alternative meanings for the dog include loyalty, service, and trust.

Dolphin

Apollo is strongly affiliated with dolphins, being able to take their shape. It was in this form, called Apollo Delphinos, that he founded the Delphic Oracle. It is interesting to note that the Greeks believe dolphins love music, and Apollo is the God of music. In their mythology, Ulysses bore a dolphin on his shield, and this king of fishes saved Telemachus.

Some of these protective, gentle associations carried over into Roman art, where figures of cherubs ride on dolphins to guide souls to the Isle of the Blessed. Native Americans also see the dolphin in this aspect and as a messenger between worlds.

For early seafarers, dolphins provided the valuable service of weather prediction. When they leapt more often, it was a sure sign that wind and storm were following close behind.

Magically, the dolphin emblemizes the breath of life, helpfulness, and the purity of joyful play. It is the child within each of us, leaping to be free.

Donkey

An English rhyme from the 1700s claims that placing a person near death on a donkey's back may cure them, since the animal was honored by Mary's ride into Bethlehem. Analogously, seven hairs taken from the mark on a donkey's back, placed in a silk bag, was said to cure whooping cough.

A slightly different version on both of these was to pass the inflicted beneath the belly of the donkey three times to effect a cure (see Chapter 21: Numbers).

In China, the Immortal of Taoist tradition known as Chang Kao-Lau delivers children on the back of a donkey. In this form the ass is an emblem of fertility and safe delivery for expectant mothers.

Sacred to Chronos and Saturn, donkeys can be used as emblems of time efficiency and plentiful gardens. Additionally, the donkey is an effective symbol for magic pertaining to health, well being, and general luck.

Dragon

Dragons are mythological creatures depicted as huge, crested snakes with wings and clawed limbs. In Latin, the word pertains to the group of tree dwelling lizards which populate Asia and the Philippines. The largest of these is the Komodo lizard, from which some of the Dragon legends may have originated.

In the Far East, dragons are a symbol of wisdom because of their longevity and potent magic. They took part in creation and were born with full ancestral memory. Dragon images were discovered here on numerous charms for bringing power to the owner. In *Feng Shui* (the Chinese art of harmonizing the placement of objects in your environment) dragons compare favorably to the imposing, protective mountains.

As an emblem of authority, dragons appeared frequently in Babylon, Egypt, China, Rome, early England and Wales. The Roman Goddess Ceres moved through the heavens in a dragon-powered chariot. Among Teutonic peoples, the word dragon meant "chief" and all the power associated with that position (notably Pendragon). Finally Hindus personify the dragon as able to manifest magic through the spoken word. This may have some connection to the depiction of dragons breathing fire (symbolizing inspiration, energy, etc.)

So, if a dragon should take a fancy to you, pay it special heed as a potent messenger from time-before-time. To fly on dragon wings in a dream definitely marks the birth of new spiritual insight and ability in your life.

Dragonfly

In many Asian cultures, the dragonfly is a great bringer of harmony and serendipity. They are never to be frightened off, but should be left to sit peacefully wherever they land. In Western society, the drag-onfly has become a symbol of dreams, luck, and ancient knowledge, both within and without the magical community.

Elemental Correspondences

Animals did not escape the human tendency towards zodiacal or elemental classification. Each creature was considered as being aligned with a particular element, frequently dependent on habitat. This correspondence was used in folk healing (a water creature to help soothe a fever, for example) and for appropriate offerings to deities. Here are some samples of traditional affiliations:

♦ Earth: Snake, rabbit, cow, gopher, deer, mole, ferret mouse, many forest-dwelling animals.

♦ Air: Most birds, flying fish, butterfly, dragonfly, ladybug, bee, and other winged creatures.

♦ Fire: Scorpion, lion, lizard, horse, desert creatures, electric eel, also creatures with a fiery sting.

♦ Water: Fish, seahorse, dolphin, seal, walrus, crab, seagull, whale, duck, beaver.

These elemental tendencies can be applied in decorating your home, altar, or sacred space, or in creating special magical items with a unique flair. A water wand, for example, would be lovely if made from willow wood and adorned with seahorses, colored sand, and tiny shells. Such a tool would function exceptionally well for any spells or rituals pertaining to the intuitive self.

Fish

The fish has been associated with the figures of the savior in various cultures. In Babylonia, Oannes was a fish-man. The first incarnation of Vishnu was birthed from a fish, and fish symbology is used throughout the story of Jesus Christ, who called his disciples fishers of men and fed five thousand with two fish and five loaves of bread.

In many seaside communities, the fish portends good luck and gratification because prosperity depends on the catch. Fish that live in wells were considered to be the embodiment of a water spirit. Some fish were even thought to be so sensitive to human trends that they would leave the area before wars erupted.

In Japan, carp swim upstream to spawn, associating them with courage, perseverance and the tenacity of true love. There is a special festival in Japan (Boys' Day) where kites and streamers of fashioned like carp decorate the land to honor these "yang" attributes. For modern magic, the fish is an appropriate symbol for times when you need a miracle, foresight, and improved fortune.

Fox

The fox is crafty, quiet, and skillful. When visiting Scotland, I learned that some Scottish families trace their lineage to foxes, either because of their physical appearance, a personal knack for facades, or the frequency of fox sightings near their home. Considering the number of sheep in this country, the animals were probably on hunting expeditions! However, a local legend claims the foxes appear to warn the families of impending difficulties.

In Western cultures the fox is regarded as a trickster, while Eastern peoples see them as shapeshifters filled with supernatural power. Native American myth also reflects this concept.

If the fox has evidenced itself in some form, take this as an opportunity to reassess your situation and see how you may covertly assert your influence.

Frog

During the medieval period, it was thought that
the tongue of a frog set over the heart of a
sleeping woman would compel her to give truth-
ful answers to her mate.

Frogs were predominantly used in the Middle
Ages for sympathetic magical cures, specifically those of the mouth and throat. In both cases,
the animal was held briefly in the mouth while spells or
prayers were spoken; then the animal was commanded to hop away with
the sickness. This is how the modern saying, "a frog in my throat" came
into being. Similar uses of the frog have been seen in Native American
rites where the shaman uses a frog as part of a cleansing ritual.

Today, you can use the image of the frog to accentuate spells involving health, honesty, and purification.

Gazelle

In Arabian cultures, meeting a gazelle is considered a bad omen, especially if it crosses your path from left to right. In this instance the
Bedouin, nomads of the deserts of North Africa and Arabia, might
shout, "Gazelle, gazelle, let misfortune vanish as well," in order to can-
cel the negative luck.

The gazelle (a type of antelope) is extremely swift-footed. They are
suited to survival in their environment and have a highly-developed sense
of smell. This gives the gazelle the positive attributes of awareness, deci-
siveness, and stamina. Try visualizing the creature centered in your third
eye when you need more conscious energy. If a gazelle has appeared in
your dreams, you may need to settle some situation or agreement sooner
than expected.

Goat

The goat has strong associations with Pan worship. As such it evoked
fear and trepidation, especially in the Middle Ages. Pan was a joyous
forest deity, portrayed as half-man, half-goat. As Christianity became
more prevalent, the Church turned Pan and the Celtic Horned God into
devilish figures to frighten people. It may be due to this fear that a goat's
foot or fur has been a talisman against evil since ancient times.

Mountain goats are adept climb-
ers and can withstand rather harsh
weather. They protect themselves using their horns. With
this in mind, use the emblem of
a goat to honor Pan, or in
spells and rituals pertaining to
reaching your goals, withstand-
ing criticism, and staying safe.

Hare

The hare was sacred to ancient Britons. A hare in a churchyard was actually thought to be the spirit of a girl who died due to abandonment in love.
Some people thought that hares changed sex every year, probably due to
their formidable procreative powers. Unlike the rabbit, a hare crossing
your path was not considered lucky, especially for pregnant women. Such
an occurrence would cause their child to be born hare-lipped!

In China, the hare is strongly associated with the moon. On the full
moon of the eighth month, they celebrate the Moon Festival with depictions of the Moon Hare. Five different platters of fruit and mooncakes
are left as offerings, along with beans, a favorites of the hare.

For your personal magical work, hares are best used as symbols of
fertility, lunar energy, and release of the spirit. If a hare has appeared in
your life, consider whether you are moving fast enough, especially away
from danger. It can also portend a time of productivity, and even children.

Hedgehog

Aristotle stated that the hedgehog, a burrowing animal, portended
changes in the wind by shifting the position of its hole. Pliny took this
idea one step further by maintaining that hedgehogs actually build two
holes, and block whichever one is necessary.

An unusual superstition about the hedgehog is that it uses its quills
to gather grapes for winter storage by rolling around in the vines. This
particular imagery could prove useful during times when you need to
reap the fruits of your labors.

Horse

The horse is perhaps the most prized above all domestic animals. To early and contemporary minds alike, it represents transportation, cultivation, and communication. In Greece, the horse was worshiped as a symbol of Artemis, and is an excellent image for those who are attracted to Her spheres. Generally speaking, a black horse was considered more fortuitous than white, as was one with a small star on the forehead, or markings that look like stockings on the feet.

In ancient Germany, white horses were kept in a sacred grove because they believed these creatures had the Gods' favor. Observing the behavior of this animal was believed to give them insight into the divine, and possibly the future. This particular scrutiny has not ceased among proficient equestrians of today: they will frequently observe their animal's behavior before going on a long ride to determine if a storm or other difficulties are ahead.

Jaguar

One of the largest cats in the world, jaguars predominate in Central and South American folklore where it is a power animal for many shamans who can be possessed by its spirit. The ceremonial stool for Mayan shamans had carvings of jaguars, and the priests often wore imitative masks, tunics, and headpieces to draw the jaguar spirit. After a shaman's death, he or she could live in this cat.

For modern magic, use the image of the jaguar as a focus if you're beginning a shamanistic path.

Lion

A lion is an emblem of the golden sun, full of might and potency. Babylonians and Assyrians trained lions for hunting. Egyptians worshiped the creature, ornamenting their doors with the depiction of a roaring lion. According to Plutarch, this was because the sun was in Leo when the Nile rose. The Egyptians also placed images of lions near their temples to watch and protect the sacred ground.

Portraits of Ishtar in Babylon depict her standing on a lion. The Sumerian Sun God, Marduk, has the lion as an emblem of complete dominion. A lion was the fourth avatar of Vishnu and guardian of the North in Hinduism. As such, the depiction of a lion in the north quarter of your sacred space would be fitting.

Among Buddhists, the lion defends the law. Buddha himself often surrounded himself with these creatures. The law is not without compassion, however, as cubs also have a place in depictions of the teacher. Bearing this in mind, when you desire strength and courage use the image of an adult lion. When you need of gentility and mercy, envision the cub.

Pig

In Valhalla, Valkyries feast on a magical sow who is reborn each day. This, combined with the traditional Celtic victory feasts of hog, may have been the source of our Easter hams. Since we celebrate Easter near the Spring Equinox, it is identified with rebirth and triumph over darkness. Thus, eating ham becomes a fitting symbol of internalizing that power.

For those who eat meat, consecrate your ham before you consume, and internalize the power of rebirth and rejuvenation, like fresh air first thing on a spring morning. If you are a vegetarian, you can choose instead to have a picture or carving of a pig in the sacred space when performing spells pertaining to inceptions.

Protection

Elder may be placed around your home to protect the animals within. For this purpose it should be kept where it will remain undisturbed by animals or human hands.

In Celtic regions, farmers passed their animals through the smoke of a Beltane fire to ensure the creature's health for another year. This procedure can still be followed in safety by lighting a stick of incense and walking sunwise around your pets. This way, you enfold them with the protection of fire and air without frightening them.

The ancient Hebrews felt that placing a dab of a white substance between the eyes of their animals offered protection from the evil eye (white reflecting the gaze back to the sender).

A contemporary means of continuing this tradition would be to beat egg whites and apply them in the same manner. The color will dry clear, but the initial visual effect is the same. Also, if the pet cleans its fur, the egg white is a healthy conditioner.

Rabbit

A rabbit's foot is considered very lucky, perhaps because the rabbit can hop so quickly away from danger (see Chapter 1: Amulets and Talismans). For visualizations, see a large rabbit carrying your problems swiftly away from you.

In Roman times, the rabbit played a large role in religious rites and was never eaten by the common people. During the Middle Ages, this taboo developed into the idea that eating rabbit meat would cause melancholy.

In Great Britain, there is a unique custom whereby you say "rabbit" as your last word before sleeping, and "hare" upon rising to receive a gift in one month. This magic is even stronger if you repeat "rabbits" three times on the last night of the month, followed by three "hares" when you awaken. In Suffolk, this varies slightly. Here it is good luck to say "white rabbit" upon waking on the first day of the month, and "black rabbit" when you go to bed that night.

My best supposition on how all this got started has to do with the rabbit's prolific nature. In the East, rabbits relate to the moon and thereby the intuitive, unseen world that includes fate. By speaking their name, perhaps the inference is that personal luck will multiply as quickly as the rabbits do!

Scorpion

In Sumeria, the scorpion protected the rising sun. It became a favorable and powerful sign in arid civilizations such as Egypt. Certain magical rituals, specifically initiation, would take place during the sign of Scorpio to ensure the blaze of deep understanding which this fire sign inspires.

Since this discernment is something we still seek in our magical work, we would do well to follow this example, if practicable. If not, the image of a scorpion could be present at initiations as a gentle reminder of the fire within which needs responsible tending.

Snake

Despite fear of this creature, the snake was sacred to many groups, including the Druids and the priestesses at Delphi. The Greeks kept snakes as pets because of the animal's association with healing deities. Hermes is a prime example of this, his staff being entwined by two snakes. Buddhism exhibits this idea again in the story of Buddha changing into a Naga (human-headed snake). In this form he healed people stricken by disease and famine. In agrarian societies, the snake symbolized the fertile earth. Because it sheds its skin it also betokens renewal and rebirth. The story of Adam and Eve adds the alternative symbolism of knowledge and sexuality.

An old bit of country weather lore states that if you toss a dead snake in the air and it lands backside up, rain is soon to follow. Since most people would find this very distasteful, just for fun you can try the same procedure with a child's rubber snake.

In England the most feared snake by far is the adder. Because it is so poisonous, if one entered the house, it was considered a sure sign that death was to follow. If it appeared in a dream, it warned that an acquaintance planned to do you harm.

Spider

It is considered very unlucky to kill a spider. This may have origins in the story of Arachne and her web-weaving skills. It is from her name that spiders get the designation "arachnids." Ancient Egyptians associated the spider with Neith, the weaver of the world. There is also the idea that one of the three Fates takes the form of a spider when snipping the thread of life and destiny.

Native Americans regard the spider as the creator of the first alphabet. Their webs are symbols of creative power and manifestation. Both the spider and its web are excellent symbols for rituals/spells centering on networking and our greater connection to all things.

In the Middle Ages, the luck of a spider might have had a little more foundation considering they ate many of the flies which carried disease. During this era it was common to lay a spider web on a cut to help its healing along. This is still considered to be a functional bandage by folk healers today.

Tortoise/Turtle

The world rests on an elephant borne on the back of a tortoise in Hindu mythology. Here the elephant is male/solar energy and the tortoise, female, bringing together the two great creative powers. The Chinese also believe a tortoise supported the world, with each of its feet representing one element or corner of the Earth.

In Taoist tradition, the shape of the tortoise symbolizes the cosmos. Among these people, it is an animal of prophetic powers, its shell being used in divination (see Chapter 1: Amulets and Talismans). Polynesians regard the tortoise with similar reverence as embodying the power of the ocean gods.

Small turtles can be purchased in many pet stores and make a good pet for children. In the home, they can remind us of the full cycle of life from the oceans to the land. Their slow, steady nature encourages constancy, and their shell teaches us how to retreat for our own good.

Whale

The Norse peoples believe that witches can ride on whales, which are themselves magical. In Japan, the whale is a sea-mount for the God of the oceans. Finally, Arctic tales say that the earth rests on the back of a whale, and when it moves, earthquakes result.

If a whale appears in your life, ponder your magic, especially those spells and rituals centering on the water element. Also, if your life has seemed shaky lately, it may be the whale spirit keeping you on your toes.

BIRDS

I hear her in the tuneful birds, I hear her charm the air.
♦ Robert Burns, *My Jean* ♦

 WHETHER IT is the desire in man to free himself from the constraints of gravity or a natural wonder at the grace of birds in flight, these creatures more than any other in history have captured the attention of humanity for developing superstition and folklore.

The word *auspice*, a synonym for *omen*, owes its origins to a Latin term meaning "observer of birds." Within actual bird auguries, not only the type of bird, but also how high it flew, the direction of flight, and whether or not the bird sang in the air were all considered.

In the Hopi culture, for example, the gift of a feather (specifically that of an owl) is a reminder of truth and honesty. The use of a quill in writing may have indicated the sacred responsibility given to those with the power of the written word.

Perhaps because of its ability to sail skyward, the bird is also affiliated with the movement of human souls. Euripides called birds God's heralds, giving them an additional affiliation with communication.

Many mythological heroes have a bird as a companion and guide. A notable contemporary example of this is the movie *LadyHawk*. The protagonist of this story has a beloved hawk companion who watches out for his welfare. Thus, if you see hawks when traveling, regard them as protective spirits (see "Hawk" listed below).

Folk medicine included birds in its healing methods. Nearly every part had some function: feathers, when burnt, were thought to aid sickness caused by bewitching, and the head of a bird wrapped in deerskin could cure headaches.

The popularity of birds as omens did not really begin to decrease until after the advent of the industrial revolution. Even in the early 1900s, superstition held that if you were to see a bluebird in spring it foretold joy, and that a red bird meant company was soon to arrive.

Today, bird feathers (as long as they are not from an endangered bird) may be used to move incense around the sacred space, decorate various magical tools, and for auric cleansing. For the latter, choose a large feather and gently stroke it through your natural energy field, moving from your skin outward. As you do this, envision tension and sickness being brushed away, even as you might sweep a floor. Visualizations incorporating birds are useful in magic where you wish to move something into or out of your life. In both instances, the bird or feather should be appropriate to the circumstances. A crow feather might be used in rituals or spells where you are desirous of news from a friend or a decision on a specific project, for example.

I also highly recommend the images of birds or feathers for the eastern point of your altar (Air element), or for any magic pertaining to releasing burdens so they can literally fly away. In the latter instance, a bluebird for happiness or the phoenix for miraculous transformation, would be fitting.

One really lovely accent for your home can be made with collected feathers, a few beads, a lace doily, dried flowers, and a small hat form. I call this a Victorian dream catcher—a variation on the traditional Native American dream catcher made of sinew.

A dream catcher looks similar to an encircled spider web, and sometimes has small crystals woven in and feathers hanging from an edge. It snatches messages and visions from the dream time when hung over the bed and helps us retain them. The feathers on the dream catcher symbolize the free movement of our spirit through this realm.

For this specific dream catcher, a hat form can be purchased for as little as 39 cents in craft supply centers, and even certain discount variety shops. Glue a lace doily on top. Draw a ribbon through the lace so that it secures at the base of the hat from which you can hang your feathers, beads, or any other items you desire. By gluing some flowers or placing an old pin into the arrangement, you can further personalize what will be both a beautiful and functional decoration.

Anka

This is a mythic Arctic bird of enormous proportions, believed to be large enough to carry off cattle. The anka lived 1,700 years, renewing itself like the phoenix through fire. Muhammad believed God created these at the time of Moses. They are similar in appearance to the Arabic *roc*, Hindu *garuda* and Persian *simurgh*.

For magic, visualize the anka carrying you to safety in times of need. Attach your troubles or bad habits to its wings and watch them move away from you.

Aspares

From Hindu mythology, these beautiful water nymphs can transform themselves into waterfowl at will. According to lore, they are the spirits of valiant warriors. As such, ducks, geese, and other water birds make excellent protective imagery and spiritual companions for safety.

Bucoros

A combination rhinoceros and bird, this creature is depicted on homes in Borneo as a bringer of luck. For this purpose the beak of the bird must always face one's enemy. The people of this region also carve the head of the bucoros on magical staffs used in imitative dance.

Chicken

Roman armies used to take chickens with them into battle, paying special attention to their behavior before a specific campaign. Based on this, chicken feathers can be hung from a magical staff or carried in a medicine pouch as a charm against danger.

The other, and most widely known, association for the chicken has less to do with the bird and more to do with its medicinal value. Chicken broth has traditionally been used as a remedy for colds and flus. If you are vegetarian, visualize warm golden broth filling you in light form to effect a similar result.

Crane

In China, the crane is thought to live for one thousand years, and its image is embroidered on the eldest family member's robe to insure his or her longevity. In Japan, the crane is not only the emblem of the royal house, but also indicative of health and fidelity. Cranes are regularly seen in a variety of forms at Japanese wedding ceremonies.

Egyptian legend tells us that a crane hatched an egg giving the earth its atmosphere. Another Middle Eastern tale indicates that Hermes was inspired to create writing after watching a flock of these birds. Since that time, the lettering he invented was only to be used for sacred purposes. Thus, runic work may attribute its early magical associations with this story.

With this in mind, depictions of the crane would make an excellent addition to any magical writer's home. Other ways to employ the Eastern symbolism of this gracious bird would be to visualize the crane rising towards the sun, taking your sickness on its wings and leaving you to rest in the warm resplendence.

Crow

In Tibet, crows are a type of messenger. What they deliver depends not only on how many there are, but also on the direction they fly, whether they land, and so on. To these people, the crow is an emissary from the gods that can communicate important messages to us. To discern their messages, observation is required. In one unusual form of divination, the querist would go out and voice his question to the winds. If he heard  the cry of a crow from the southeast it meant an enemy was coming. From the south, it meant a visit from a friend; from the west meant a great wind was soon to come; and from the southwest it was a sign of unexpected profit. In all cases, the time, direction, place and sometimes intensity of the cry were important in the divinatory interpretation.

Also included in Tibetan texts were ways to interpret crows while journeying or if encountered in the nest. Thus, a crow feather is a good token to carry with you before traveling abroad, or when you are waiting for answers to specific situations.

Cuckoo

The cuckoo is a welcomed sign of spring. Sussex legend has it that on April 14, many years ago, an old woman, out of kindness, released several of the cuckoos whom she tended. Since then, it has been fortunate to hear the cuckoo on April 14 if you have change in your pocket. It means you will have a prosperous year thanks to that woman's generosity.

Since the cuckoo only stays for a short while, the English thought they changed into sparrowhawks when winter's chill arrived. Hindu mythology portrays them as having magical traits such as foreknowledge. In Greece they are a symbol of wedlock, because Zeus turned into a cuckoo when he pursued Hera to win her love. For modern witchcraft, the symbolism of the cuckoo can be applied for personal transformation, developing second sight, and benevolence.

Dove

Because of its white coloring, the dove
became a symbol of peace and love, as well
as a symbol for the Goddesses Venus,
Aphrodite, and Astarte. Ancient
Egyptians released doves to the four
winds at special celebrations to carry good
news to the country and the Gods. People so
widely esteem doves there that they appear in
portraits of the tree of life, like a special fruit, to inspire faithfulness.

The Oracle at Dodona, the oldest oracle founded by Zeus, was a
dove who lived in an oak tree, and related its messages. According to
Strabo the messages came in the form of movement by the birds or the
subsequent rustling of leaves in the trees.

Psalm 55:6 portrays the dove as a symbol of freedom, rest, simplicity, and constancy. Perhaps this is why a dove came to Noah bearing an
olive. It announced God's peaceful intentions and the hope of land
ahead. Later, in the New Testament, doves became the embodiment of
the Holy Spirit, a healing, gentle power.

The image of a dove would work well in meditations for getting past
blockage, easing hardship, and improving inner accord.

Eagle

Many traditions, including Egyptian and Zoroastrian, depict the Sun God as an eagle, or as a
disk with the extended wings of an eagle. This
may owe its origins to an ancient belief that
eagles can stare directly at the sun without blinking. Eagles are also sacred to Jupiter/Zeus and
considered bearers of luck. Virgil called eagles
God's weapon-bearer. This may pertain to the
many portraits of an eagle with a lightning
bolt in its talon. This symbol returns again to
their being under Jupiter's or Zeus' dominion.
For this reason, Romans referred to eagles as
storm-bringers.

In Imperial Rome, rulers adopted the eagle as an emblem of their authority and power. When an emperor died, the attending priest released an eagle to symbolize his soul rising to the next life.

The Navaho regard this as the wisest and most powerful creature, the symbol of their highest ideal, and the protector of their villages. The eagle's power of protection was later translated into the eagle being the national bird for the United States. To this day, the eagle's image appears on American currency, homes, mailboxes, and many other items, as if the portrait itself somehow invokes that shielding power.

Feathers

The Greeks and many other cultures used feathers as a type of miscellaneous omen. Their system was based not only on the feather and type of bird it came from, but also the position in which the feather was found and its color. If you happen to find a feather, try using the list below to see what it predicts for you (remember to wash your hands carefully after handling a feather you find as it may carry disease:

- ◆ Red: good fortune.
- ◆ Black: death or bad news.
- ◆ Orange: promise of delight.
- ◆ Black and white: trouble averted.
- ◆ Green and black: fame and fortune.
- ◆ Yellow: false friends, be wary.

- ◆ Brown and white: joy.
- ◆ Green: adventure.
- ◆ Gray and white: a wish comes true.
- ◆ Blue: love.
- ◆ Gray: peace.
- ◆ Blue-white and black: new love.
- ◆ Brown: good health.
- ◆ Purple: exciting trip.

Goose

Romans considered the cackling of geese to be a warning of impending raids or other dangers. As such the goose is suitable for any protective magic. Use the goose down from pillows or comforters as part of protective charms, amulets, or incense.

Ovid called the goose "wise." In Greece this bird was a household protector and kept as a pet because of its association with Hera, the Queen of Heaven.

Geese were sacred to Juno. In Egyptian mythology it was Gengen Wer, a goose god, who produced the cosmic egg and birthed the universe. Amun was sometimes known to appear in this form, to accentuate his power as a creator. These tales reveal the goose as an emblem of invention and new beginnings.

Hawk

In the Egyptian pantheon, Ra was sometimes depicted as hawk-headed. In Greece and Rome the bird's speed connected it with Apollo and Mercury as a messenger of divine information. Similarly, in India a hawk brought *soma* from heaven. Soma was a divine beverage which was so healthy it could bestow immortality.

Use the hawk when you need to rise above present circumstances and gain insight, or move swiftly with sharp vision.

Hummingbird

The feathers of a hummingbird when given to another comprise an ancient love charm. This is because of the unusual way the creature collects nectar from flowers, using its long beak. In similar manner, the feathers of the bird open the nectars of another's heart. Additionally, both American and Basque folklore tells us that hummingbirds never lie, allowing love to remain likewise true.

Magpie

In Sweden this bird is a witch who has important errands to attend to quickly. In other areas of Europe, two magpies flying together are lucky; one alone is a warning.

In the East, the magpie is a bird of joy and fortune, especially if you hear it chatter. This portends good news. Conversely, in the West a talking magpie signifies trouble between husband and wife. To avert this, you can spit at the bird or carry an onion in your pocket.

For magic, the image of the magpie is best employed for swift, but cautious decisions, or in visualizations where you need to forewarn someone, unreachable by other means, against coming difficulties.

Owl

Images of Athena, the Goddess of Wisdom, show her with an owl for a companion. Because of this, the owl has strong associations with sagacity and as a messenger from the Gods. Sacred to Demeter in Greek myth, the owl is also a prophetic creature.

Hopi folklore claims that if you give someone an owl feather, they will be unable to lie to themselves. Thus this plumage makes an excellent addition to your medicine pouch to keep yourself honest.

Navaho tradition tells us that if an owl hoots three times within your hearing, or flies near you, it is a sign to check your behavior and motivation.

Peacock

Arabic legends tell us that the peacock allowed the devil to enter the Garden of Eden. Since that day, he has been given the task of warning all descendants of Adam to take shelter when storms approach. Hence, to this day the harsh cry of the peacock foretells rain, and peacock feathers can be used beneficially in rain-related or safety spells.

On a more positive note, Ovid calls the peacock a bird who carries the stars in its tail. From this, the beautiful creature obtained the symbolism of immortality. In Persia, it represents royalty; in the Far East it portrays dignity and authority. Buddhism credits them with compassion.

Phoenix

This legendary firebird may owe its origins to the Egyptian *bennu*, or bird of the sun. This creature was worshiped at Heliopolis, where it rose from the ashes of a great conflagration. It was also strongly associated with Ra (the Sun God). In Australian aboriginal myth, the kestrel also rose from the ashes of a bush fire to protect warrior spirits.

Asians believe the phoenix is so ancient and long-lived that it witnessed the creation of the universe. Exactly how long the it stays alive is debatable. Albertus says it is 350 years, while the Talmud places the life span closer to one thousand years. Because the phoenix makes a nest of incense and flames to prepare for its death, and then rises from them with reborn youth, the modern symbolism of the phoenix is one of miracles and resurrection. To be rejuvenated, the phoenix must immerse itself in flame. This imagery in visualization is very potent during times when your personal energy is lacking or when you feel you need a totally clean start.

Raven

A raven met before battle portended a victory. Ravens also were believed to guide travelers, especially sailors, to their destination. This may have been because of the large bird's natural tendency to head toward land.

Norse and Germanic texts show that much credence was given to understanding the language of the birds, especially the raven, and using them for counsel. This particular perspective is even reflected in their language: the Nordic term *gauldra*, which means chanting or spells, is also applied to the cry of birds.

It is believed that if all ravens leave an area suddenly it is a sign that draught or famine is soon to follow.

For personal magic, allow the raven to be a spirit guide in your dreams, a protector and a strong link to the natural world. Through this bird, the ancient understanding of winged creatures and perhaps even of other animals, may eventually be reclaimed through patient meditation and ritual.

Robin

In England, when a robin pecks on a window, it means that an unborn soul is about to be conceived by someone inside. There is also a charming story about how the robin, out of compassion, once a day tries to take a beak full of water to quench the fires of hell. In the process he singes his feathers and hence bears a red breast. This allusion can be utilized in any magic pertaining to compassion and fertility.

Rooster

Sacred to Apollo, the Sun God, the rooster has the privilege and responsibility of announcing the dawn and commanding the return of any shadows to the Underworld. A rooster's feather is a good charm to carry when you need the phantoms in your life to flee or for use in spells pertaining to the illumination of a perplexing matter.

Stork

Egyptians believed storks cared for their elderly, making them an emblem of filial responsibility. They also revered the stork as a lawgiver.

Greek mysteries portrayed the stork as the great Mother Goddess, filled with nurturing, devotion, and loyalty. It is from this image that our modern myth of the stork bringing children into the world originated.

Use the stork in rites of Eldership and Croning to show your respect to those who have walked the Path for many years. In other magic, consider it an emblem of the Mother aspect of the Goddess, who cares tenaciously for Her young.

Swan

The swan was dedicated to Apollo, who also happened to be the God of music. It was long believed that when swans died, they sang a special song to Him. Thus it was that the term *swan song* came into use to indicate a final farewell.

Ancient Norse legend tells us that the thirteen maids of Odin (also the number of lunar months) took the forms of swans. Combined with the white color of the bird, this gives it a strong association with the moon and lunar magic.

I have also always held a personal fondness for the story of the ugly duckling and the small bird's transformation into a beautiful swan. This tale reminds us of many important lessons pertaining to inner beauty, self-confidence, and the amazing transformations which can occur if we are patient and trust in our hearts.

White Bird

Among Indonesian natives, when a tribal member is in trouble they use a great drum to call on their ancestors for aid. The spirit arrives in the form of a white bird, and if the petitioner's motives are good, it will leave through a different window to set about its task. For magic, the symbolism of a white feather thrown to the winds as a plea for help, or to indicate the presence of a ghost, might be an appropriate substitute.

Wren

Long believed to be the wife of the robin, the wren was a sacred bird to the Druids. Wren feathers are a traditional charm against drowning. A contemporary use might be to carry one in your car to prevent accidents.

4 BODY DIVINATION

A solemn air, and the best comforter to an unsettled fancy.
♦ Shakespeare, *The Tempest* ♦

ONE OF the most interesting areas of folklore is the use of physical features to determine personality traits. Just as the behaviors of different animals were interpreted as omens, scrutiny of bodily idiosyncrasies, quirks, and other physical characteristics was thought to expose an individual's demeanor and his or her future.

This science was known as physiognomy. The Greeks relied upon this system to determine a person's fitness for public office. It is probably because of this tradition that we now look for a person's character in his or her face.

For adept physiognomists, this was not a simple science. They considered everything about their patients, including the shape of the nose, personal carriage, age, sex, any resemblance to animals, etc. Final determinations came after making these observations.

Handwriting analysis is sometimes used today by businesspeople and police. However, like any form of divination, it should be noted that the exterior signs are only one part of the overall reading. When combined with keen intuitive sense, physiognomy can be very accurate. I think that for the most part it should be looked at for entertainment value instead of a "carved in stone" interpretation of qualities or future potentials.

Eyebrows

Eyebrows which meet across the nose are signs of a brooding character. In Iceland, Germany, and Greece, they were considered the mark of a shape shifter.

In Scotland, eyebrows which lay close together on the face are a sign of a lucky individual.

Eyes

A person with two differently colored eyes, deeply set eyes, or closely set eyes, was considered likely to administer the evil eye (see Chapter 18: Magic and the Supernatural).

In *Daemonologie* by Nitomes, and in Shakespeare's *Othello*, the itching of an eye portends specific things. If the right eye itches, it means sadness, while and itchy left eye indicates joy. In some rural English folklore, however, this symbolism is reversed. The change may have to do with the general misgivings about the left side of the body

In his *Natural History,* Pliny says that anyone with two pupils in one eye is surely a sorcerer. Gypsies regard squinting eyes as a sign of evil.

Feet

Anyone born with an extra toe was considered very lucky. Flat feet, however, were a sign of poor fortune. Children born feet first were thought to have special healing gifts, especially with sprains. In Scotland it is bad luck to meet someone with flat feet when you're going fishing or on a Monday morning.

Finger

If an individual's second finger was longer than the first it was a sign of dishonesty. Extra fingers, as with toes, were a token of luck. Crooked fingers spoke of a crabby temperament, and large half moons on the fingernails were a mark of longevity.

If spots suddenly appeared on a thumbnail, it was thought to betoken a gift soon to come, and on the forefinger, the arrival of a friend. Yorkshire lore claims that the number of times your fingers crack when pulled equals the number of sweethearts you will have in your life.

Hands/Palmistry

Palmistry is based on the belief that hands hold the secrets to the true self. It has been practiced for around five thousand years. Greek classical literature has hundreds of references to hand divination, as does an untitled German treatise on the subject printed in 1448 by Hartlieb. In all three settings, students of the hand placed great importance on the shape of the limb and its thumb, which was purported to indicate willpower. Since many of the older sources of information on the origins of this art have been lost, much of what we now consider palmistry comes from its resurgence in the late 1800s.

Palmistry over tea was a very common sight during the Victorian era. As a matter of fact, it was so popular that in 1889 the English Chirological Society was founded to bring the study of the hand to a scientific level, to promote palmistry, and to try to protect the public from flim-flam artists.

According to a popular book entitled *Complete Book of Fortune* (Crescent Books, 1936), resilience of the skin is a sign of potency, energy and adaptation. An accomplished reader would next examines the shape of hand and the fingers. Broad hands versus long tend to be people of strength rather than breeding. Pointed fingertips seem to occur on artists, tapering fingers on excessive personalities, and round or flat fingers are generally found on people who consider themselves nature-lovers.

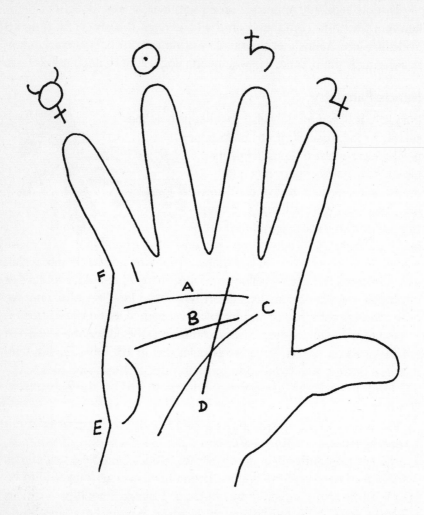

Palmistry chart

A. Heart line   D. Fate line

B. Head line   E. Intuition line

C. Life line   F. Children

Other things to look for in reading palms:

♦ Knotted hands—a mind for ideology.
♦ Smooth fingers—an individual of insight and inspiration.
♦ Long center bone in thumb—rationality.
♦ Short top bone in thumb—lack of resolution.
♦ Square hands—sensibility.
♦ Long tapering fingers—an aesthetic and creative temperment.
♦ Long hands and fingers—sensitivity and naiveté.
♦ Life line high on the hand—zealousness.
♦ Life line circling into palm—benevolence.
♦ Broken head line—frequent sickness.
♦ Head and heart line join—spontaneous, unpredictable nature.
♦ Heart line crossing palm entirely—emotionalism.
♦ Short heart line—unsuccessful relationships.
♦ Full fate line—achievement, charming demeanor.
♦ Fate line stopped at head line—hindrances to success.

Handwriting (Graphology)

Graphology is the study of handwriting. It is a complex task; the adept graphologist studies everything, including the size, shape, and texture of the subject's hands.

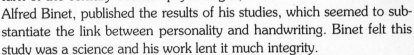

More popular in Europe than in the United States, by 1906, a well-known turn-of-the-century French psychologist, Alfred Binet, published the results of his studies, which seemed to substantiate the link between personality and handwriting. Binet felt this study was a science and his work lent it much integrity.

Should you desire to look at someone's handwriting to see how accurate the interpretations are, here are a few things to look for.

- ◆ Level direction of written lines—composed behavior.
- ◆ Right sloping lines—person full of life.
- ◆ Downward slope—lethargy and lack of motivation.
- ◆ Upward slope to excess—imprudence.
- ◆ Signature slanted up—aspirations which lead to success.
- ◆ Letters in words upright—inner fortitude.
- ◆ Letters slant right—gentle kindness.
- ◆ Letters slant left—respectful demeanor.
- ◆ Small lettering—inquisitiveness.
- ◆ Medium lettering—forthright approaches.
- ◆ Fine handwriting lines—discretion.
- ◆ Large lettering—punctual.
- ◆ Connecting lines which hook—tenacity.
- ◆ Connecting lines which dash—determination.
- ◆ Large well-formed capitals—self-respect.
- ◆ Printed capitals—reserve.
- ◆ Exaggerated capitals—love of formality.
- ◆ Capital separate from word—laid-back person, relaxed.
- ◆ Capital connected to word—sensibility.
- ◆ Rounded letters—loving.

While most of the characteristics noted in this chapter are ones genetics alone can predispose, handwriting analysis may offer an avenue for mystical applications. In any spell where there is a written wish or component involved, you can try forming your letters using the guide above, according to the goal of the magic. If you are performing a rite to help improve your self-esteem, use large, well-formed capitals, all of which connect to each other to encourage the attributes of respect and reasonableness.

Another application might be through doodling. Since both ink and writing have been used for divination-related arts, you could close your eyes and sketch randomly while focusing on a question. When you feel finished, review the drawing for significant symbols and images, and interpret accordingly.

Moles

Divination by moles was practiced by the ancient Greeks, but did not become popular again until the late 1700s. Even so, Greek writings on this subject acted as a foundation for all that would follow.

Generally, the potency of the influence of the mole was based on its size, shape, and color. Round moles of light coloration and good size were all good luck. Next in consideration was placement. A mole on a man's forehead is a sign of happiness, and for a woman it predicts power. Close to the eyebrow of a man or woman, a mole predicts a joyful marriage. When on the bridge of the nose, they portend extravagance; on the nose, a sign of travel; and on the lips a mole betrays gluttony. Other associated personality traits are as follows:

- Round—kind heart, positive spirit.
- Angular—a dichotomy of personality.
- Oblong—material prosperity.
- Light colored—a sign of good fortune to come.
- Black coloration—trials before success.
- Belly—self indulgence or gluttony.
- Buttocks—lack of ambition, laziness or poverty.
- Chin—great character and personality, many good qualities, possible wealth.
- Finger—tendency toward embellishment and lies.
- Forehead—mental power.
- Foot—a wanderer, or much travel.
- Front of throat—good luck.
- Ear and neck—good providence.
- Lip—eloquent speech.
- Shoulders—unhappiness, unsettled nature.
- Chest—meagerness.
- Hands—productivity, especially in regards to bearing young, also artistic talent.
- Ankle—on a woman a sign of fortitude.
- Under right arm—attentiveness.

- Back—beware of hidden secrets.
- Navel—yearning for children.
- Wrist—economical and cunning, lively mind.
- Left knee or hand—many children to come.

To these (and even more detailed descriptions which existed), some people added whether the mole appeared on the left or right side of the body, the right being more favorable. Further exactness was given by ascribing signs of the zodiac to positions of moles appearing on the face, the attributes of which were then used in the reading and/or prediction.

The greatest advantage to this type of system is the fact that anyone can enjoy attempting it from a distance, then see how accurate the folk-beliefs are!

Phrenology

Phrenology, the study of bumps on the head, was first developed by Franz Joseph Gall in Italy around 1796. In 1832, a young student named Orson Fowler became fascinated with this new science. He and his brother, Lorenzo, took their studies on the road, creating quite a public interest in this new and unique activity. They were so successful that by 1836 they were able to open a New York office, where they also operated a museum and produced the monthly *American Phrenological Journal*.

While their magazine centered mostly on phrenology, it also focused on psychology, science, home education, and agriculture. By 1842, they started to teach hopeful phrenologists at their school, slowly developing a special phrenological chart that identified how the human head could be representative of certain emotional predispositions.

Today, though, phrenology is considered less a science and more an amusing anecdote on the pages of American history.

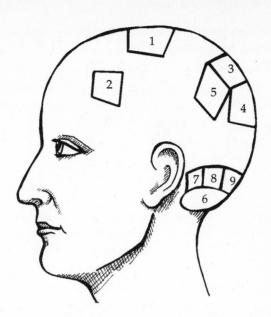

Simple Chart Key

1. If this area is well-evolved it portends beneficence, consideration and goodwill. If overdeveloped, it warns of a tendency to worry so much about others that personal welfare is overlooked.

2. Joy and general good humor are indicated in this region. This person is very pleasant and has the capacity to laugh at his or her difficulties. If the area is overdeveloped, the individual is probably the proverbial class clown, and is rarely taken as sincere by those in close association. Conversely, if the area is undercultivated, a very serious nature is indicated.

3. This area is associated with concentration and the ability to reason. If large, it is an indication of bullheadedness; if the area is underdeveloped the individual is wishy-washy and rarely can make a decision without being swayed by others' opinions.

4. This region corresponds to a developed sense of self and knowledge of one's own worth. When tending towards the large side, it is a sign of egotism and false pride. Underde-

veloped, this person has a bad self-image and is dubious about his or her own potential.

5. This is the responsibility center. When large, obligations always take priority, even over the needs of self. Underdeveloped, it may signify a person who is undependable and disinclined to be accountable for anything.

6. This represents love. If overdeveloped, the individual is unrealistically sentimental and frequently wears rose-colored glasses. If underdeveloped, it may warn of a person who finds relationships and trust very difficult.

7. This area governs fortitude. If large, it indicates courage without focus or vision of the possible aftermath. Where this area is lacking, it shows a timid personality who is afraid of anything other than absolute security.

8. This region corresponds with yearning for marriage or serious relationships. An overdeveloped area means an impractical search for the perfect mate, often tainted by jealousy and selfishness. Underdeveloped indicates a person who is more hermetic in nature, and perfectly happy alone in the wilderness.

9. This shows the love of youngsters. An overdevelopment in this area may indicate a person with too many children who are undisciplined, while the underdeveloped may remain without children by choice.

5 CELESTIAL OBJECTS

Thou lingering star, with lessening rays
that lovest to greet the early morn.
♦ Robert Burns, *To Mary in Heaven* ♦

IN THE early years of human existence, celestial occurrences amazed us. When the sun rose, there was warmth and light with which to hunt; come nightfall, darkness snatched this security away. When a great streak of light fell through the sky, a storm followed. Simple observations like these led to animistic ideas about celestial bodies.

So much was this the case that the sun, moon and stars gained divine attributes. Eos was the Goddess of Dawn, Selene the Goddess of the Moon, and Aeolus the Wind God in Greece. Amaterasu was the beneficent Sun Goddess in Japan. In Hindu tradition, Agni controls rain and lightning, while in Rome the Goddess Luna controlled the lunar sphere.

The best-known philosophers of the greatest civilizations have all pondered the meaning of heavenly objects. Plotinus, in the *Enneads*, explained that everything is connected with celestial bodies in a web of living inspiration. This included magic and prayer working together to send specific signals over the network, thereby achieving results.

Astrology also played a role in the network, but was only one part of a greater picture. Many other natural occurrences taking place in the universe also grant insight and motivation. Astrology as a science, however, would develop closely on the heels of astronomy before having true popularity in its own right.

Astrology

In considering astrology among folkways, it is important to know that versions of this science occur all around the world. It most likely began as a road map for travelers in Babylonia.

In Arabic, an astrologer is called *murajjim*. It is not uncommon for the children of this culture to call upon a true star or lucky star for good fortune. Mesopotamian priests connected the sun, moon, and planets with divine visages, believing each represented orderly structures in the universe. The Greeks and Romans later substituted the names of their own gods and goddesses throughout this framework. In Rome, this model of the universe was called *mathesis* or "the learning." The Mesopotamian methods also moved to Egypt, Syria, and India. By 300 B.C. the Babylonians divided their charts into twelve houses, and the Egyptians followed suit.

Aristotle supplied some principle philosophies for this art during his life by speaking of heavenly bodies as being responsible for, or promoting actions on, Earth. The Divine Spirit used the heavenly bodies as a way to influence things below. Aristotle was emulated by Egyptian astronomer Ptolemy (2 A.D.). While Ptolemy's theories did not gain wide acceptance until the sixteenth century, his *Tetrabiblos* details how celestial objects can affect life in complex ways. This power was not considered absolute, however.

Until this time, the more popular superstitions regarding celestial objects centered around the moon (the most easily seen and night object) and its phases. This heavenly guidepost was consulted for everything from hair-cutting to planting cycles. This tradition continued into the early 1900s in the United States (see Chapter 12: Gardening and Farming).

The arrival of serious natal astrology came much later. Certain writings, dating to 5 B.C., contain bits of information on the natal influences, but these are not referred to until a Greek astronomer, Eudoxus, in the fourth century A.D., reintroduced the concept. At this point it was not taken very seriously. Books on customary astrology, however, were quickly being circulated throughout the Roman world.

The stoic philosophy of astrology believed that this, and other divination techniques, fit into the network of life, being joined by sympathetic bonds. Posidonius further supported this idea by linking moon phases with the movements of the sea. In Greece, Ptolemy hypothesized that heavenly bodies near to us would have abundant influence on our lives. These ideas have remained ever since.

As late as 1930, French farmers often harvested by the waning moon and planted with the new moon to stay in harmony with celestial motion and rhythm. In the early 1900's that the very first daily astrological column was printed in an English newspaper. Now astrology is a popular pastime, even for those who do not believe in the magical influence of the stars.

While a detailed study of astrology would be too cumbersome for this book, people interested in working with the appropriate signs to enhance magic should seriously consider getting a few books on the subject. One excellent guide for lunar work, *The Moon Sign Book,* is available through Llewellyn Publications on an annual basis.

Astrological Signs

As spoken of above, the heavens were divided into a kind of map for early civilizations to travel, plant, and harvest by. More than that, however, was the feeling that the celestial bodies played a key role in defining the rhythms of life on the Earth below.

While what we know now as natal astrology is relatively young branch of the original science, it has become one of the most popular forms of divination. Professional readers with a keen knowledge of the stars, and planets, create charts that are sometimes amazingly accurate. Generalized readings can often be found in the daily paper, but because one particular sign covers a full moon cycle, these cannot be considered precise on an individual level.

It is interesting, just for curiosity's sake, to read the temperaments associated with each sign to see how accurate they are. During your examination, remember that those born close to a change in the zodiac are considered to experience at least some overflow from the previous or coming sign. These traits can be translated into magical use by working spells for courage during Aries, for example, or inscribing the symbol of Cancer on a pink candle when performing a rite to improve romance in your relationships.

The emblems can also be combined. An artist with a creative block might try a special ritual held during Gemini in which they write the image (in star or emblematic fashion) of Pisces on the top of their artistic medium to encourage versatility and imagination.

Astrological Sign Chart

Sign	Symbol	Associations
Aries 3/22-4/21	♈	Fire, positive, courage, spirit, leadership skills, aptitude.
Taurus 4/22-5/21	♉	Earth, poetic, love of beauty and nature, common sense.
Gemini 5/22-6/21	♊	Air, versatility, intelligence, divided attentions or interests.
Cancer 6/22-7/21	♋	Water, timid, tenacious, sensitive, romance, endurance.
Leo 7/22-8/21	♌	Fire, ardent, loyal, courageous, dignity, bravery.
Virgo 8/22-9/21	♍	Earth, discriminating, calm, practical.
Libra 9/22-10/21	♎	Air, balance, justice, harmony, decisions, perspective.
Scorpio 10/22-11/21	♏	Fire, contradictions, magnetism, energy, intense emotion.
Sagittarius 11/22-12/21	♐	Fire, frankness, sincerity, will power, optimism, tolerance, equity.
Capricorn 21/22-1/21	♑	Earth, patience, persistence, hard work, self denial, objective.
Aquarius 1/22-2/21	♒	Air, idealistic, generosity, humane, empathic.
Pisces 2/22-3/21	♓	Water, rich imagination, vision, romance, quiet persistence, endurance, compassion.

Aurora Borealis

Individuals with a gift for seeing auras say that the aurora borealis (also known as the northern lights) closely resembles the energy given off by the human body. While science tells us that the actual cause for the aurora has to do with stellar radiation interacting with the earth's atmosphere, on a spiritual level this beautiful exhibit might be likened to the earth's auric field in full display. These lights also appear over the South Pole, where they are called aurora australis

The Inuit explain these beams of color as dancing spirits, full of joy. Thus, to see them in this form is good luck.

In northern England and certain Arctic regions, a deep red aurora is said to portend war, famine, or the death of a great hero. Some people were so afraid of the display that they would not venture out until it was over.

Constellations

In addition to acting as markers on ancient road map, figures of certain constellations appeared in the architecture, jewelry, and art of civilizations dating as far back as ancient Egypt. This was done to encourage good fortune based on the myths of how the constellations came into being (see "Astrological Signs" listed above).

For example, Orion was the son of Neptune and a skilled hunter. Diana wished to marry Orion, but her brother did not approve. So, one day when he was in the sea, Diana's brother pointed out a dark spot in the waters, challenging her adept skills with the bow. The spot was Orion's head. In her grief, Diana placed Orion in the heavens where he could hunt for eternity. Thus, an image of Orion can become the focus for magic concerning observational skills and personal searches (symbolized by the hunt). If depicted with Diana, the couple symbolize love.

Another illustration comes from the story of the Pleiades. These were the seven beautiful daughters of Atlas. When Orion amorously pursued them, they prayed to Jupiter to change their form for protection. He first turned them into pigeons, and later allowed them to fly into the heavens, becoming constellations. A sketch of the Pleiades is a fitting accent for spells of safety or in thwarting undesired romantic advances.

Below is an abbreviated list of some of these constellations and how they were interpreted and/or used. Today, similar artistic efforts might

be attempted to decorate altars as a focus for certain spells or to adorn the home.

♦ Ursa Major, Ursa Minor, and Draco combined into jewelry or carvings in the home would render the user watchful, flexible, and strong.

♦ Hercules symbolized victory, especially in battle.

♦ Cygnus the swan represented all functions of the mind, improved monetary position, and aided in curing fevers.

♦ Andromeda was a symbol for protection from disease, and reconciliation of marriages.

♦ Aquilla the eagle symbolized protection of personal honor.

- Delphinus (the dolphin) showed good fortune in fishing (figurative or literal).
- Pegasus represented swift but alert decisions and movement.
- Orion protected you from your enemies.
- Centaurus maintained health and fertility.
- Hydra represented prudence and good fortune.

Eclipses

In Sanskrit writings, solar and lunar eclipses were believed to be caused by an ancient dragon so large its image hid the face of the sun or moon when it flew. For magic, an eclipse marks a very potent in-between phase when neither night nor day really exists. Since magic itself takes us beyond traditional space/reality constructs, working spells or rituals during an eclipse can increase their potency.

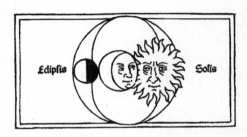

Falling Stars/Meteors/Comets

Falling stars are believed to portend the death of a great person, or the birth of another, and it is lucky to wish on them.

Pieces of meteors (moldivite and malachite) are often worn or carried by the contemporary magician to increase personal connection with universal energy.

Halley's Comet is a semi-regular visitor to our solar system, appearing approximately every seventy-five years. Its movements were discovered and predicted by E. Halley, an English astronomer living in the late 1600s. Comets were usually thought of as portending calamity. This idea may have easily evolved by happenstance considering that Halley's Comet appeared before the battle of Hastings, the demise of Herod, and while Queen Elizabeth took to her deathbed. However, there is conjecture that this may be the same object spoken of in the Bible as the Star of Bethlehem.

Moon

The belief in the moon's influence over human behavior is the source for the word *lunatic*. The word *luna*, is Latin, meaning the moon.

Modern medical research of mental illness does show a correlation between severity of the condition's symptoms and the full moon. The reason, however, remains a mystery.

In the Middle Ages, medicines were often administered according to moon phases. The symbolism of the moon's birth, growth, and decline was very powerful to these people; its continued use in modern magic, shows the impact strong these beliefs have had on our psychology. Many activities, such as sewing crops, waging war, marriage and even cutting hair (see Chapter 22: Personal Care and Chapter 12: Gardening and Farming), were frequently timed accordingly. It is well to note at this point that physicians only two to three hundred years ago might still have cast a horoscope for an ailing patient to try to determine a restorative.

In ancient Rome the worshippers of Diana would go to the temple at the first sighting of a crescent moon. Not to do so was considered irreverent. This slowly developed into the idea that a crescent moon first glimpsed as a reflection brought bad luck.

To see the moon over your right shoulder means you can make a wish. Turning your purse by the light of a crescent moon will double your money by the next crescent (twenty-eight days). It is not surprising to also discover that the moon is personified as Diana riding in a chariot, bearing a quiver, and followed by dogs.

Any of these superstitions may be tried and mixed with an incantation to test their validity. More important to the modern practitioner, though, are the lunar phases mentioned above. The waxing moon is commonly applied for magic involving growth and development; the full moon for fertility, productivity, and imagination; and the waning moon to banish, or turn away negative energy and bad habits.

Each month, on the first night after a full moon, the sun and moon will often appear together in the sky. This was long believed to be the best time to create any type of charm, and for enhancing the quality of balance in your life. In some months there will be an occurrence called a "blue moon," or two full moon cycles. The phrase "once in a blue moon" comes from this phenomenon, based mostly on timing, and is considered a very lucky lunar aspect as well as a powerful time for magic.

A person with the moon predominant in his or her astrological chart is said to be somewhat of a dreamer, religious and dualistic in nature.

North Star

The North Star has been associated with Ishtar and Venus. Since it is frequently the first star visible in northern climes, to wish upon it was actually a supplication for this Goddesses' favor in ancient times. Children and adults alike can still be seen outside as dusk falls, watching for that first sign of starlight to which they can whisper their desires.

Perseid Meteor Shower

On or near August 11, a large meteor shower lights up the sky with shimmering fire. Sometimes as many as sixty meteors an hour can be viewed. Every year since about 830 A.D. people have been able to observe this wonder in the constellation Perseus.

Count the number of meteors you see. As you do, focus your mind on a question. At the end of the shower, look up your final count on a list of numerological correspondences for its meaning. If the count is too large to be listed, add the digits together and use that number as the basis of your interpretation.

Perseus was the focus of several Greek legends. With Athene's help, Perseus killed the Medusa and created the Atlas Mountains. He also rescued Andromeda from a sea monster and made her his wife. Because of his great feats, he was made a constellation.

Planets

Tied in with astrology was the predominant belief that people born under a specific ruling planet would take on certain characteristics ascribed to that planet. In similar fashion, planetary movements guided planting and harvesting, as well as folk healing. Here are some of the qualities attributed to each (the modern planets, Neptune, Uranus, and Pluto are not included here):

Mercury—Associated with the swift messenger of the Gods, Mercury is personified as a young, slender man with winged feet, beard, and caduceus. This planet is associated with communication and knowledge. It is especially favored by merchants, who, possessing bothskills, can vastly increase their wealth. Individuals who have this planet predominant in their astrological readings usually have good memories and writing skills, but are often too dependent on other people's opinions for their sense of worth.

Mercury is an excellent planet for teachers or speakers to use to improve their effectiveness.

Mars—Personified, Mars is depicted with a banner and lance, mounted on a horse. Because of its strong association with the God of War (being the color of blood), Mars is a planet of victory. People born with Mars as a ruling planet tend towards valor and have a strong drive for success. It is the best sign to work under for illnesses pertaining to the blood, or blood mysteries (menstruation).

Jupiter—The medical profession's abbreviation *Rx* may have found its roots in the symbol for this planet, because Jupiter was long believed to protect medicine. It may have been carried or written as a charm to ensure success of the treatment. Magically, this symbol could well be used in any spell or ritual pertaining to healing. Personified, Jupiter appears as a seated individual, sometimes in a chariot holding a staff and a spear. The planet is frequently associated with personal honor and decorum. Most people born under Jupiter will be incredibly moral, but somewhat suspicious of other people's motivations.

ħ **Saturn**—Personified, Saturn is depicted as an elderly man with a beard holding a scythe. Saturn is a planet of power and energy. Individuals with Saturn as a ruling planet tend towards intense ponderings and contemplation. In magic, Saturn might best be used to improve the force or focus of any spell.

♀ **Venus**—Depicted as a beautiful woman with a dress and shawl, holding laurel in one hand, Venus is the planet of love, success, and protection from drowning. The personality traits governed by Venus are love of the arts, creativity, and difficulty in resisting temptation.

Besides the basic personality traits, you may use planetary symbols to create a unique set of runes, embroidery on various magical cloths, as signs for your magic circle, etc. as appropriate to your goals.

Sun

In early times, sun worship was natural. The glowing disk in the sky represented a welcome relief from the dangers of the darkness. Since it moved unaided and inexplicably through the sky, it became the emblem of a powerful spirit. We see this reflected in many solar associations for the ancient Gods', including Osiris in Egypt and Apollo in Greece.

In many northern regions, December 25 (or thereabouts) commemorates the birthday of the sun. This is when the long nights of winter begin to grow shorter. Thus, when Christianity came on the scene, it was natural to place Christ's birth on this date.

At the turn of the century, people considered the presence of the sun at special occasions a sign of God's approval. Because of this, many movements followed the direction of the sun (clockwise) to draw in divine favor. A Victorian lady wishing her bread to rise correctly would stir the ingredients clockwise! In contemporary magic, we continue to follow this belief by performing ritual dances sunwise. Reversing this direction is a means to banish or turn back unwanted energy.

Representations of the sun include a disk with rays (Egypt) and a man in a horse-drawn chariot (Greece). Such characterizations will aid in the success of the hunt and bring achievement. Additionally, in Egypt the morning sun symbolizes immortality. Depictions of it on amulets protected the bearer from all evil. Also, gold rings, because of their color and shape, are attributed powers similar to the sun.

Someone with the sun figuring significantly in his or her astrological spread will often be wise, noble, and giving and possess a strong sense of independence. When the sun and moon are seen in the sky on the fourteenth day of any month, it portends glad hearts and joyful times.

If you wish to draw solar qualities into your life, carry stones aligned with the sun. These include amber, opal, garnet, and gold pyrite (see Chapter 7: Crystals, Gems and Metals). Better yet, create a representation of the sun in splendor (shown on page 77) to carry with you so the light of day energizes your desires.

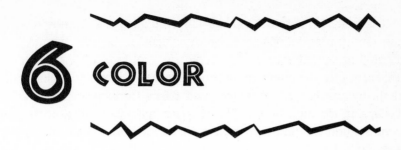

6 COLOR

My heart leaps up when I behold a rainbow in the sky.
♦ William Wordsworth, *My Heart Leaps Up* ♦

COLOR HAS the amazing ability to act on the unconscious mind. Many of our reactions have been bred into us over countless generations of living in a wild and harsh environment. Black, for example, usually brings with it a sense of fear or foreboding, because when the blackness of night came, early humans were most susceptible to the elements and predators.

Blue was a welcome, comforting color. When it filled the sky, blue signaled the end of the terrible darkness and offered light with which to hunt. Yellow was also a very pleasing color, as it represented warmth. Green was the pigment of many foods and thus associated with nourishment. These and other related color associations remain strongly ingrained in the human pysche.

This type of subconscious awareness is what scientists now refer to as ancestral instincts and codes. A common experience repeated again and again by early humanity, would become so much a part of staying alive that it was no longer thought about, but a natural part of daily routines. It was then taught to the children by example, making it natural for them too. There is some supposition today that such deep-seated responses have slowly been incorporated into human genetic structure over thousands of years of repetition.

So, when we consider the beliefs surrounding colors, most of which have strong associations with moods, places, or sounds, we must also realize that these folkways had some very real foundations in our own distant past. It was only natural for the growing, inquisitive mind to find creative ways to apply feelings about colors through myths, lore, and perhaps most important to the modern magician, religion. In most instances you will find that these feelings are very familiar to you and seem quite normal. This is because you, like your forebearers, have been taught through observation and direct experience to respond in certain ways to various hues.

Since these subconscious and conscious responses are second nature to us, color becomes a marvelous medium for magical work. Color symbolism can be applied in many ways, including:

♦ The candles, altar cloths, or robes we choose.

♦ The pigment of plants we incorporate in our incense.

♦ The tone of our ritual space decorations.

♦ Getting different-colored light bulbs for the four quarters or for special lighting during a specific ritual/spell.

♦ Choosing uniquely painted wall hangings (paper or cloth) or decorative rugs to accentuate the goals of your magic.

The idea here is to allow the subtle messages of the color(s) to improve the overall effect of the magical rites and hopefully have a little fun in the process.

Black

As the color of night, black represents foreboding, fortitude, and consistency because of the need to "make it through the darkness." In the Middle Ages, this color was also associated with Saturn, Saturday, the hog, and the number 8.

Black cats and hares were most frequently considered to be familiars, and a black ox was sacrificed in ancient Rome to satisfy Underworld gods.

In Madagascar, a black stone is placed in each of the four directions on top of a new grave to represent the power of the dead. In the British Isles there are stories of a black dog which is part fairy and part ghost, who, if seen, brings ill temper to the unfortunate individual gazing in his direction.

For magic, black is sometimes used as a protective color for magical tools. It is the most appropriate color to use when trying to banish a bad habit, turn negativity, or make drastic life changes.

Blue

Considered the color of wisdom, thoughtfulness, and celestial regions, blue's traditional day is Friday. Identified with Venus, the number 6, and natural sciences, a feeling of youthfulness fills this color.

Blue was a color sacred to the druids. On August 18 during the Eisteddfod celebration in old Wales, druids wishing to attain the office of Bard would wear green to the observances. The winners of the coveted title received permission to read to the gathering from a rune book, were blessed by a sword and presented with a knotted blue ribbon (see Chapter 16: Knots). From that point forward, the new bard joined the ranks of those so honored in Wales.

The God of the Jews commanded the Israelites to make the fringe on their garments blue (Numbers 15:38). Christian tradition associates blue with Mary. In Scotland, people don blue garments to restore circulation, and in northern Europe (circa 1600), a blue cloth was worn around the neck to avert sickness.

Blue is affiliated with the throat chakra and sign of Capricorn. If you want to know if someone is telling the truth, watch for blue in his or her aura.

The shade of blue can sometimes influence its deeper subconscious association (as is true of all colors). Sky blue tends to bring patience and tranquillity. It is aligned with the season of spring, and the sounds of wind chimes or bells. On the other hand, midnight blue is the color of dreams, aspirations, midnight, the season of winter, and sounds of celestial harmony, such as the instrumental arrangements often used in planetariums.

Asian cultures believed that wearing or carrying a blue item would avert the evil eye. In Eastern cultures, blue is called the auric envelope which contains and sustains life.

In contemporary magic, blue is an appropriate color for the western point of a sacred space. It is an excellent hue for peacefulness, and if used as paint for a meditation room, can help increase the individual's ability for profound reflection.

Gold

Gold represents the color of the sun, the astrological sign Leo, adolescence, joy, fruitfulness, and nobility. It has long been the most popular metal for a ruler's crown and other symbols of office in the belief that the energy of the sun belonged in the hands of the leader, chosen by God/dess.

Gold as a precious metal retained all the attributes of solar power. In England, rubbing it on the chest of a child was a common cure for colds. In the Middle Ages, healers prescribed water or liquors with gold leaf as remedies for eye sores and life-threatening illnesses (see Chapter 7: Crystals, Gems and Metals).

Associated with masculine energy, gold is used to connect with the attributes of strength, leadership, and vitality. In visualization, the image of the sun pouring golden rays into your skin for revitalization seems to work for many people. This impression is also useful when you need to refill the wells of strength by allowing gilded water to permeate your mind's eye. From there, the golden light pours into the fountain which is your inner being.

Green

Hope, joy, delight, growth, and change are all aspects of green. It is associated with the planet Mercury, Wednesday, the fox spirit, the number 5, the heart chakra, and the sign of Cancer.

Forest green is connected with fertility, the body, courage, and classical music or wilderness sounds. Ivy green represents the emotional aspects of humanity, coping with grief, cliffside ponderings, and hushed music or silence.

Many hospitals still use pale-green in patients' rooms, stemming from the ancient conviction that this color aids the healing process.

Spiritual healers claim that green is the best color of light to visualize as they work. Envision this healthful light flowing delicately down from above you, then through your arms and into the recipient. The color should be similar to the pale green you see on new shoots of grass and sparkle as if it were filled with dew. Keeping this firmly in mind, place your hands on (or for the sake of propriety, near) the afflicted area, and simply allow the warm energy to flow out.

When working with healing energy, make an extra effort to be sensitive to personal space and the individual's auric energy. The aura (usually located no more than a foot from the body) can give you many important clues to other physical problems the afflicted person may have. These signs include an itching in your palms, drastic changes in temperature, auric color, and/or spots which seem to have more or less auric field than the rest of the body. It will take time to recognize such differences, but as you become more conscious of them your aptitude in healing arts will improve dramatically.

Orange

The golden orange of Leo is located at the second (sexual) chakra. Orange is attuned to warmth, friendship, abundance, spirit, will, principles, theory, and alertness. It is associated with passionate music, the rustle of autumn leaves, and natural sounds at dusk or just after a storm.

Orange candles are good to use in rituals for kinship and prosperity, bearing the color of a fall harvest. They are also handy for any time when you are studying your magical arts, to help keep your mind attentive. If you don't have a candle handy, try a pale orange tablecloth, flower, etc.

Purple (Violet)

Considered the color of royalty, purple is associated with judgment, industry, religious thought, Jupiter, Thursday, the bull, the number 3 and old age. A color sometimes ascribed to the Crone along with black, purple is aligned to the crown chakra. It corresponds to the signs of Virgo, Sagittarius, and Gemini.

Violet is the color of spirit, etheric realms, higher esoteric learning, ancient wisdom, and mysteries. It is along the same vibration as many magical songs or other deeply spiritual musical pieces. It is the best color to have available any time you are working magic to improve your understanding of deeper mysteries.

Use violet as your focus specifically for spiritual centering and awareness in meditation. Begin by burning a purple candle or focusing your eyes on another object of similar color (a scrap of fabric will do). Try, as you concentrate, to feel the energy in that hue. Sense its texture and even a smell, if you can.

Next, close your eyes and visualize concentric circles of purple-white light moving towards your third eye. At first you may feel a little dizzy, but as the light settles, it will naturally move towards your center of gravity, helping to create profound symmetry.

You may experience "visions" or get spontaneous ideas while you meditate. Try not to be so surprised that you loose the images. Instead, relax and flow with them. Have a pen and paper handy to write them down immediately after you are finished. Many of these flashes of insight will prove very useful in the days ahead.

Red

Red is the power color. It is associated with command, Mars, Tuesday, pride, anger, the number 9, bravery, strong emotions. It is also sometimes attributed to divine love, Aries, Scorpio, and the base chakra.

Bright red is fire, inspiration, vitality, purification, arid places, aggressive music (especially drumming like a heartbeat), and storms which include lightning.

Faerie caps and magicians' hats were often described as being red, and ghosts were sometimes seen draped in red flannel. Red in folk medicine was used to treat rheumatism or fever. In some instances, herbs were wrapped in red cloth and tied to the head in the belief it would cure a headache.

Red was particularly obnoxious to evil spirits, so in China parents blessed red cloth and braided it into their children's hair or stitched it into their pockets. The English wear red rags at their neck to keep away the spirits that cause colds. In Japan, children afflicted with smallpox remain in a totally red room, clothed in scarlet to hasten healing.

Red is regarded as the best color to ward off danger. Wear a red robe during a spell or ritual for protection. Also use red when working spells to commune with the Fey, improve your personal energy levels, for any blood-mystery rites, or to enhance your motivation.

White

The color of purity, white represents friendship, the moon, infancy, the number 7. Japanese traditions consider it the color of mourning.

Crystal white is the color of sincerity, divinity, transformation, and singular focused sounds such as a gong or bell. You will notice that many ancient temples and churches were made of white marble or painted white wood.

White is also the color of the Goddess, so a white candle dedicated to Her on your altar is an excellent touch. Each time you light it, in some small way you are asking for Her blessing on your work.

Yellow

Another version of gold, yellow is frequently the color of friendship, goodness, and faith. Aligned with the solar plexus (third) chakra, yellow works well with the signs of Libra and Taurus, bringing a fresh congruity.

Golden yellow, specifically, is the color of charm, trust, summer, the beach, bright sounds such as children laughing, and upbeat music. Pastel yellow tends more towards spring, psychic endeavors, and creativity. It is the sound of a fresh breeze across the meadow. In China, magicians wrote their charms on yellow paper to improve their potency. Here, yellow was an imperial hue and was associated with the sun.

Yellow is one of the most popular colors today for in children's rooms and in nursery schools. For magic, it is a terrific pigment to improve balance, self-esteem, charisma, divinatory efforts, and creativity.

Planetary and Astrological Colors

Each planet and astrological sign is thought to be sympathetic with a particular color. It is considered best for your mood and luck to decorate your home with appropriate astrological colorations in some manner.

In most instances the corresponding color is fairly logical. To better accentuate the energy of a specific planetary or astrological sphere in magical rites, use these color associations for your altar cloth, candles, decorations, robes, etc.

At the time these associations came into popular usage, certain planets were, as yet, undiscovered. Thus Pluto, for example, does not appear herein. Also, some discrepancies appeared in associations when comparing sources. For your reference, the variations are included on the following page:

Planetary Colors

Sun: orange yellow   Moon: white
Mars: red   Mercury: light green
Venus: blue   Jupiter: purple
Saturn: black/dark blue

Astrological Colors

Aries: white   Libra: violet
Taurus: yellow   Scorpio: red brown
Gemini: red or purple   Sagittarius: orange or purple
Cancer: bright green   Capricorn: brown or blue
Leo: golden yellow or orange   Aquarius: dark blue
Virgo: pale blue or violet   Pisces: white or purple

To further complicate these correspondence, there are also colors considered most advantageous to wear on specific days of the week: Sunday is orange; Monday, white; Tuesday, red; Wednesday, green; Thursday, purple; Friday, blue; and Saturday, dark blue.

So how can you combine all this? If the moon sign is Aquarius, with Saturn somewhere in the picture and it happens to also be Saturday, all of your color sympathies are towards a deep blue to empower your magic. The more consistency you have, the stronger the influence can be. Since getting all these particulars to work together isn't always easy, especially in our nine-to-five world, consider combining colors to honor each planetary, astrological, and daily aspect.

7 CRYSTALS, GEMS, AND METALS

Thy heart alone is such a stone.
♦ George Herbert, *The Altar* ♦

PROBABLY FIRST attracted to crystals, gems, and metals because of their variety and resplendence, humanity has had an almost child-like wonder of them for millennia. Each stone and gem quickly accrued bits of lore that were used for the creation of amulets and talismans (see Chapter 1: Amulets and Talismans). Shells and seeds were for a long time considered in the same category as stones, and were frequently used in jewelry because of the good spirits abiding in them. Luminescent pieces, such as moonstone and sapphire, encouraged these animistic superstitions. The moving light shining from the heart of the stone lent this gem a life-like quality. Some of the earliest stone carvings take the rough form of a human body to induce the beneficent spirit to stay.

When Arabs swept through the Roman Empire in the seventh century, they learned the attributes for the crystals they found. This knowl-edge returned with them to the Middle East, was refined, then passed back to Europe during and after the Crusades. The stones placed in the tops of modern magical wands may be a modern development of the portrayal of the fairy godmother in some Arabic stories.

Crystals were employed during the Middle Ages for almost everything from protection, sleep, and pleasant dreams to fortunetelling and ending dissension. In some instances they were considered useful in the medical field as well. Paracelsus was a Swiss physician who first introduced the use of metals for medicine including lead, arsenic, iron, and mercury.

Up through the mid-1600s, it was firmly believed that stones could become ill, turning rough or pale especially if their owner was going to die. So strong was the sympathy between owner and object that some stories told of crystals fracturing in grief upon the death of their possessors. Thus the use of crystal amulets for men going to battle became common.

Part of the power of crystals was credited to their pigment and/or shapes. Red related to blood or passion; a yellow stone might be used in a treatment for jaundice. Some of the earliest magical formulas from Sumerian texts are careful to include gems in their instructions. Here, alabaster and dolomite figured predominantly, sometimes being carved into the form of an animal to enhance the crystal with attributes of that creature. These two stones were often used to protect the owner from the evil eye.

Greek lore as late as the nineteenth century suggests that much stone magic was done for sailors. Carbuncle and chalcedony, when put together, guard against drowning. Beryl kept the men aboard from being afraid, and coral was thought to keep a ship safe from wind or waves. Other magic with stones focused on longevity and health.

So powerful, it seems, were these crystalline spirits that they were actually believed to possess a life essence. In Borneo, you can still sometimes find a fisherman preserving every ninth pearl in a bottle with two grains of rice. The tradition was started with the notion that these pearls would help breed others, and the rice was food to help the process along.

The love for stones has recently been rekindled. Fostered by the New Age movement, there is a growing recognition that stone legends have an important level of truth to them. Many people now carry small pouches of stones to help improve daily activities while still others have one or two around the house for decoration and/or meditation.

Crystals may be employed for their color, shape or purported magical association as part of altar decorations, in jewelry, baths, gardening, and probably a hundred other activities, limited only by your imagination. The only word of caution is to remember that a crystal, gem, or metal only has latent energy. You are the enabler of that energy. In itself, a stone is merely a stone; you are the one who can give it that magical sparkle and special meaning for any occasion.

Agate

Eloquence, intelligence, and truthfulness are enhanced in those who carry an agate. It means special luck for people born under the sign of Gemini, and is used to bring good harvests to gardeners. Agate was predominantly a stone of love, victory, and strength during the Middle Ages. It was also thought to safeguard against lightning, cure insomnia, and increase personal confidence.

A special type of agate known as sylvester is banded with two colors. This stone is given to a child born on the last day of the year to signify both the end of the old year and the beginning of the new. Gray agate is a talisman against colic, and green agate is believed to protect women against sterility.

In the 1700s, a Brazilian priest living in Vienna developed an idea for an airship that used coral agate with iron in the overhead section. It was believed when the coral agate was warmed by the sun's rays it would become magnetic, thus drawing the ship skyward.

Amber

Born from the nectar of the setting sun and cooled by the ocean, amber is a good amulet for traders and merchants because of its workability. In Denmark, pieces found with depressions in them are thought to be the resting place of spirits. In Norway, amber carved in the shape of animals improves its power.

Amber is actually fossilized tree sap. In its original form, it is gummy, so amber often houses insects and bits of grass or leaves. Because of this, folk healers felt amber was the best stone to lay against an afflicted area of the body to entrap sickness.

An amber piece tied to a child imparts great protection and is favored by many magical people for unbroken necklaces, to symbolize the sacred circle.

Amethyst

Spiritual ideals and virtue are in this stone. Shrewd business decisions, protection for soldiers, and prevention of drunkenness are all ascribed to the amethyst. The last superstition may have come from the fact that certain types of amethyst found in early days had a reddish hue. Larger pieces were fashioned into drinking vessels, making them appear as if they were filled with wine, even if only water was poured inside. In French poems, the color of this stone has been attributed to Bacchus, God of Wine. When angered one day, the god vowed to avenge himself by venting his ire at the first person he met. So, he hid some fearsome tigers in his train, hungry and ready to attack. Unfortunately, the first mortal to happen by was a lovely maiden on her way to worship at Diana's shrine. When the beasts sprang toward her, she prayed for Diana's protection, who turned her into a white stone. Recognizing his error and feeling sorry for his brutality, Bacchus poured his wine over the maiden, thus giving the amethyst its purple coloring.

Beryl

Carried most frequently to bring harmony in relationships, beryl can also be an amulet for legal battles, improved mental agility, and physical energy. In German and Anglo-Saxon superstition, beryl is used as a cure for laziness.

Birth Stones

The dedication of each month to a specific gem for luck dates back to the writings of Josephus in A.D. 1 and St. Jerome in A.D. 5. Both of these writers associated the calendar months with the stones of the Hebrew high priest's breastplate (of Old Testament fame), said to contain twelve precious stones which represented each month of the year. While not actually adopted into popular use until the 1800s, another biblical reference aided the designation of natal stones, namely those mentioned in Revelations as being the foundation stones for the New Jerusalem. There is some evidence that the earlier custom was not only to own the stone for your birth month, but to have all twelve to wear, each in its appropriate month, to bring beneficial energy all year. You can continue this idea, or perhaps use the stones pertinent to each month to help enhance your spell and ritual work.

The most common stones given within ancient and modern texts for monthly associations follows:

- January—garnet, hyacinth.
- February—amethyst, pearl.
- March—jasper, bloodstone.

- April—sapphire, diamond.
- May—emerald, agate.
- June—cat's eye, turquoise, agate.
- July—onyx, ruby, turquoise.
- August—carnelian, moonstone, topaz.
- September—chrysolite, sardonyx, zircon.
- October—beryl, opal, aquamarine, coral.
- November—topaz, pearls.
- December—ruby, turquoise, bloodstone.

If you have children, a marvelous calendar can be made for them using gemstones. At the beginning of each month, give them a stone from those listed (or an item of appropriate color if the gem is too costly) and tell them about its significance. They can then place their treasure in a special pouch attached to the calendar, and at the end of the year use the stones for Yule projects or as keepsakes.

Birthstones can also be used to decorate altar cloths by placing small gems in a circle around your central area and sewing or gluing them in place. This way, the entire wheel of the year is represented—no matter the season.

Bloodstone

In the Leyden Papyrus (reprinted in *De amuletorum apud antiquos usu*, 1907) the bloodstone is highly praised. The writer says that it grants wishes, keeps the wrath of kings at bay, and provides its owner with believable speech. Victory in battle, protection, and luck to those born under Pisces is what this stone represents. When placed in water, its colors reflect to make the liquid appear as though the sun itself has turned blood red. Because of this, some ancient civilizations thought this stone could cause tempests. This belief eventually translated into people carrying bloodstone to improve their ability to divine by the signs of a storm. This also makes it appropriate for weather magic.

The bloodstone is associated with health matters and admiration, and is thought to act as a guard against deception.

Carbuncle

The Koran states that the fourth heaven is fashioned from this blood-red stone. Its color, being akin to human blood, led to the conviction that it could act as a heart stimulant. Carbuncle was once believed to be the material within dragon's eyes. With these associations in mind, the carbuncle is a stone for wise perception, health, and connecting with celestial energy.

Carnelian

This stone stands for luck, protection from evil, and when engraved, for hope. It is good for improving verbal skills and bringing bold speech. The great prophet Mohammed was thought to have worn this stone as a ring, thus making it popular among his followers and many Middle Easterners.

In powdered form, carnelian was sometimes administered as a cure for foreboding, and also protects a person from injury from falling objects.

Coral

Red and pink coral are favored to slow bleeding from wounds and for protection, especially for children. As an amulet, coral cures madness and brings wisdom. It is most powerful when used in a natural formation as cast up by the sea. In this form, it is considered a treasured gift from the gods that rule the waters. It is also thought best to wear it conspicuously. If it is ever broken, its spirit leaves and it is no longer useful for protection.

Coral in general, along with kelp and sea shells, make an excellent addition to any water-based magic, perhaps most especially that pertaining to healing arts.

Diamond

Diamonds stand for invincibility, purity, strength, and courage. This is a gem of reconciliation between husband and wife, and in this form has become popular today for engagement rings. Once thought to have been formed by a thunderbolt, lightning was long considered the only natural force which could destroy this stone.

The Talmud indicates that a diamond was used by the high priest to decipher guilt or innocence in one accused. The Hindus credited four types of diamonds with bringing power, youth, success, and good fortune. The Arabs, Persians, and Egyptians followed suit, using the diamond as a luck stone that could bring spiritual well being and physical fortitude.

In Sanskrit the diamond is called *vajra,* which means "thunderbolt" or "storm fire." It is assigned by Hindus to the planet Venus, the most brilliant object in the night sky other than the moon. If we substitute the Goddess of love for this planet, this association may have given rise to the use of diamonds as a token of deep affection.

According to tradition, the diamond must always be acquired as a gift to retain its amuletic powers. If you cannot afford such a luxury, a Herkimer diamond is a much less expensive substitute which can be employed for spells/rituals involving durability, success, and harmony in relationships.

Emerald

A rabbinical legend states that the emerald was one of four stones given to Solomon as a sign of his wisdom and the power of a king over creation. (The other three stones were probably carbuncle, lapis, and topaz, to represent the four elements.) Another Egyptian and Greek myth, recounted by Albertus Magnus in his treatise on stones, herbs, and creatures, claims that the emerald was originally discovered in the nest of a griffin.

During the Spanish conquest of South America, a huge emerald was found in Peru known simply by the natives as "the emerald goddess." It was adored by these people and only shown on high holy days. The monks of the region managed to keep it safe from invaders, its actual resting spot being a safely guarded secret to this day.

With these stories in mind, it is not surprising that the emerald has come to symbolize foreknowledge, faith, truth, mental agility, resourcefulness, and insight. To foretell the future, it is to be placed under the tongue while posing a specific question, before casting your runes, pulling a card from the tarot, or employing another divinatory tool.

Feldspar

Feldspar is a hard green stone made up of aluminum silicates with sodium, potassium, or calcium in a crystalline form. In Egypt this was carried to prevent headaches, sunstroke, and nosebleeds. More currently, it is associated with the Goddess of love and fertility, and the ability to see faeries.

Garnet

The stone of loyalty, faithfulness, health, and charity, the garnet was used frequently in the Middle Ages to protect against nightmares. It is an appropriate addition to any youngster's room, as a gift between hand-fasted couples, or in magic pertaining to beneficent action.

Hag Stones

Also known as "witch" stones or "mare" stones in Scotland, these little pebbles with holes neatly through them are scattered across the English countryside. If found by the sea, they are also known as "holy" stones and all are considered very positive omens to find (see Chapter 27: The Sea). If carried or hidden in the house they are protective amulets.

Some larger versions of these stones (see Chapter 28: Sacred Sites) have been used in very creative ways. The Woden stone was a place for weddings, where a couple was considered married if they clasped hands through the center. The swearing stone was used to bind agreements, and other holy stones were used in healing (see Chapter 13: Health and Medicine).

If you are fortunate enough to find such a rock, affix it to a necklace, wand, or staff, or carry it in a medicine pouch to accentuate the virtues of honesty, harmony, and devotion.

Hematite

Hematite was first praised in 63 B.C. by Azchalias of Babylon in a treatise written for King Mithridates. According to Pliny's recounting of this, hematite carries the energy of attraction and charm. It can also improve human destiny, especially in matters of law.

As an iron ore, hematite is under the dominion of Mars. Because of this, warriors would rub their bodies with hematite to invoke this God's favor. Hematite may be a valuable aid to auric work in the hands of a trained healer. Its dark color makes it symbolically acceptable to collecting "disease," yet its luster implies the light-filled energy so important to spiritual well-being.

Hyacinth

In Sanskrit writings, hyacinth is connected with the dragon. Purported to be so large that it hides the sun or the moon when it flies (see Chapter 5:

Celestial Objects), the dragon bears tremendous power. Anything associated with such potency would be an emblem of safety; thus hyacinth became an amulet against misfortune. It carries all the wisdom and power of the mythical dragon.

Described as a blue gem in ancient times, hyacinth may be another name for the sapphire. What we call hyacinth today is a reddish-brown variety of zircon, a semiprecious stone.

Jacinth

This stone was favored by ancient travelers for protection against injury or sickness and to improve hospitality wherever they went. For this particular function, a bit in your shoe is suggested. It is also a proof against lightning when imbedded in a part of your home and a sleep inducer if placed under the pillow.

Jade

Sacred to Asian sea goddesses because of its green color, jade was used as an amulet in China. The ancient kings and emperors of this land adorned themselves with beads of jade to indicate rank. Confucius was reported to use different tonal qualities of jade for a musical instrument to soothe the mind.

If you are fortunate, you may be able to locate some low-quality jade through a gem and rock exhibit. If you can, purchase several pieces of differing sizes, to carry different tonal qualities. Drill a hole in the top of each. These can be then strung around a circle of wood, or hung off the boughs of a tree to make a serviceable Confucius-style windchime!

In China, almost every important event was commemorated with jade. During the Ming dynasty, the monarch's girdle was decorated with various colored jades depending on the ritual being held. Coming of age was represented by a jade phoenix, newly married couples would receive a carved unicorn and rider (a sign of children to come), and the jade butterfly was an icon of successful love often given to a fiancé upon engagement. Indeed, the jade stone itself was believed to be the melodious essence of concentrated love. It is still a popular amuletic stone in China today, and is definitely suitable to any love enchantments you may have brewing.

In New Zealand, a special family treasure was formed out of jade with the aid of a specially-trained wizard. Once the jade was found, it was carved and worn by the head of the family. This was then passed down through the generations in the belief that each recipient would share in the wisdom of the ancestors. When the family line died out, the amulet was buried with them. Many such stones could be found in burial sites as recently as a hundred years ago.

Jasper

Jasper has rather diverse abilities, including encouraging rain and protecting its owner from snakebite. Because of its wide variety of colors and patterns, jasper has a many applications for sympathetic magic. For instance it is a rain-bringer in England, and in eleventh-century Germany, healers placed it on snakebites to attract the venom.

For the uses of jasper, first look to its color and then refer to Chapter 6: Color. Next, observe any patterns in the stone that immediately evidence themselves. Between these two observations and your own sensitivity, you should be able to discern its best application to your personal magical goals. For example, a piece of jasper with circular blue patterns could become a meditation tool. For this purpose, place the stone over your third eye and visualize the circles moving inward to bring peace and centering.

Jet

Popular in Belgium, Switzerland, and among the Native American Pueblo culture, this stone was also a Victorian symbol of mourning.

Early rosaries in North Umbria were created from this material, sometimes known as black amber in the sixteenth century. In Ireland, powdered jet is burned to protect a mate who is traveling away from home. Today, jet is accepted as a stone which can give us strength through trying times, helping to absorb our sorrow into its perfect blackness.

Language of Stones

During the eighteenth century, it was the custom in France and England to make jewelry that by its ornamentation alone carried a certain sentiment to the recipient. Although exactly how certain stones became associated with particular messages is unknown, one can assume that much of this list pertains to much older beliefs. The original listing is rather extensive, but here is an abbreviated version for your consideration.

- Faith: fire opal, tourmaline, topaz, amethyst.
- Hope: opal, pearl, emerald, hematite.
- Charity: cat's eye, amethyst, rose quartz, jade.
- Luck: gold beryl, diamond, obsidian, onyx.
- Forever: onyx, emerald, ruby, opal.
- Regard: garnet, diamond, rock crystal, amethyst.
- Long Life: zircon, sapphire, sard.
- Mitzpah: moonstone, peridot, hyacinth, aquamarine.
- Friendship: pearl, sard, pyrite, feldspar.
- Love: opal, lapis, moonstone, emerald.
- Eternity: alexandrite, emerald.

If you feel like getting really inventive, choose among these messages and have a special gift made for someone. For example, give a friend a necklace fashioned from pearl and alexandrite as a token of your abiding kinship.

Lapis

Used to increase psychic or magical energy during meditation, lapis was also popular in Babylonia and Egypt to cure fever and melancholy. In some cultures it is believed to endow the owner with the joy of the Gods.

Lodestone

Also known as heraclean, this was first discovered in the area of Lydia around 400 B.C. As early as the fourth century A.D., its magnetic qualities were being revered for their ability to keep mates faithful and improve all aspects of personal "attraction." In the East Indies, it was traditional for the monarch to have lodestone as part of his crown to improve his charisma, and thus ensure his acceptance by the public.

Alexander the Great reportedly gave this stone to his men to protect them from the Arab *jinn*. Lodestone being so fond of iron, and iron being the bane of any fey, the *jinn* would be hard-pressed to fight such power.

A woman's beauty has often been compared to the magnetic ability of lodestone, sometimes called the "loving stone" because it draws its true sweetheart (iron) near to its side. Even one of the great foes of magic, Augustine, admitted his belief in the amazing power of this stone.

Lodestone cut in the shape of a heart and bearing the image of Hecate was believed to protect a necromancer from any summoned soul. This symbol of respect for Hecate as the Crone and Goddess of the Underworld combined with the strength of the lodestone may well improve one's charisma.

Lodestone can be used to help attract any type of energy necessary into your magic.

Malachite

A type of meteorite, when attached to a cradle this stone protects the infant within and brings quiet nights of rest to the parent. It is most powerful when inscribed with an image of the sun. If trouble is approaching, the malachite is reported to shatter, warning its owner ahead of time.

Metals

The largest volume of information we have on magical metal theory came through the alchemists, who were in some ways medieval versions of modern chemists. They claimed that since everything of this world could be broken down into the four elements of earth, air, fire, and water, these elements could also be recombined to form higher types of matter, namely gold and silver. They also believed that any such work was best done during a waxing moon for a purer product.

Picking up odd pieces of metal (especially horseshoes) and carrying them home was thought to encourage good fortune in the Middle Ages,. Small bits of metal can be part of your medicine pouch for just such a purpose. They can also be symbolic of your connection to the earth, the place of their birth.

- ◆ Flint: This was the first rock to be made into tools because of its durability. It is a favored tool to harvest magical herbs (iron, conversely, can harm mystical qualities and frighten away faerie folk). Flint is an excellent stone to bring to Midsummer celebrations, when magical herbs are most potent for reaping
- ◆ Iron: Ancient Roman wedding rings were made out of iron as a symbol of the union's strength. Commonly related to the planet Mars, iron is also used to counter evil spirits.

Scotsmen of the Highland region frequently buried a corpse with iron spikes laid crosswise on the chest to prevent the soul from wandering, and in the Canadian woods an iron knife is sometimes placed in a nearby tree to keep away fireflies, linked in their lore to the devil. Iron harms the mystical qualities of magical herbs and will scare away fairy folk, but as a tool to keep mischievous spirits away, it can be an excellent addition to the sacred space.

♦ Gold: Attributed with the masculine aspects of the divine, gold is the symbol of the sun, fire, and success. Historically, it adorned magical wands and was a symbol of authority.

♦ Copper: This metal is associated with the element of Earth, the planet Venus, and conduction, which is why it is a good balancing influence, focus for energy, and often part of magical wands.

♦ Silver: Often associated with female intuition, the moon, and water, silver is the balance to gold, reflecting the unseen world and creative energy. Silver is often used for ritual cups and other containers for herbs set aside for magical use.

♦ Lead: Noted for its heaviness, lead is for foundations. People with a tendency to daydream should put a little piece of lead in their shoe to help keep one foot on the ground. Lead is also associated with the planet Saturn.

♦ Tin: Tin is a metal of serendipity, aligned with Jupiter.

♦ Quicksilver: Attributed to the planet and God Mercury, this metal helps with communications and swift action.

Moonstone

This sacred stone of India is only displayed on yellow cloth, a holy color to the Hindus. It is believed to inspire passion and aid in foreknowledge if held in the mouth when the moon is full.

The name moonstone might have come from an old legend which claims that the white line of this crystal waxes and wanes with the phases of the moon. Either way, this is a very suitable stone for any magic which marks the movement of the moon, or draws on moon-related energies.

Obsidian

Favored throughout the ages as a base for magic mirrors, this stone is dedicated to Hecate because of its black color. This stone holds a razor edge. The Aztecs and Mayans used obsidian to make ritual knives.

Onyx

Onyx is used to create discord or dissension. One positive application for this stone, however, is to reduce the intensity of love. If you are feeling as if things are moving too quickly in a relationship, give a blessed onyx to your partner (white and gray are best for a cooling effect).

Opal

Associated with fire and the memory, opals are good fortune for those born in the month of October, , but are unlucky for others. If you are not superstitious about this stone, they are good to carry when you need to accentuate your cognitive abilities.

Pyrite

Also known as fool's gold, this glittery stone is often part of the Native American medicine pouch. In Mexico, it was put to the abundantly useful function of being polished into mirrors, partially as a way to reflect God to the self.

In Burma, pyrite is carried to protect the owner from crocodiles. Taking this symbolism a little further, this stone may be good to carry when people's tempers are biting or when falsehoods are prevalent.

Quartz

The Chinese Emperor Wu sometimes used quartz or rock crystal to build great houses for the Gods and eternal spirits so that the doors would always allow sunlight to flood inward, keeping them happy. In this part of the world there is also a popular belief that quartz is actually ice which has been solid so long it can never melt. In Japan, small quartz crystals were thought to be the breath of the white dragon, in which the perfect powers of creation were embodied. Because of this, it symbolizes purity and infinity. The notion of quartz as an ice product makes it an excellent choice to hold or restrain specific energies.

To the Cherokee, it is a stone believed to improve hunting and divining skills, and as such is wrapped in fine buckskin, hidden in a sacred cave, and periodically fed with deer's blood to help retain its potency. (Again, we see the belief that certain stones have a life force and need to be tended in specific ways to keep then functional as amulets.)

One of the largest spheres of quartz was produced in Madagascar early in the 1900s. It measured just over six inches in diameter and sold for $20,000. Quartz is probably the most popular of New Age stones because of its natural electrical quality and variety of size and color.

Religious Uses of Crystals

Crystals and precious gems have played important roles in the myths of many world religions.

The earliest documentation of the religious use of precious stones comes to us from the Egyptian *Book of the Dead*, where jasper engraved with various hieroglyphs was inlaid into sycamore wood and left in a tomb to protect the spirit of the deceased. The most common form for this amulet was that of an *ab,* or heart, where the Egyptians believed the soul resided. About the only image not commonly used was the hieroglyphic symbol ascribed to truth; this was reserved for a high priest.

Hebrew high priests had breastplates with twelve jewels, each representing one month of the year. In Buddhist lore, precious stones (especially the diamond) were used by monks in allegorical tales told to their leaders as a way of subtly teaching purity and wisdom.

Gems were also a means to implore the Gods for favor. In Sumeria, archaeologists discovered a five-inch carved ax of onyx, dating around 2000 B.C., inscribed with supplications to the Sun God. In India, similar traditions existed: for example, sixteen very specific stones were used for worshipping Krishna. Of these, rubies insured the supplicant of power; emeralds, knowledge; and diamonds guaranteed the faithful giver of the most difficult attainment, Nirvana.

Today, much of this veneration has fallen into disuse, except where we periodically see the adornment of older church relics. This is partially due to the costly nature of most of the stones considered suitable for divine temples, as well as to the modern mind's ridicule of what might be considered antiquated practices. In New Age circles, however, there seems to be a reawakening sense of honor given to these folkways.

Round Stones

Perfectly round stones are considered lucky, as a symbol of the full moon, fertility, and the circle. This may be why marbles were originally made from crystal or pure glass.

Ruby

Most valued by the Hindus, the ruby is considered the king of all precious stones and the color of a lotus. Its bright hue contributes to the superstition that there is a fire within it which cannot be quenched. Any cloth wrapped around this stone is said to eventually burn away; if tossed into water, the liquid will boil. Such power has given rubies the reputation of being excellent for mental and physical health, as well as peacekeeping. For this purpose, it is most influential when worn on the left side of the body in a brooch, ring, or bracelet.

In Burma, the ruby offers soldiers invulnerability, but only when set directly into the flesh. A good alternative might be to have a ruby chip mounted for a pierced earring.

Sapphire

A verdant beacon for divine favor, the laws of Moses were once thought to have been carved from a giant slab of sapphire. This story led to its becoming the favored gem for ecclesiastical rings. Beyond this, the sapphire is also a magician's aid for understanding omens and, in powdered form, was even used as an antidote for many poisons.

The star sapphire was considered most potent of all, bearing the image of a sun in splendor to bring luck, victory, and faithfulness. The three lines of the gem represent faith, hope, and fortune, making this version of the sapphire a stone of destiny. So commanding is the magic of the sapphire that it was purported to continue to influence a person even after it changed hands in a sale. It is also strong protection against fraud and treachery.

Sard

Carrying a sard will offer protection against magic, improve your wits and bring renewed joy. Try carrying a sard when you are studying your craft, or when you need an emotional boost.

Selenite

Believed to be sacred to the moon and faerie folk, this stone grows in caves. If you happen to find some selenite, take a small piece and plant it in a flower pot by the light of the full moon, leaving an offering of bread and honey to encourage faerie guests.

Serpentine

The name of this gem comes from its appearance, which is similar to that of snakeskin. With this visage, it is not surprising that its sympathetic magic pertains mostly to protection from snakebite. However, to this function, ancient tradition has it that it must be in a natural, uncut state, because any iron tool will ruin its power.

Turquoise

Also known in earlier times as *callais*, turquoise was given the same attributes of most blue stones. The ancient Aztecs regarded gem-quality turquoise as the only stone befitting as offerings to their gods. Later, turquoise developed a reputation as being a guard for both horse and rider against fall and injury, and it was especially favored for this purpose in Persia and Turkey. So attuned is the stone to horse and rider that it is reported to sometimes crack and break in its owners stead when a serious accidents occurs. A more modern version of this application is to keep a piece in your car to help avert accidents.

In the 1600s, turquoise came into fashion in Europe for men's jewelry. In Persia it was thought most fortunate to see one's reflection in the stone. Mexicans used turquoise extensively in their burial rites, and the Navajo associate it with rain, and marksmanship if affixed to a bow. For men, turquoise is a good stone to use for improving the sense of sight at deeper levels of awareness.

In Buddhism, the turquoise is considered a stone of protection and power. One story recounts how it aided the Buddha in destroying a loathsome creature. Carry one as a safeguard anytime you feel you might be under psychic attack.

Unlucky Stones

Just as many crystals had good qualities, others were regarded with caution and sometimes even terror. Opal, being of a luminescent nature, was considered very favorable in the Orient; contrarily, the Western mind thought it unlucky except for those who wore it as a birthstone. This attitude may have developed because of the opal's fragile nature and the fact that it loses its luster after some years.

In Hindu cultures, a flawed diamond was considered as dramatically negative as a perfect one was positive. If the blemish was part of a three-sided stone, it would bring quarrels; a four-sided stone delivered fear, and a five-sided one, death.

Another interesting superstition regarding the diamond was that to swallow one, or its dust, would bring death because of its sharpness. More than likely, however, it was not the stone, but a greedy individual causing death in order to obtain this valued prize.

In the Middle East, the onyx is considered a stone of apprehension, and its Arabic name means sadness.

Weekdays and Hours for Stones

Certain stones are favored for each day of the week and hour of the day. One type of stone was to be worn daily for protection and luck, and another for creating more potent amulets. All of these associations can be used to further accentuate your ritual and spell work. For example, if you are doing a ritual with your cat familiar, you might want to work on Thursday, wearing a cat's eye.

Obviously, some of these items are very costly, so a stone, candle, or cloth of similar color and meaning can be substituted.

Days:

- Sunday—wear topaz, sunstone, or diamond; use pearl in creating any talisman.
- Monday—wear pearl, moonstone, or crystals; use emerald for amulets.
- Tuesday—wear ruby, star sapphire, or emerald; use topaz.
- Wednesday—wear amethyst, star ruby, or lodestone; use turquoise.
- Thursday—wear sapphire, cat's eye, or carnelian; use sapphire.
- Friday—wear emerald or cat's eye; use ruby.
- Saturday—wear turquoise, labradorite, or diamond; use amethyst.

Hours (A.M. and P.M.):

- One—jacinth, morion.
- Two—emerald, hematite.
- Three—beryl, malachite.
- Four—lapis, topaz.
- Five—ruby, turquoise.
- Six—opal, tourmaline.

- Seven—chrysolite, sardonyx.
- Eight—amethyst, chalcedony.
- Nine—kunzite, jade.
- Ten—sapphire, jasper.
- Eleven—garnet, lodestone.
- Twelve—diamond,

White Stones

In Celtic regions, white stones found near a sacred well are considered the best with which to build a prayer mound. If the stones are collected and prepared just right, sometimes the faeries will appreciate the sight and play soft music or sing.

Zodiacal Influences

A great British astrologer, Alan Leo, proposed some of the following stones as lucky for people born under various signs of the zodiac (see Chapter 5: Celestial Objects). This concept actually has far older origins. There are therefore many differing opinions on the subject, evidenced on Page 111, and the variations from what we now consider traditional birthstones.

Certain gems were also assigned to aid healing in persons born under its corresponding sign.

- Aries—diamond, amethyst, garnet; crystal bloodstone for health.
- Taurus—emerald, moss agate, ruby; sapphire for health.
- Gemini—aquamarine, beryl, sapphire; agate for health.
- Cancer—black onyx, ruby, agate, beryl; emerald or health.

- Leo—diamond, ruby, topaz; onyx for health.
- Virgo—hyacinth, pink jasper, magnets; carnelian for health.
- Libra—diamond, opal, jasper; chrysolite for health.
- Scorpio—topaz, malachite, beryl, garnet; aquamarine for health.
- Sagittarius—turquoise, carbuncle, emerald; topaz for health.
- Capricorn—moonstone, white onyx; ruby for health.
- Aquarius—sapphire, opal, amethyst; garnet for health.
- Pisces—moonstone, chrysolite; amethyst for health.

For magic, you can choose the stone you prefer and employ it when working during the various astrological phases. This enhances positive energy. Alternatively, carry the stone associated with your birth sign to facilitate health and well-being.

Ancient cultures also assigned various stones to specific planetary influences. This list is rather extensive, but for reference purposes I have listed some of the more commonly available crystals and correspondences below. The planetary influence is considered most important to how the stone is eventually employed (see Chapter 5: Celestial Objects):

- Jasper—Venus, Mercury.
- Beryl—Venus, Mars.
- Amethyst—Mars, Jupiter.
- Agate—Venus, Mars.
- Hematite—Mercury.
- Garnet—Sun.
- Jet—Saturn.
- Magnetic stone—Mars.
- Carnelian—Jupiter, Mars.
- Sardonyx—Saturn, Mars.
- Topaz—Saturn, Mars.
- Pearl—Venus, Mercury.
- Turquoise—Venus, Mercury.
- Lapis—Venus.
- Amber—Sun.
- Quartz (clear)—Moon, Mars.
- Pyrite—Sun.
- Opal—Sun, Mercury.

8 DANCE

Around fires burning towards the moon
with pentacle and candles bright
are we in working magicks be
as dancers in the night.
♦ Marian ♦

DANCE PLAYED a significant role in many early civilizations. Our ancestors regarded dance as a fundamental element in such rituals as marriage, death, and the coming of age. It also played an integral part in the worship of their god(s). Dancing to the powerful beat of the drum helped spirits rejoice, food grow well, and give comfort to the injured heart.

Historians believe that dancing became important in most ancient cultures not just because of its religious application, but also because its role as imitative magic for the hunt. This type of folkrite was central to the well-being of entire communities.

The movements of early dance were not just happenstance. In certain Egyptian drawings, we can easily see where the placement of the arms, hands, legs, or head is specific. Leaping and jumping accompany dances for the hunt, with the dancer taking on characteristics of the beast. Therefore, the intention behind the dance takes form in external expression for religious folk dances to be effective.

Rhythm is inseparable from dance in many cultures, including those of Arabia and Assyria. Provided by percussion instruments like cymbals, drums or hands, this beat added another expressive dimension to the dance. In ecstatic dancing rhythm was integral because it provided growing momentum needed to achieve an altered state of awareness.

In considering how customs grew in dancing, it is important to remember that many early cultures believed anything that moved was inhabited by some spirit. Human action in the form of dance was a means to honor this power. The dances that mimic animals were sacred because many creatures were associated with a divine image. The Greeks even thought that the Gods themselves taught humans to dance as a means of venerating them.

Sacred dances were done for many reasons. In some instances a dance was a type of offering to please or implore the Gods/desses into action. Most often requests were for immediate necessities such as a good harvest or protection in battle. In other examples, the movements of the dance were designed to bring about an altered state of awareness where the individual could become a conduit of divine power for healing, or to prepare a holy beast for sacrifice.

A wide variety of folk dances are still enacted around the world, the origins for many of which are no longer known. Dancing continues to mimic the movements and weavings of the universe, animals, and, in subtle ways, fate itself, each intrinsic to the particular country of origin. These dances frequently recount the culture's folktales which so often go hand-in-hand with its celebratory activities.

Sufi dancing is a modern attempt to return to a form of sacred motion. This type of dance reveres the Creator and creation, in the belief that consecrated movement (such as moving joyfully sunwise) will renew human awareness of the natural order. This will then bring healing to the earth as well as to the dancer's body and spirit.

One important function of ritual dance is as a rite of passage, specifically for deceased spirits. While unique to each culture, many mourning and burial rites have strong links to one another seen in dance.

In some countries, the rhythmic stamping of feet accompanies the memorial speech. Among Sephardic Jews (Spanish and Portuguese), mourners move around the body seven times while reciting prayers in a chant-like style (see Chapter 21: Numbers).

Chinese and Irish cultures have comparable burial rites. Each culture uses a circle of dancers to mark the line between the living and the dead, world and not-world.

Another purpose of death dances was to bring peace to both the living and the dead, and hopefully keep restless souls from wandering about. In Greece, for example, a burial dance for one's enemy was performed to bind the angry spirit and keep it from taking revenge.

In many cultures there is a strong belief that the ancestors of the recently deceased come to act as guides during the mourning rite, and actually join in the dance to bridge the gap between life and death. I think this idea is quite lovely. To apply this effectively in modern Wiccan Summerland rituals, simply invite the ancestors to join the sacred space along with the spirit of the departed for one last celebration together.

Dance of Phantoms

This dance takes place in Australia on January 8-9. The participants wear scary wooden masks and colorful costumes to drive away evil spirits and bless the grain for the coming year.

If you happen to have a garden, January 8-9 is a good time to bless your seeds by carrying them sunwise in a personalized dance of thankfulness to the God/dess (with or without a costume). I tried this for the first time recently, leaving my seeds on the altar until planting in May. The results were wonderful. The tomatoes' yield seemed larger than previously, as did that for the chives, carrots, and radishes.

Geerewol Dance

The *geerewol* is a tribal custom in Nigeria that celebrates the end of the rainy season. This is a festival of beauty and grace, where dance, clapping, and song help bring the participants luck, and often mates. Quite practically, this is the tribe's way of bringing life and resplendence to the wastelands.

For modern magical families, a *geerewol* dance before the Great Rite might be a lovely touch. The actual steps or movement of the dance should be inspired by what you are comfortable with, and should also accentuate rhythm and beauty.

Another version of this would be to dance through an area of land that needs replenishing, weaving in and out of trees and stones, sharing your magic with the earth to bring renewal.

Ecstatic Dance

Widespread among civilizations was the ecstatic dance. Religious zeal was physically expressed, often ending in a semiconscious or unconscious state. The ultimate goal of such movement was to achieve an altered level of awareness and oneness with the Divine. This particular state of awareness was so revered that the art of gyromancy (divination by the utterings of someone after ecstatic dance) was very common. Ecstatic Dance is still very much a part of many cultures. For example, the South Indian Devil Dancers, Bodo priests and indigenous peoples of the Fiji islands include ecstatic dance as well as self-laceration in religious rites. In all instances, self-laceration is considered an act of devotion, believed to allow the spirit of God/dess to dwell within the individual. This possession lasts long enough to cure disease, create oracles, and impart courage before battles. In the latter instance, certain taboos were usually added for warriors before battle, including abstinence from sex.

Dervish dancing is a type of ecstatic dance performed by members of a Sufi order in which altered states of awareness are sought through dance. The dervish's methods compare with those of early Israelite prophets for gathering divine knowledge and inspiration.

There is some indication that ecstatic dances were performed when grave emergencies arose, requiring immediate divine action. The dancing dervishes of Egypt are a remnant of such beliefs, as are the Malbus

of Saudi Arabia who, to this day, consider dance as a means to achieve mystical experiences.

Ecstatic dances are not as common in magical traditions today probably because of our sense of propriety and inhibition, although a certain level of the ecstatic dance can be experienced when a cone of power is raised.

Harvest and Victory Dances

These are dances of celebration and thankfulness. The Hebrews had the Feast of First Fruits and the Feast of the Tabernacle in which certain fields were used for celebratory dancing. An offering from the harvest to the Gods was presented to thank them for providence. The Romans had corresponding festivities, with the minor variation that the dates were not set but performed according to the state of the crops.

The differences between harvest dances and those of victory are relatively small, except that victory dances also honor warriors and any protective divine entity credited with their success. The victory dance is frequently preceded by the blowing of horns, and sometimes followed by the eating of a sacred beast for renewed vitality. There is also an underlying indication that victory dances were held to bring peace to the restless spirit of any villager slain in the battle.

Modern harvest festivals in most magical traditions include some type of dance and song. As you enact your celebration, remember that you are continuing a great tradition of gratitude to the universe. Allow yourself to feel a connection with the ages and rejoice!

Marriage Dances

Feasts, dancing, and music are still important aspects of the marriage tradition. These items, however, have roots dating back to antiquity, when various dances were performed at joinings to ensure the acceptability of the bride and the bride price, for protection of the couple, and to aid in fertility. More elaborate dances were also performed to please the patron God or Goddess and invoke Their blessing on the marriage.

Among Bedouins, the wife will perform an exquisite dance with candles before the home of her new husband, turning in all four directions to cast away any shadows that might impede their future happiness. Analogous to this is the Henna dance of Malay, where the bride must turn over the cup holding the Henna without allowing adjacent candles to go out. The hand of the bride is then anointed with the substance to protect the union. In many lands the couple being wed is regarded as king and queen of the celebration, and the dancers are therefore there to entertain them. This custom probably dates back to ancient fertility rites and the idea of the sacred marriage between God and Goddess. Partially, this change in status to royalty is also considered an effective disguise so that any malevolent magic might thus be averted.

After the marriage dance has occurred, in almost all instances, some type of physical change is made on the bride to mark her new status. Her hair, headdress or even the people she is seated with may reflect the marital status. So, in this respect, the marriage dance also marks the transformation from one life into another, from child to adult.

Any one or all of these festivities can easily be adapted for hand-fastings according to the couples' desires, with the additional possibility of eliminating the gender-related roles and perhaps having the bride and groom dance with, or for, each other.

Masks for Dance

Many cultures use masks as an integral part of their dance customs and lore. In Malay, villagers dance wearing masks to bring their lives back into balance after someone in the village dies. Most often the masks are those of animals, hunters, or trees.

The people of this region see life and death as part of one great dance. After the mourning and burial dances are performed, the shroud is kept by the family as a gentle reminder that death is part of living.

Animal masks make a wonderful project for children and adults alike. Fairly complex versions can be made in papier-maché, but really a simple cardboard backing, fabric, and a little creative flair will do. Masks portraying natural creatures and objects are appropriate to rituals where you are calling for a familiar or questing for a totem. The mask is your way of honoring their environment. Just remember to keep your goal in mind as you prepare your mask.

Processional Dance

This type of dance was best illustrated in the Old Testament where, to honor Jahweh, the Israelites would dance in cavalcade before the ark of the covenant. This procession was frequently led by the king. In certain Egyptian communities, the processional dance was extended to barges traveling in succession down the Nile. Comparable rites were done in honor of Baal, and continue to be exhibited among Bedouins today, sometimes accompanied by offerings.

Among the Greeks, there was a prevalent belief that the gods and goddesses would dance for their worshippers when they were pleased (and vice-versa). So much was this the case that some of the roads in Greece were laid specifically for processional dancing! A slightly different version of the processional dance was seen in a special Greek rite for young girls (from five to ten years old). This seems to have been an initiation of sorts, or an introduction to the Gods before puberty.

An Etruscan processional dance was performed to aid the movement of the stars on their courses, and even Brahman worship indicates that an offering of dance was seemly and encouraged. In Central America, dance takes on the form of a supplication that can last several days. The dancers' movements make them appear as if they are limping to invoke, to invoke the pity of the Divine and inspire quicker action.

Today it might be fun to create processional dances for erecting the Maypole, preparing for a handfasting, introducing a new coven leader, or puberty rites, for example. For a puberty dance, it is appropriate to have children interweave themselves between the arms or legs of adult coven members as a symbol of connection to adulthood and a type of rebirth.

Sacred Objects

Perhaps the most common type of ritual dance throughout the world, movement around a sacred object was part of many ancient belief systems in ancient days. First, this dance was a type of worship. Second, it acted as a form of consecration to sanctify either the ritual space or the object encircled by the dancers. Last, in instances where a well or grove was chosen, the dance may have been performed to renew waters or crops that had failed.

The most common central objects were an altar, sacred well, tree, or sacrificial item. One of the most popular times of the year in England for well dances was on May Day, when the wells were decorated with ribbons, flowers, and bells.

An important element of this dance was the dancers' physical connections each other. The unity of bodies and spirits, while circling the object sunwise, was believed to magically draw holy energies into play.

We still see this belief prevalent in almost every modern magical tradition. For example, while dancing at Summer Solstice during and open gathering in Pennsylvania, everyone joined hands around the fires. The dance moved in a clockwise circle at first, then later broke off as people wove among one another to symbolize the network of life.

Promenades around sacred objects were often accompanied by an offering (which was probably on the altar during the dance to make it acceptable). If the sacrifice was an animal, it was believed that the spiritual essence of the creature went to the Gods, while the material parts would be totally used by the worshippers. To waste any part of an accepted sacrifice was considered an insult to the divine. While the actual purpose of this offering may have varied, the goal of the dancing was the same: that of preparing, blessing, and cleansing the sacred space and the offering for a divine presence. It is no less so for our magical circles today (see Chapter 18: Magic and the Supernatural).

Weather Dances

Weather dances, most commonly known to Americans today through the Native American traditions, are also a routine sight in other cultures, especially those living in harsh regions. Fire is often used to invoke more sun. If rain is needed, water may be poured out to the earth as a type of representative magic.

Weather magic should be approached with caution, but the dance can certainly be used today. Generally you want to move your dance into the direction where the change of weather or wind is needed (see Chapter 30: Weather Lore). To illustrate, if there is a drought in a region west of you, sprinkle water while you dance, moving yourself toward the west to draw positive energy in that direction.

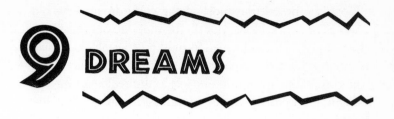

9 DREAMS

Oh, what land is the land of Dreams!
♦ William Blake, *The Land of Dreams* ♦

 THE OLDEST surviving text of dream interpretation dates back to 1350 B.C. in Egypt. The Bible has many examples of dream interpretation, especially for prophetic or allegorical visions. Plato called dreams "prophetic visions," and many civilizations took dreams very seriously, including the Chaldeans, Chinese, Hindu, and Greek. So much was the case that, by A.D. 2, dream books were showing the deeper meanings of these images to the literate public. In the sixteenth century, dream interpretation advanced to include the social status and physical health of the dreamer as considerations for interpretation.

The mystical nature of dreams may owe part of its origin to superstitions about sleep itself. Being so much like death, anything seen in this state was apt to be taken more seriously, perhaps even regarded as divinely inspired.

Dream lore has an important place in folklore because its symbolism often comes from that source. For example, many of our interpretations of dreams depend on a play on words. The aphorism "an apple a day keeps the doctor away" may mean that one who dreams of eating apples might want to take care with his or her health!

It should be noted that most of the early dream keys did not cite their sources or connections, nor do the majority of modern collections. Therefore, some of this information must be speculative. Similarly, since the connection between dreams and their meanings is subjective, personal interpretations must often be left to the realms of faith.

Today, a dream diary can be insightful. It can provide clues to your past lives, help in problem-solving, and sometimes teach important mystical principles by serving as a record of a reappearing spirit-guide or recurring metaphorical sequence. The longer you keep a record of your dreams, the better you will come to understand the symbolism within them. Use recurring symbols from your dreams in meditation to focus and inspire special responses in your behavior. For example, if you find you are having trouble with productivity, try visualizing yourself as a rosebush with hundreds of blossoms opening. Or if you need to overcome something, meditate on a hammer and take that strength with you to break the barriers you face.

There are some people in the New Age community using such meditations to help develop what is called "programmed dreaming." Here a set of symbols or suggestions are repeated before sleeping in the attempt to bring about a specific vision related to spiritual growth or quandaries. While I believe this approach has great merit, please consult someone with more expertise in these realms before trying this yourself. The actual effect that our dream time has on waking reality is a very new psychological study; therefore caution is prudent.

Dream Dictionaries

The papyrus from 1350 B.C. spoken of earlier this chapter shows that the ancients used symbolic adages, like those employed in modern psychoanalysis. The only difference was the addition of incantations to ward off bad dreams. Slowly, dream dictionaries moved into fashion. Popularization began in Greece around 400 B.C., with evidence of strong public use in many lands by 2 A.D.

Much later, and moving more into modern history, Carl Jung, Swiss psychologist and psychiatrist, wrote that dreams were a storehouse for remembrances, reflections, and conceptions. Jung's work with dreams helped to bring dream interpretation back into popular use.

The premise is that the mind becomes more open to spiritual impressions, subconscious needs, and feelings during sleep. Considering

this, lists of symbols were compiled into dictionary form for any arm-
chair philosopher and diviner to try to apply. Some of the more popular definitions include:

- Anchor: disillusion-
  ment, something
  holding you back.
- Apples: longevity and
  many descendants.
- Arrow: writing a letter
  which you
  may rue.
- Bath: vitality, long
  life, early matrimony.
- Blooms: productivity.
- Canary: a delightful
  house.
- Cherries: pleasure
  and enjoyment.
- Clock: missed oppor-
  tunity, lack of inven-
  tiveness.
- Cornfield: wealth,
  certainty.
- Doves: success
  in love.
- Faerie: flights
  of fancy.
- Fan: rivals in passion,
  an argument.
- Feathers (black): loss
  and failure.
- Fountain: laughter.

- Gloves on the hands:
  honor.
- Hammer: victory.
- Hearing hymns:
  solace.
- Iron: a good
  transaction.
- Kitchen: success and
  advancement.
- Leaf: impending
  change.
- Milk: peace in the
  home, possible
  pregnancy.
- Needle: family
  squabble.
- Nightingale (singing):
  faithfulness.
- Oak: steady increase.
- Sage: wisdom and
  caution.
- Snow: hidden circum-
  stances.
- Thread: tangled
  situations.
- Tied hands: difficulty
  in getting out of
  trouble.
- Wall: obstacles.

You may continue to use this list as a very abbreviated guide; however, also consider the more contemporary symbols that fill your life. If you have experienced a dream that seems significant somehow, write it down and review it from various angles. First look to the emotions involved, and the basic scenario itself. Look at dominant items and colors for clues. You will find a hint of a theme that will slowly develop and make sense.

Some dreams are obvious in their meaning. To illustrate, if you happen to be a woman dreaming about being pregnant, you could be hoping for a child in the future, pregnant, or worried over a moment when caution was tossed to the winds. These types of modern considerations need to be added to any older text of dream interpretation to make it more readily applicable in current settings.

Dream Keys

Similar in form and function to dream dictionaries, dream keys were lists of symbols considered as important representations to the individual. Much of the character of these items was actually quite logical in meaning. For example, an abyss was danger that could be averted, bathing in clear water meant an improvement in business and clarity of decisions, and dreaming of a cold cinder was a sure sign of a relationship's demise.

Dream keys can still be found today; however, remember that interpreting your visions is a personal matter. Books cannot always reach this level because of the wide expanse of human nature. Consider first and foremost your own instincts on the meanings of your dreams and then consult the written guides for additional perspective. The following are examples of interpretations found in *The Complete Book of Fortune* (Crescent Books 1936).

- Accident on the road: You're trusting others too much.
- Aircraft: Courage and ambition will help you achieve your goals.
- Axe: Strength of character brings rewards.
- Baby: Joy.
- Ball: Playing with one means good news is on the way.
- Candle burning: Letter with good news will arrive soon.

- Dancing: You will get a surprise gift.

- Diving: Into water means good luck in investments.

- Dragon: Change of residence.

- Drums: Family quarrels ahead.

- Eyes: If inflamed or closed, a the loss of friends.

- Glass, clear: A successful future.

- Hounds, following: Lucky sign.

- Ivy: A sign of faithful friendships.

- Jade: Returning to health.

- Lamb: Peacefulness.

- Lion: Powerful affiliations.

- Mirror: Scandal or disappointment.

- Mouse: A busybody interfering with your affairs.

- Ocean, calm: Reconciliation.

- Olives, gathering: Accord and harmony.

- Rat: Powerful enemies, usually unknown.

- Running: A journey that is helpful.

- Silver: A pending marriage.

- Teeth, aching: Sickness is coming.

- Watch, winding: Lack of independence.

- Witch: Making useful discoveries.

Dreaming True

In Iceland the practice of gaining visions through dreams is called "dreaming true" and is still taken seriously. Before the arrival of Christianity, both the Celtic and Germanic people depended upon, and believed deeply in, the power of prophetic dreams, evidenced clearly in writings of Julius Caesar and Tacitus. There were similar convictions among the Norse, who felt that supernatural women visiting their sleep were bearers of luck or guardians of some kind. These women may have been a derivative of the fertility goddess, guardian angels, or even the more modern spirit guides.

Today it is said that if you wish to have visionary dreams, invoke the appropriate protective powers and place a sachet of ash leaves, bay, cinquefoil, and holly beneath your pillow. Settle yourself into a calm, meditative state of mind before drifting off to sleep, and be certain to keep a diary handy. Note anything you recall as soon as you get up; then read through it later to consider its meaning.

Dumb Cakes

The traditions of dumb cakes originated in England. They were prepared to induce dreams of future love. No sound was uttered during preparation. Once prepared, the cake was marked with the persons initials and laid on the hearth or under the his or her pillow. This was done Friday night for best results.

Fruits

Like almost everything else in the natural world, different types of fruit in dreams were thought to have special divinatory meanings. Apples portended wealth; cherries signaled unhappy love; figs meant an inheritance; lemons symbolized a quarrel or souring of relationships; oranges stood for infidelity; and a strawberry was believed to be the sign of a trip to the country. Some of these symbols have spilled over into the magical attributes ascribed to fruits (vegetables too). For more information on foods and their emblematic significances, read Scott Cunningham's *The Magic in Food,* (Llewellyn, 1990) and *Kitchen Witch's Cookbook,* (Llewellyn 1994).

Garters

In England on St. Agnes' Eve, if a young woman knits her left garter stocking to the right and repeats a charm, it is believed that she will dream of her future husband that night. The knitting in this particular bit of folklore is strongly linked to superstitions regarding knots (see Chapter 16: Knots).

Gemstones

One of the first notable writers on this topic was the Roman Artemidorus who prepared *The Five Books of the Interpretation of Dreams and Visions*. These books became the basis for many modern dream keys. Artemidorus believed that ornaments and gems appearing in dreams were especially favorable signs for women, each stone carrying a different message. This sentiment was echoed in A.D. 8 through an Arabic text, laden with heavy Hindu influences.

As dream oracles, the vast amounts of folklore already identified with gemstones (see Chapter 7: Crystals, Gems and Metals) certainly contributed to their interpretations. Here is a sampling:

- Agate: journey by land.
- Amber: voyage by sea.
- Amethyst: protection.
- Beryl: joy.
- Carbuncle: wisdom.
- Coral: recovery.
- Garnets: end of a mystery.
- Onyx: joyous marriage.
- Opal: prosperity.
- Pearl: friendship.
- Turquoise: abundance.
- Lapis: faithfulness.
- Diamond: victory or love.
- Jasper: love reciprocated.

Incubation

Incubation, or sleeping alone at a sacred site, was long considered the most trustworthy method of procuring a dream or vision to effect a cure. Most commonly known at the temple of Aesculapius in Greece, principle shrines were set up inside specifically for healing dreams. The supplicant would pay a fee, then spend the night within. Some of the dreams reported included God pouring ointment into the eye of a blind woman, who woke up able to see, and someone afflicted with lice dreaming of being swept down by a divine broom. These two images are still potent for visualization pertaining to both health and cleansing.

This type of procedure was also enacted in other countries. In the Orient, for example, the emperor would have a special dream chamber available to him in a cloistered city, where he could confer with the gods on important matters of state. Even the oracle at Delphi was thought to have originally been a dream incubation site before the followers of Apollo took over and changed the procedure to use menstruating women as seers.

Today, the best way to effect dreams of a spiritual nature is to meditate quietly in bed before going to sleep. You may burn incense of jasmine to encourage vision and insight, and even ask for a dream from your patron God or Goddess. Keep a dream diary handy to record your dreams when you wake up.

Nightmares

Thyme tea drunk before bed and a string of garnets left around the neck is an ancient JuJu tribal charm against frightening dreams.

Since garnets are fairly inexpensive and widely available, this ritual can be used today. When you have guests come, give them a garnet piece as a way of welcoming them and blessing them with a restful stay.

Numbers

Numbers in dreams had slightly different interpretations than those attributed to numerology (see Chapter 21: Numbers). One represented a skill obtained; two, a business difficulty; three, ideas coming into reality; four, security; five, discovery; six, love; seven solutions to problems; eight, pleasant affection; and nine was a warning of caution. These numbers could appear alone or be represented by a count of identical items, or even the number of times the dream occurred.

Why these numbers had a slight variation in dream lore from regular numerological interpretation must be left to conjecture. I believe that those who studied dream analysis might have felt that the subconscious message of a number was altered by the human dimension more than the study of numerology.

A spell or incantation can be repeated a certain number of times according to this symbolism or that in the numerology section. Another creative way to apply this information is in making incense. For example, you might place seven grains of frankincense on the altar to cleanse your sacred space and help give you insight for resolving a situation.

10 THE ELEMENTS

Earth and Air, Fire and Sea
I call you all, come dance with me!
♦ Marian ♦

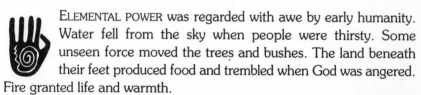 ELEMENTAL POWER was regarded with awe by early humanity. Water fell from the sky when people were thirsty. Some unseen force moved the trees and bushes. The land beneath their feet produced food and trembled when God was angered. Fire granted life and warmth.

In modern magic, a great deal of time and space is dedicated to the the four directions, winds, or elements, the basic natural powers of this world—earth, air, fire, and water. From these all things are created and to them all things will someday return. This alchemical axiom is one that deeply influenced both ancient and modern magical practices.

The applications of elemental superstitions are as rich and varied as the elements themselves. However, one element will probably call to you more strongly than the others as the best vehicle for your personal work. For example, I am a water person. Most of my visualizations for myself involve water, as a place of peacefulness and strength. It seems to me that from these silken drops my essence begins, flows, and ends in a never-ending aqueous circle.

I find that I am drawn to freshwater sources when distressed; and it is there that I discover the greatest personal energy. Other people might feel similarly when standing in the wind, in the midst of an electrical storm, near a roaring fire, or when working the land. This is not to say that a water person cannot use a fire-based spell. I do believe, however, they will do so with less intense results than a "fire" person might achieve, simply because it is not their strongest element.

Another use for the elements in magic is in understanding others better. Inevitably, a fire person will feel a little ill-at-ease with a water person because of that underlying difference. Earth is nervous around air because it tends to uproot earth's strong foundations and closeness to its first love, the Mother. Air excites fire; earth with water makes for very muddy relationships.

Of course this generalization is not accurate all the time because most of us have other trace elements as part of our personalities. Even so, this is good information to remember if you meet someone for the first time and can't quite figure why you were immediately defensive.

Air

Mostly connected with wind lore, the element of air was the most elusive of all natural spirits. It would come and go as it pleased, carrying sun or clouds and granting a sense of life to each tree it touched. The howling of the wind was once considered either a restless spirit or a sign of impending trouble, and true enough, a storm would likely follow, giving strength to the folk belief (see Chapter 30: Weather).

In modern practice, the element of air is most commonly associated with mental theory, learning, the signs of Gemini, Libra, and Aquarius, pastel or yellow colors, and all flying creatures. It is considered a difficult element to work with because it can change direction or die altogether.

Even so, many people like to use a southerly wind to empower magic pertaining to energy and vitality, a western wind for creativity and emotions, a northern wind for physical nature and growth, and an eastern wind for psychic matters. For this type of magic an item is often released into the chosen breeze to carry the force of the spell. Feathers, flower petals, colored sand, rice or anything else light enough to blow away can be chosen as appropriate to your work. For example, a crow's feather can be released to impart a message to a friend, or rose petals dispatched on a quest for love. Please note that feathers are best found, not taken. If someone sells feathers, try to be certain of their source.

Other items to be released should be chosen for their safety to the environment (no balloons, for example, which animals can choke on).

Earth

Geomancy is based on the belief that the patterns which already exist in nature, and which are not created by mortal hands, are the best and least biased oracles.

In the Far East, handfuls of dust were tossed in the air and their patterns inspected for astrological and other symbols to predict future events. An alternative to this is where the querist randomly pokes holes in the ground, and their configuration determines the interpretation. A straight line of four holes, for example, meant travel, a road ,or open way, and was also identified with the astrological sign of Leo.

Soil has been used in many cultures to aid healing. For this, soil taken from holy ground is most effective. One practice was to bury the sick up to his or her head in earth, simulating death and fooling the evil into leaving. Mud packs are another medicinal use of earth, most commonly employed for insect bites and beauty aids.

In contemporary magical practices, earth is considered the best element for grounding energy. I frequently use rich soil and seeds as a focus for spells pertaining to personal growth. Fertile soil scattered to the winds can act as a blessing of land and gardens.

This element is frequently represented in the northern point of magical circles usually by a stone, dirt, flowers, the colors brown and green, or other natural objects. In the Far East, earthquakes are really an ancient dragon jumping up and down demanding an offering, so the northern point of your sacred space can also be occupied by a dragon image—especially if you live in California!

Fire

Fire meant not only warmth and light, but also the difference between life and death. Because of this, many superstitions developed pertaining to anything with a flame. With candles, for example, a blue flame is an indication that a spirit is present. One side burning down on a candle is called a winding sheet and foretells death or drastic change, while a bulge in the wick means a mysterious stranger or gift to come.

These folk tales illustrate pyromancy, a form of divination that can be easily attempted by modern practitioners. A question is posed while watching a candle flame's movement. A high or dancing flame is a positive answer, while a low flame or the candle going out is a negative response. Another belief has to do with open fires or fireplaces. When a cinder is thrown from the fire, wait for it to cool. The pattern of a circle equals a purse and money, an oval symbolizes a baby or fertility. When fires burn fiercely and roar it is a warning that some type of storm (emotional or physical) is on the way. An old Mexican custom says if your loved one has gone away, you can see them in the well-tended fire of your hearth and know if they are well.

For modern magic, a fire is used as a hub in many outdoor gatherings and is a favored element for scrying. It is best to use five different woods for your scrying fire (representing the five points of the pentagram and all four elements plus spirit/ether), and to light it with natural flint instead of matches. Then settle in a comfortable position and look to the flames with a specific question in your mind. The flames will probably become blurry, which is fine. You are not really paying attention to the fire itself, but the images that will form within the flames. When you feel tired, or your eyes hurt, stop and make notes of your observations. Try to be patient. Good scrying skills take time to develop, but they will come.

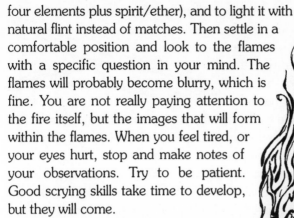

Fire is also a good place to burn away your anger, leave problems, and help improve personal energy. It should never blaze fiercely, but burn steadily, or it will extinguish itself.

Fire is placed at the southern point of our magical circles and is frequently represented by a candle, the colors of red and orange, hot spices or anything else which embodies that intensity. It is also associated with the smoke of incense, which carries our prayers to the God/dess.

Water

In ancient Mesopotamia, guilt or innocence was determined by throwing the accused in into the divine river. If the accused floated, he or she was retrieved. (This was a much kinder version of this trial than that given by the seventeenth century witch hunters.)

Thankfully, many of the superstitions associated with water are not quite so macabre (see Chapter 27: The Sea).

In Egypt, water was considered the father of the Gods, and Babylonians felt the waves were the dwelling place of the divine. Since Ea and Hapi were the two gods associated with water in these cultures, and these figures represented a source of wisdom and knowledge, many techniques of divining by water were used in both regions.

Most frequently these oracles used the surface of water, sometimes stained with ink, as a focus. The magician would usually employ a spell or incantation of some kind, walk around the querist, and ask him or her to look in the water (or the magus would). The images would be described and an interpretation given. A less costly alternative was tossing a pebble into water and counting the number of ripples. An even number meant a positive answer.

One of the more interesting pastimes regarding water is the art of dowsing. Here, a forked branch, usually about eighteen inches in length and one-half inch in diameter, is used in the attempt to locate water. Most who practice this technique believe that it is passed on through family lines, father to daughter or mother to son, and that the dowser acts like a sonograph, with the wood as a needle.

The druids were known to create a potent potion by extinguishing the coals of sacrificial fires with spring water. The remnants were infused with all types of magical power and were suitable filling for the ritual cup. You may want to try a personal alternative to this by quenching your own charcoal with spring water and then using the remaining liquid for herbal tinctures and so on. Do not ingest this.

Native Mexicans regard the river as a symbol of the Mother Goddess. At sacred banks, they leave offerings to Her and other honored ancestors to invoke blessings on them and their houses. This particular tradition would be a charming way to truly honor the spirit of Gaia. Today, since no specific time was given for the offerings, we might want to choose spring, when the icy grip of winter looses its fingers and waters start to run freely, refreshing the earth.

The element of water is placed at the western point of magical circles and is represented by a cup, vase, or bowl, the colors blue or seagreen, a beach stone or shell, or sand.

11 FAERIES

Who, then are the masters, and who of us serves still?
Who, then are the wise ones and where be Faerie hills?
♦ Marian ♦

ORIGINALLY KNOWN as the Fair Folk and *Sidhe* (pronounced she), faeries as we think of them today are not evil creatures, only pranksters. They enjoy tricking country folk, especially those lazy in nature. Faeries cannot stand messes. Some slothful humans will sometimes find their clothes on the floor and small bruises where the creatures were trying to pinch them to get them moving.

In the past, no one would ever uproot a thorn bush, for fear they would find it in their bed. Thorn bushes housed fairy folk. Many milkmaids would leave bowls of honey or cream to befriend the fey in hopes their chores would be done when they awoke. Another tradition, known mostly in England, was to leave a farthing on the edge of a large field you were about to cross. This was a gesture of good faith so that you would not be pixie-led and go astray.

Many plants, such as rings of mushrooms and foxgloves, are associated with the faeries. Throughout history people have gathered or planted specific plants to either attract the wee folk or protect them selves from them. Elder leaves offer safety, while rue, ivy, fern, and straw attract. If you have a window box or small garden, you might like to add a few appropriate plants to encourage faery guests.

These elemental creatures exist throughout the world in various forms. In Arabia they are called *jinn*; in Hawaii, *menehune*; and in France *fee* (a close derivative of our present form of the word *faerie*). Generous humans and lovers attract faeries best, and most frequently they are sighted during transition hours such as noon, midnight, and dusk.

Although the modern mind has, for the most part, relegated these elemental creatures to the storybook shelf, I tend to believe that there is at least some level of truth to the tales. Historically, the fair-folk and *Sidhe* did exist in Celtic regions as real people with strong magical backgrounds. The folklore that grew around them had much to do with their magical adeptness. Why they eventually became depicted as small, winged nature spirits remains a mystery perhaps never to be unraveled.

Even so, the stories remain an important part of our childhoods and cultures; the belief in unseen worlds grants our imagination great richness and calls us to look beyond the surface world. If we remember this lesson in our spiritual quest, we will learn to see much more than the fey; we will also begin to discern the divine self.

Brownies

Described as small, shaggy men with dark-brown skin and wrinkles, brownies stand about twenty inches tall. They adopt homes and enjoy doing various household chores in return for cream and cakes with honey. In Scotland, they are special assistants to brewers. If you are thinking of making ritual wine, you might want to leave a small offering to encourage their assistance.

Elves

Known in Old French as *auberon*, Old English
as *aelf* and Norse as *alfr* (all words meaning
white), elves are very pale in color. Their
ghost-like appearance made them respected
and feared. Among early Germanic peoples,
elves were powerful and frightening. Their depictions show slight-figured people, with pointed ears
and a magical disposition. Depending on their
mood, they could be beneficent or terrible to
humans. Most medieval folklore portrays them
as mischievous and having many subclasses
including dwarves, and gnomes. All traditional
ways of appeasing or protecting oneself from the
fey will work on these creatures.

Faerie Islands

Many places, including the Land Under the Waves and Tir Nan Og, have
been marked on maps as islands of the fey, but they remain undetected
by any explorer. Even more important to these legends is the fact that the
islands are visible only to those who are ready or need to find them. It
reminds me of the old adage: a teacher will appear when you are ready,
only in this case the faeries will only return to humanity when we are prepared to live in harmony with nature. Then, we will see them.

Faerie Loaf

This is a heart-shaped fossil, properly called micrasta. It was food for the
faeries. As such, anyone fortunate enough to have one in their home would
never want for food, especially bread. This pebble symbolizes abundance.

Faerie Mounds and Rings

The faerie mound is an underground fort where these elementals reside.
It is cautioned you should never fall asleep on one as you will slumber a
hundred years. It is unwise to even walk on one without leaving some
type of token for the fey to show your good intentions. A sprig of grass
from such a place would be excellent in an incense to bring relaxation.

Walk around a faery mound nine times during a full moon to find its entrance. While going in is considered dangerous for a mortal, you might wish to place an ear to the ground and listen for the bright music of their celebrations. Take care, however, as these sounds have an hypnotic effect that can lull you unwittingly into slumber for many years.

The faerie ring, a circular collection of mushrooms, is also a very magical place where the wee-folk dwell. Eating these mushrooms (with permission from the faeries) will improve psychic ability. However, be cautious and check the type of mushroom very carefully. Some are poisonous and can cause severe illness.

Faerie Paths

Any section of wood or glade where a straight line of grass appears to be an especially vivid green, or a different shade of green from the surrounding area, is the site of fairy processionals.

Such areas make a good place to meditate on your life's course and goals. Sit comfortably beneath a tree and visualize a goal. Think of it as a path towards tomorrow and envision yourself walking on it. As images and ideas move by you, allow the magic of the faerie path to give you new insight and direction. Make notes of your experience.

Faerie Stones

These small staurolite stones grow naturally in the shape of an equidistant cross. They are though to be formed by faerie tears. Faerie stones were known to the Norse as *gyfu*, meaning "divine gift." With this in mind, carrying a staurolite might be a good way to connect with perspectives and understandings of the higher self.

Gnomes

In Greek, the term *gnome* means earth dweller. Included in this category of faerie are brownies, elves, and dwarves. These creatures are linked directly to the Earth and all that dwell on it. Each flower and plant has its own gnomish spirit to attend it, often abiding there, and sometimes taking on the empathic appearance or attribute of the plant. For example, those that tend a rose would likely be very handsome, while those bound to nightshade are described as thin and pale.

The ancient magi always warned not to betray the trust or selfishly gain power over these creatures. To do so was considered a crime against nature and reaped dire consequences. The lesson from these faeries is really about the web of life and the connections we have to all things. The spirit of creation is all around for those who stop and look.

Goblins

The olive-skinned, pirates of the faerie world, the goblins' favorite time of year is Halloween. Goblins love to snitch things and successfully pull off malevolent pranks. Yet, not all goblins are evil. Those who live in mines are neutral and sometimes helpful.

Miners in Cornish regions claim the goblins (properly called knockers) knock on the walls to tell them where rich veins are. In Germany, they are called *kobolds*, and the Welsh name is *coblynau*. Sometimes the knocker teases miners by making faces and dancing; but if it is given a bit of food, the minor's luck will improve. The best treat to give is a bit of crusty bread with a long shelf-life. This might make a suitable component for luck and prosperity magic.

Horses for Faeries

Faeries are claimed to be able to make serviceable horses for themselves by uttering incantations while sitting upon a sprig of ragwort. This notion has strong resemblance to the superstitions regarding witches and brooms. Thus, the symbolism of ragwort may be used in any spell where you desire movement or progress.

Leprechauns

The word *leprechaun* comes from a term meaning one-shoe-maker. These are solitary creatures who love to work on but one shoe, never pairs. To win over the leprechaun, you must spy him first, because they disappear quickly. Additionally, leprechauns are tricky, roguish, and tenaciously independent.

One story claims that these faeries, so fond of gold, like to hide beneath dock leaves. Carry a dock leaf when you effect prosperity magic to capture this chap and keep good fortune always in your pocket.

Living Spaces for Faeries

Besides the traditional faerie mound, a bed of thyme is a favorite home of the fey. As mentioned earlier, they also seem to be attracted to a number of other plants, such as primrose, ragwort, and foxglove.

If you have a large tree in your yard, especially a thorn, you can create a welcoming faerie circle by planting a circle of annual flowers and foxgloves at its base. Smaller, indoor versions can be set in window boxes with the additional benefit of scenting your home.

Other appropriate additions to please the wee-folk include silver bells or ribbons hung on trees and bits of apple and honey bread left out as a snack.

Names and Faeries

Most country folk would never speak the proper name of a faerie for fear the wee-folk might get angry at the impropriety and cause mischief. Similarly, one would never tell his or her true name to a faerie. To do so would give them great magical power over you. These beliefs go back to the superstitions about names (see Chapter 24: Pregnancy and Children).

Pixies

Residents of the Dartmoor district of Cornwall, pixies are another group of carefree fey. They love to steal horses and toss pots and pans at kitchen girls. If left bread and cheese, though, they will gladly thresh corn and finish other chores.

In the woods of Ireland, pixies can lead you astray. If you step on sod, you will suddenly find you have lost your way. If this happens, turn your coat or other item of clothing inside out to turn the magic.

Protection from Evil Faeries

Protection from goblins was seasonal work. In winter the holly bush was brought into the home; come spring it was replaced with boxwood. Next, by the height of the sun, a yew branch would come into the house, and in the fall, bay. It should be noted that the Yule log itself was never burned to ashes, but kept for kindling as a powerful ward against these creatures.

Other recommended forms of protection from the fey are very similar to those used to change bad luck, mostly because troublesome circumstances were often blamed on the invisible little folk. These methods include turning your clothes inside out, sprinkling salt, wearing bells or daisy chains, carrying a twig of broom, and hanging St. John's wort.

If you happen to feel plagued by a mischievous spirit, it would not hurt to try a bit of this folklore. Holly, boxwood, yew, and bay are still all considered good woods for protection, and in powdered form make a good incense. To this you might add daisy petals, St. Johns Wort and a dash of salt (see Chapter 23: Plants).

Salamanders

Salamanders are those joyous fire spirits who jump and leap until the fires of their lives die. They can also manifest themselves through the smoke of specially prepared incense. They are also believed to be the cause of such wonders as St. Elmo's fire and will-o'-the-wisp. Known properly as *ignis fatuus*, will-o'-the-wisp is a phosphorescent light that hovers over swampy ground. "Friar's lantern" and "foolish fire" are two other names for this phenomena.

Salamanders live in the southern quarter of the world (an area of heat) and have influence over all things of fiery temperament. They are included in human beings as part of our emotional nature, evidenced in the form of body heat.

The salamander offers you an opportunity to hone your observational skills the next time you are sitting quietly by any fire source. Use a soft focus, take a deep breath, and welcome its presence. Watch each tongue of flame for the life within and see what wonders your inner sight reveals. Listen to the crackling, smokey voices as each ember sings, and experience a portion of elemental life that may be totally new to you. With time and careful study, you may discover you can even understand the language of salamanders (or other elementals), who share their perspectives on the natural world with your attentive ears.

Seeing Faeries

In the late seventeenth century, a pastor wrote a recipe to help see the fey. A revised version of this preparation uses one pint of salad oil, rose and marigold water prepared from flowers gathered in the east at early morning. Include buds of hollyhock, thyme, hazel and marigolds plucked from near or on a faerie hill, and a sprig of grass from the knoll itself. Do not use the greens from the flowers. If you can also find a four-leaf clover, all the better. Let the mixture sit in the sun for three days. Strain the oil. Lightly apply to the eyelids for enhanced sight. Before you meditate use this oil on pulse points, chakras, or a small amount on your eyelids to improve your visionary abilities (caution: keep this closer to your eyebrow so that it doesn't get on the surface of your eye).

Sylphs

Invisible, intangible air elementals with gossamer wings, sylphs live in clouds and on the tops of mountains. This is the most commonly pictured faerie. In some folklore, sylphs are assigned the duty of protecting humans from evil spirits, and do resemble guardian angels.

A sylph's duties include gathering clouds and making snowflakes, using each breeze as a vehicle and never growing old. These creatures may have had some direct influence on ancient oracles, particularly the speaking oak of Greek legend (see Chapter 23: Plants).

They are associated with the east, as our sacred space honors the air. They represent mirthfulness, and are considered the perpetual gypsies of the universe. Sylphs, in this regard, are excellent assistants to air magic, along with any matters of joy, daydreaming, or travel.

Times of Visibility

Several times of the year have always been considered best for faerie sightings and antics. On Midsummer's night, Faeries can speak the human tongue, and twelve flowers bloom in their honor, all of which grow in faerie rings.

On Twelfth Night in Italy, a good faerie blesses homes and fills children's stockings with sweets. This is an excellent day to welcome the spirit of the kindly fey into your home or circle to bring good fortune. On the eve of May Day, Victorian women would bake sweet cakes and place them in a garden near the thyme. The next morning they would rush out early and see if the sweets had disappeared. If so, it was a definite sign that the little people were pleased.

There is no reason why you can't try this procedure yourself. Use a biscuit-like recipe that would please the fairy folk and your neighborhood birds alike.

Undines

Undines are water elementals whose essence is fluid, natural beauty. The embodiment of grace, they almost always appear as female—one form is the commonly known mermaids (or *merrimaid*, a term possibly derived from the one of the ancient names for the Goddess of the Sea, Myri).

Undines are special friends to fishing villages and families, whom they enjoy serving. Although they are emotional beings, they appreciate any true, unaffected loveliness. They are associated with the west.

12 GARDENING AND FARMING

The fields which answered well the ancients' plow.
♦ Abraham Crowley, *To Mr. Hobbs* ♦

 MUCH OF the folklore surrounding gardening and farming grew out of the need to survive. When crops failed for whatever reason, people relied on their wits, wisdom, and superstitions to try to recoup their losses the following season.

Folk methods for fighting insects, effective growing, harvesting and storage techniques, fertilization, irrigation, and so on, developed through trial and error. Farmers looked to the weather signs and the moon's phases to help them know what type of season it would be, what best to plant, and when.

For the magical gardener, these bits of wisdom are very useful, especially for those of us who prefer chemical-free cultivation. This approach is not only better for Gaia, but also more appropriate for spiritual applications. Additionally, old-time gardening suggestions follow astrological guides. This gives modern green thumbs many more options for their personal efforts.

These ideas are fun to try in your apartment with window sill boxes or small planters placed strategically in well-lit areas. You will find that puttering with soil can be relaxing, teaches you a great deal about natural cycles, and has many other benefits, not the least of which are fresh herbs and vegetables for your kitchen.

Beating the Bounds

In ancient Rome, once a year there would be a procession performed around the land you owned, the town you lived in, or both, to bless the soil. Called beating the bounds, the holiday corresponded to another festival, Terminalia, and was performed with a sprinkling of water or garlands of flowers to insure the land would be safe and rich for the coming year. This action drew a protected spiritual sphere around the village and its inhabitants, and is very suitable to recreate just before your own growing season.

Blessing the Land and Seeds

This festival is commonly held just after the first thaw, or just before planting. Predominantly a rural festival, it brings divine favor to the land and all the crops sewn therein. One example comes from China, where civil and military officials go to the fields in procession and make offerings of grains, fruit, meat, and wine on southern-facing altars. After the presentation, the highest ranking official prays to the Gods with careful humility. This same person then plows several channels in the fields, digs in the ground nine times, and finally returns to town (see Chapter 21: Numbers).

Another example is Ceralia, from Rome. In honor of the Goddess Ceres, Roman farmers danced around their fields with torches on April 13. Generally the farmers wore white, Ceres' color, while blessing their crops and land. In later years these movements were translated into folk dances throughout that region.

A third illustration is the Roman planting festivals that took place in late January. One week apart, Romans held two separate planting festivals known as *Feriae Sementivae*, or the "feasts of sowing." These honored Tellus, who presides over fertile soil, and the Goddess Ceres, patroness of agriculture. Ceres was specifically represented by poppies, chariots, and depictions of dragons.

Corn

Corn has long symbolized the life of the land. Corn husks are used in a diversity of folk arts to bring prosperity, protection, and fertility to the home. Most common are corn dolls, made in a variety of forms. Human shapes encouraged plentiful harvests, while an animal construct was to protect the livestock for the next year. The traditional corn ornaments are made from the last tuft of corn gathered.

Corn dolls do not have to be fancy. You can make some very ornamental pieces by wrapping husks around a scented sachet, tying with a ribbon, and hanging in a window to bring fresh aromas and prosperity.

Corn sachet

Navaho and Seneca tradition incorporated the use of popcorn as a form of divination by throwing a few kernels on the fire. The reading was determined by observing which direction they flew and how many popped. This might be fun to try at home on a cold fall night. Kernels to the right are a positive answer; to the left, a negative response. The number of them coming out of your hearth usually indicates a time frame in which the situation will be resolved (weeks or months).

Finally, Cherokees always plant their corn with beans and squash due to a legend that claims these three are sisters, never to be separated. We now know that these three staples provide a high quantity of protein in the diet.

If you are planning your own magical garden, perform this dance either beforehand to bless the ground, or afterwards to encourage your seeds. In both cases move in a sunward (clockwise) direction, during a waxing moon, while offering rice or bread crumbs to the winds so that the sympathetic elemental energies are invoked. The actual steps performed are of little importance; do what feels right at the moment and rejoice with your handiwork. This movement is not just a way to coax your plants, but also to thank the Great Spirit for continuing providence (see Chapter 8: Dance).

Fertile Fields

A twelfth-century German manuscript describes a magical way to make a barren field fertile again. For this, the individual must awaken before dawn and pull four clumps of land from each quarter of his or her property. Oil, milk, honey and blessed water are sprinkled over the soil while reciting in Latin "Be fruitful and multiply and fill the earth." After that, the rest of the day is spent in prayer and supplication until sundown, when the soil is returned to its place, and the land is considered renewed.

This is a lovely ritual that can be used with modern magic. You may wish to change the incantation to something more personally appropriate. This rite is also suitable to times when you need rejuvenation. In this instance, the soil represents you, is blessed, and then be returned to the ground, allowing the energy to grow. Keep a pinch of this soil in your medicine pouch.

Grafting

Grafting entails taking the bud or shoot from one plant and inserting it into another to grow permanently. This often produces higher quality fruit. According to lunar gardening techniques, the best time to cut for a graft is during Capricorn (December 22 to January 21), then attach the sprig during the fruitful sign of Pisces (February 22 to March 21).

On a spiritual level these signs bode well for planting specific virtues in your own life.

Growing Aids

Moss agate is the farmer's best friend. Worn on the right arm and fastened to the plow, it will bring abundant harvests. Therefore, wear moss agate while working your own garden for times when you need to reap the fruits of your labors.

In much the same manner, moonstone aids the growth of plants and trees in an orchard or garden setting. In this case, the stone is to be placed in the ground, but not completely covered, so that it can reflect the beneficial rays of the moon to the nearby greenery.

Harvest

Top-growing crops such as corn and tomatoes are best harvested between the hours of 10 A.M. and 3 P.M. for freshness and longevity. Root crops, on the other hand, should be taken late in the afternoon to preserve flavor and firmness. This probably developed because farmers regarded root crops as "dark" and usually planted them at the New Moon. Top-grown crops are more solar and thus reactive to the hottest hours of the day (10-3). The only exception to this rule was peas because they grow counterclockwise.

Spiritually, when you are trying to improve your foundations, perform your spells or visualizations in the afternoon, whereas fruit-bearing efforts can be done between 10 A.M. and 3 P.M. to follow this symbolism.

Harvest of Magical Herbs

Magical herbs are most potent if harvested on midsummer's day. Draw a magic circle around the plant with a double-edged sword or flint knife before cutting it so that its energy is protected. A small bit of wheat cake should be left as a way of giving back to nature for what you have gathered.

Magnetism

Magnetism can help plants grow and bear a higher yield. It is recommended that a copper wire be strung around the boundaries of the garden or field (slightly off the ground), with one end of it planted in the soil.

Copper wire can be employed in the sacred space to help ground energy after an intense ritual, or could be placed around the outside of your home to help connect you with the earth's abundant power. (This second option would be especially beneficial for those who have a tendency towards daydreaming or flights of fancy to keep their feet on the ground.)

Moon Signs

Strict students of moon sign agriculture believe there is a precise time for each gardening activity. A rural saying tells us that, while nonchemical gardening teaches us how to work with nature, astrology gives us a guide as to when. Here is a brief review of some of these rules:

- ◆ Aries: Arid and stark, really only good for planting onions or garlic.
- ◆ Taurus: Semi-fertile, fairly prolific. The earthy quality of this sign makes it good for any root crops such as potatoes. It is also reliable for leafy vegetables.
- ◆ Gemini: Dry and barren. Do not transplant or plant during this time. Instead concentrate on weeding and cultivation of plants already growing.
- ◆ Cancer: The most productive of all zodiac signs for gardening. Excellent for grafting, transplanting, sowing, and budding. Yields under this sign should be increased visibly.
- ◆ Leo: The driest least fertile sign of the zodiac. The best time to rid the garden of undesired insects.
- ◆ Virgo: Moist, but almost as barren as Leo.
- ◆ Libra: Damp and fairly productive. Flowers, root crops, vines, lettuce, corn, vines, and hay all do well.
- ◆ Scorpio: Second most productive sign; good not only for growth, but also strength of vines.
- ◆ Sagittarius: Tends towards the arid, but considered productive for onions and hay crops.
- ◆ Capricorn: Similar in nature to Taurus but a bit more arid; plant tubers and other root crops.

- Aquarius: Dry, barren. Cultivate and turn your soil, get rid of any unwanted pests and weeds.

- Pisces: Productive, fruitful. Plant anything that requires good root growth.

At the turn of the century, some still believed plants carried a physical resemblance to the planetary sign ruling them. These associations can be very useful when you are working magic governed by a specific planet. To illustrate, a spell to improve your intuitive sense would be considered under the jurisdiction of the moon; therefore, a willow branch or lily would be a good spell component. Here are some sample correspondences:

- Sun: orange, saffron, chamomile, sunflower, rosemary, marigold.
- Moon: melon, pumpkin, water lilies, lettuce, willow.
- Mercury: carrot, marjoram, caraway, parsley, fennel.
- Venus: tomatoes, periwinkle, violet, apple, strawberry.
- Mars: tarragon, garlic, onion, pepper, radish, basil.
- Jupiter: clove, anise, oak, nutmeg, sage, dandelion.
- Saturn: elm, pine, barley, cypress.

This list is further complicated by the four phases of the moon. The rule of thumb is to plant underground foods in the last phases of the moon, and above-ground plants while the moon is waxing.

- First quarter: Best for leafy annual plants, especially green ones, with above-ground yield, such as broccoli, cauliflower, celery, parsley, spinach, asparagus, lettuce, and leeks.
- Second quarter: Similar to the first quarter, only best for rounder objects, such as cantaloupe, eggplant, peas, peppers, squash, tomato, cucumbers, and beans. Plant with the moon in Cancer, Scorpio, or Pisces for best results.
- Third quarter: Bulb and root crops, any vegetation with yield in the ground. Beets, garlic, potatoes, carrots, turnips, and radishes all do well, as do most fruit bushes.

♦ Fourth quarter: The time of rest. Turn your soil during the barren signs of Leo, Virgo, and Gemini to help rid yourself of weeds and pests. Good time to harvest, especially if combined with the signs of Aquarius, Aries, Gemini, Leo, or Sagittarius.

So, how do you put all this information together for magic? Well, obviously you could just use it for gardening, but there are hundreds of other creative applications for spell and ritual work, too. For example, use the moon sign of Aquarius during a waning quarter to rid yourself of bad habits, or the sign of Scorpio with a waxing moon to improve your personal strength.

First consider what the basic meaning of the moon phases are (see Chapter 18: Magic and the Supernatural), then add to that the significance of the signs. Between these two you should be able to find a personally meaningful time frame for working most of your spells, visualizations, and rituals.

Planting and Sowing

Planting and sowing are most commonly done during a waxing moon, because the growth of the lunar sphere should also help the vegetation prosper. Two interesting exceptions to this rule are runner beans and peas which, because the vines climb counterclockwise on a pole, are planted during the waning moon.

Our ancestors also paid close attention to the subtle signals their own crops gave them. Simple growing charts were created to note when the seeds came up, and under what weather conditions. These types of tabulations helped decipher what items were best to plant, when to plant them and how to do what is called stage planting to attain the longest growing season. I have recently tried this method and am learning much about the earth and her communications to us.

Seeds

A way to discover the order of future events is to plant five seeds in five different planters named after five circumstances. Make sure the soil receives the same amount of light and water, then watch to see the order in which they germinate. The first to sprout will be the first event to come to pass.

Seeds are often used in growth, change, and prosperity related magic because of their symbolism. In most instances they are planted or carried to allow the energy to germinate and blossom like the plant itself.

Soil

According to farming tradition, seed soil is thought best prepared (ie, fertilized, turned, in February, under the sign of Aquarius, and during the last quarter of the moon. If this time of year is too cold, then wait until it warms enough and follow the same directions.

Similarly, this is a good time of the year to consider ways of enriching your own life, and beginning an activity to help accomplish that goal.

Tools

Rubbing bear fat on your tools makes them impervious to mildew and rust. Since this may be difficult for some people to do today, an alternative is to periodically clean your gardening and magical tools (metal ones only) with an anointing oil of your own preparation. I personally like frankincense and myrrh in an almond oil base because of its cleansing quality. Oiling the tool serves dual functions. It keeps the tool free of rust, and using magically prepared oils dispels any unwanted residual energy.

To prepare this oil for yourself, work during a waning moon (the idea is to banish the rust). Take a teaspoon each of powdered or crystallized frankincense and myrrh (or other herbs of your choosing) and place them in oil which has been warmed. If you do not have almond oil, good olive or safflower oil also works well. This bottle needs to be left in sunlight and shaken daily for at least a month before use.

When the oil is not in use, continue to leave the container in the light to improve the incorporation. When you reach a half bottle, pour in more oil and a few grains of fresh herb to help renew the scent. This oil is also an excellent anointing compound to use in preparation for any magical working, as well as a personal perfume or cologne.

Wheat

The last sheath of wheat in many country traditions is called the *wheat maiden.* It is taken in the house and kept until the following year to ensure bounty (then returned to soil). In autumn, harvest festivals are given by farmers to workers as a way of sharing their wealth so they will never want.

Keeping a bit of wheat in your home prevents poverty. Place a sprig on your altar whenever finances are difficult, or carry it in your wallet. If actual wheat isn't available, there are several commercial cereals on the market that are "wheat puffs" that you can substitute. Remember, it's not the fanciness of your spellwork but the sincerity of intention that is important.

Yule Log

The ashes of a Yule log scattered in a field or garden will prevent your root crops from rotting. These ashes are also considered a very strong protective agent for your home. Scattering a bit in your sacred space, around the house or in any area that you are blessing will bring positive energy. Always keep a bit to burn with the new log next year so that the good fortune is carried over.

13 HEALTH AND MEDICINE

The feeling of health, the full noon trill
the song of me rising from bed and meeting the sun.
♦ Walt Whitman, *Song of Myself* ♦

SICKNESS WAS one of the most difficult aspects of life for early humans to understand. Until science began discovering the physical causes of disease, people figured out their own reasons, frequently blaming malignant or angry spirits.

Some learned to control these forces, spurring the development of the shaman and medicine men. People were awed by medicine men because of their apparent power over sickness. The more often a cure worked, the more popular and trusted a specific healer became. Being both priests and physicians, these individuals developed ceremonies and rites to incorporate into their position, making it more elite. Remnants of these rites may still linger in some of our approaches to health and folk medicine today.

Unlike modern doctors, early healers assumed no responsibility for their work. Diseases and cures were matters left to the Gods. The Gods gave and took these gifts as they saw fit. Because of this, for many generations healers had no reason to discover the real cause of disease and its prevention.

Egyptians evoked their gods, administered plant substances as guided by divine wisdom, and performed a bit of crude surgery. The Greeks treated healing as a science, but it was not maintained at that level. Anglo-Saxons called upon Woden in their healing rites, while the Christian monks relied on the "Father, Son, and Holy Spirit."

Hippocrates changed this by separating religion from healing and placing responsibility for medical treatment with the practitioner. He observed and recorded the symptoms of disease, supplied philosophy and ethics (the Hippocratic oath), and began to classify sickness. His attention centered on both the patient and the disease to affect cures.

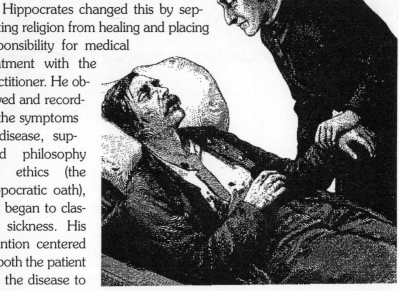

This did not eradicate superstition or folk medicine by any means. These remained deep-seated until around 1920, lingering on the edges of mainstream medicine. This was due to short life spans and the inaccessibility of trained medical professionals for most people. Consequently, the folklore remained. Some of these superstitions centered around ideas about how the body works, and others related to specific cures for ailments.

Many contemporary folk healers combine medicine and magic into a singular, flowing system. They harvest their herbs by lunar, planetary, and star cycles. They might pray, intone, or recite incantations as they prepare the ingredients, and they frequently give credit for their skills not only to practice and the knowledge of their ancestors, but also to the Great Spirit.

This allows the modern magician a whole new approach to personal and family care—the ability to blend the power of faith with tecnical information. If, by way of example, you have a cold, you can combine eucalyptus leaves, which are proven to help this ailment, with a dash of blessed pepper in your tea for cleansing. Another example would be to wrap a sore muscle in scrap cloth, then remove and bury the cloth to likewise bury the pain.

If you are contemplating using folk medicine for personal care, and blending it with magical rites, you should use caution and a healthy amount of common sense. Folk remedies cannot replace the advice of a trained healthcare provider. It may only give you peace of mind, but it is a serenity well worth the cost of an office visit.

One other word of caution. If you begin to practice folk medicine in your home, inevitably people will ask you for teas or recommendations on their own conditions. It is fine to help, but do so with care. Advise people that what you share is based on lore, and that it cannot always be proven medically effective.

Amulets for Health

To relive pain, touch the affected area with an amulet created from a poultice of red coral and ash leaves. Bury the amulet under an oak tree. Similar methods were used to rid the body of warts. A potato was applied to the wart, then buried. For any health-related magic, coral, ash leaves, oak leaves or a piece of potato makes an excellent focuses or components.

Arthritis

One teaspoon of chopped garlic twice daily with water is reputed to ease arthritis symptoms. This folk remedy may have come from the belief that garlic aids the blood circulation. Other options include wearing charmed belts or blessed cords of wool near the afflicted area.

Athlete's Foot

Saltwater soaks and cornstarch powder dusted on the feet daily work against the fungus that causes athlete's foot. In ancient Greece, you may have been given powdered orris root. This not only helps keep your feet dry, but also relieves odors.

Bee Stings

Plant leaves are the common denominator in methods of relieving the pain and itch of bee stings. Turks apply wet tobacco leaves directly to the sting. In other cultures, various types of plant leaves or petals are used, including burdock, dandelion, and marigold.

Burns

The three most universal aids to spread over a burn are damp baking soda, honey, or aloe. Any of these might also be metaphorically applied in a spell to ease fiery anger. Rub the substance over a picture of the individual who is irate.

Colds

A tea made of lemon juice and honey in warm water is soothing, and hot tar smoke is thought to relieve and prevent coughs. If you put seven beans in your pocket and throw one away each day, by the end of the week your cold should be gone (see Chapter 21: Numbers). This can be further assisted by eating horseradish.

Constipation

A daily cup of licorice and senna tea works to relieve constipation. These herbs are also excellent magical ingredients for spells to overcome an artistic block or any other barrier.

Cramps

Ginger and pepper combine for a good hot drink to ease stomach cramps.

For muscle cramps, wear a garter of corks near the afflicted muscle or place it between the springs of your bed and the mattress. This last idea may have developed because, when a cork is taken from a bottle, it releases pressure with a pop. Consider employing this symbolism any time you feel constrained or limited.

Diarrhea

Peppermint tea is one of the best-known remedies for this uncomfortable condition. An alternative drink is ginger tea with two teaspoons of vinegar and a dash of salt.

Dog Bite

The bite of a mad dog was once thought to be cured by eat-
ing some of the creature's hair boiled or
fried with rosemary. This was how the
saying "hair of the dog that bit you"
came into being and is an excellent early
example of sympathetic magic. Thus,
when people drink alcohol for a hang-
over, they are using the "biting" item to
effect their cure.

Eyewash

Rinsing the eye with the water used for steeping a lapis stone is said to
relieve itching eyes. One word of caution: be sure the lapis and water
are both clean and free from impurities. Lapis water blessed beneath a
full moon can also enhance psychic vision.

Fever

Goldenseal tea and a teaspoon of lemon juice taken every four hours
reduces fever. Another recommendation is to take clippings of your fingernails and mix them with warm wax which is then bound to a tree or
rock so that the fever is attached to something other than you.

Similar symbolism can be used when you are feeling angry and out
of balance. In a symbolic sense, you are literally disengaging the negativity from yourself.

Gemstones

The use of gemstones in remedial work was closely tied to their color,
planet of influence, and other commonly associated superstitions (see
Chapter 7: Crystals, Gems and Metals). Red stones, for example, were
frequently considered helpful for blood conditions, green stones for all
types of healing, and blue for improving emotional disposition.

Gems were used in a wide variety of ways not only as curatives, but
also to ward off sickness. In many instances, the individual was
instructed to wear or carry the stone in a specific manner, frequently
near the center of the prevailing problem. This was done so that the
stone could collect any illness.

An alternative to amuletic work was the gem elixir. These may or may not have actually been made from gemstones, considering the expense involved and the cleverness of many healers. Instead, solutions likely had the appearance of a particular stone in coloration. The other option was to place a particular stone in any liquid for a duration of time to allow absorbtion of its positive remedial qualities. Some of these costly cures include diamonds and emeralds for an antidote for poison, jade for kidney disease, jasper for stomach ailments, ruby for flatulence, topaz for the plague, and bloodstone to stop hemorrhaging.

Crystalline elixirs are used by many people in the New Age community today to internalize specific aspects of a stone. Usually the gem (or crystal) is steeped in spring water by the light of the sun or moon, depending on its intended use. The stone is removed afterwards and the liquid drunk.

To make your own drink, refer to the section on crystals and find the attribute you need. For example, if you are giving a speech soak an agate for eloquence. Rinse the stone under running water, then add it to your spring water. In this instance, set it in the light of both the sun and moon to give your speech power and creativity.

Headaches

An amethyst, warmed by the rays of the sun, wrapped in silk, and then bound lightly to the temples eases the pain of a headache. Wearing rings of lead or quicksilver also prevents and soothes this difficulty. These suggestions are likewise applicable for psychically caused pain as experienced from overexertion in a reading, or returning to normal awareness too quickly after meditation.

King's Evil

This is a disease of the lymph glands thought in the Middle Ages to be cured only by the touch of a reigning monarch. The first instance we see of King's Evil is during the time of Edward the Confessor (A.D. 1042-1066). Most likely, this superstition was invented by the court to improve the king's esteem in the eyes of the populace.

Since kings are not readily available these days, a supplication directly to the king and queen of the heavens can be made to reduce the swelling of the lymph glands. Or wear a piece of blue flannel tied nine times around your neck. The warmth of the flannel, combined with its peaceful color was considered a powerful combination (see Chapter 6: Color).

Laryngitis

When your voice leaves you, try gargling three times with a combination of vinegar, rainwater, and honey. Salt and garlic water are also effective. In England, country physicians recommend the juice of a boiled cabbage with honey.

By adding a little incantation, such as "through the gums and past the lips, my speech is strengthened with each sip," you can also use these concoctions before a speaking engagement to empower your presentation. While the incantation may seem a little silly, it is easily committed to memory and has a meter which allows for rhythmic repetition.

Laying on of Hands

Great power and reverence has always been given to the hands of the healer. They are the conduit not only of divine energy, but also, more immediately significant, of relief from pain. Many religions and even modern science speak of the amazing power of touch to calm, reassure, and grant emotional relief on a temporary basis. Many healing methods have developed from the simple laying on of hands, for example, acupressure, shiatsu, and reiki. In these methods, pressure points, massage, and touch are incorporated to improve circulation, ease pain, perform auric cleansings, and even cure hiccups.

Melancholy

To cure a case of melancholy in India, healers suggested wearing lapis lazuli around the neck and keeping busy so there wasn't time to think about troubles.

Pain

Jade or lapis worn on any afflicted area is thought to relieve pain. Once the pain is gone, the stone should either be thoroughly cleansed in salt-water or buried so the pain isn't returned the next time the gem is handled. For emotional pain, place the stone over your heart.

Prescriptions

Medicinal prescriptions have been found in cultures dating from ancient Mesopotamia, Egypt, Greece, and Rome. These first prescriptions included clearly written instructions and pictures. These images were not only for the illiterate, but also were believed to help improve the effectiveness of the folk cure. (Considering the handwriting of many contemporary physicians, they might want to consider doing likewise.)

More seriously, we can continue this tradition by adding appropriate runes or other personal symbols to any written spell.

Sand Paintings

One of the more interesting healing traditions is that of sacred sand painting practiced by the Hopi culture in the southwestern United States. Here, it is regarded as a kind of magic, where the ancestors and the Gods are called in to aid the patient.

When the shaman finishes the painting (usually a two-day process), the patient sits on one portion while the shaman chants and blesses him or her. Eventually, some indication is given to the healer that the work is complete, and the sand painting is destroyed with the remains being given to the to the winds.

In our own healing rituals, sand could be used in a similar manner. Personally significant symbols can be sketched with various colors of sand, then given to the afflicted person to hold. He or she should then direct all aches and pains to the grains of sand while releasing them to the winds. This will carry the sickness away.

Scapegoat

The term *scapegoat* dates back to the time when animals were used for disease transference (see Chapter 2: Animals and Insects). Here, one particular animal would be chosen to bear the sickness of the entire community, and would then be ritually killed, burned, or buried to cure the people.

Most magical people today disdain such activities as disrespectful to the animals involved, so a kinder alternative should be considered. Inanimate objects such as the sand illustrated above can be substitute for a creature with equal effectiveness, since symbolism is the most important factor in sympathetic magic.

Skin Disease

Tenth-century Anglo-Saxons used a basic preparation of goose fat mixed with elecampane, bishop's wort, cleavers, and a spoonful of old soap, lathered it onto the skin at night to relieve skin problems. Additionally, a little blood taken from a scratch on the neck was released into a flowing stream to magically carry the sickness. While it moved away, the afflicted person would say, "take this disease and depart with it" three times, then return home by an open road, going both ways in silence.

Sneezing

The sneeze was considered a message direct from God or a bit of the soul being released. In Scotland, parents waited impatiently for their child's' first sneeze to prove there was no fairy hold over him or her and that the child was thus of sound mind.

There is also a form of divination by sneezing: if you sneeze after dinner it means good health; three sneezes in a row portend gifts or a letter; two, a wish; five, silver; and six, gold. Perhaps it seems a little silly to try, but if you are performing prosperity magic, you might keep a little pepper handy to see if the sneeze helps empower your spell!

Sympathetic Magic

Sympathetic, or symbolic magic, whether called by that name or not, is common throughout various cultures. For example, the patient would have a string attached to the affected area and the healer would place the other end in his mouth to suck out the sickness; to break curses or mark transitions from the sickness to health, the patient would be moved through a fire or wreath.

Similar versions of sympathetic magic can be seen in prescriptions calling for a wool string to be worn around the neck to a cure cold, red glass beads worn as a necklace to prevent nosebleeds, placing medicine on an object to help cure a wound it inflicted, and making headaches disappear by sleeping with scissors under your pillow.

The marvelous part about sympathetic magic is the wide variety of creative approaches it offers. Consider what it is you are trying to accomplish, an appropriate symbol of that goal, and finally what magical procedures you want to follow, and you have just originated a personalized spell or ritual.

Toothaches

A nearly universal treatment for toothache is clove oil. In Kenya, wax or chewing gum is used for temporary fillings. Another interesting superstition is that a wedding ring touched to an aching tooth will relieve the pain because of the power of love.

Toxins

In Scotland, a poultice of onions is applied to the stomach and armpits in order to help the body sweat out any toxic materials. This might be a good folk remedy to try when you are going through a personal purification or attempting to rid yourself of a physically addictive habit such as smoking.

◆ ◆ ◆

A final word of caution to those readers with a history of allergies or other recurring medical problems. It is best, in your case, to consult your doctor before trying any folk remedy. Please be prudent, careful, and wise.

14 HOLIDAYS

If St. Paul's Day be fair and clear
it doth betide a happy year.
♦ Monk's rhyme ♦

EVERY CULTURE has special days set aside for gathering people together to celebrate or commemorate specific events or ideas. Most of these festivals include processionals, dancing, feasts, and games, to help give the community a greater sense of history and tradition. Any time such observances are shared from generation to generation, superstition and folklore are almost sure to follow. This, too, is part of the society and part of what makes each gathering unique.

Magical rites are filled with custom and traditions, some of whose origins we can only begin to ponder. Those of our own ancestors alone comprise a rich heritage to share, but many holidays initiated by other traditions can also benefit our magic in important ways.

This chapter explores the lore behind magical holidays and other festivals commonly held around the world.

April Fool's Day (April 1)

The origins of this holiday are uncertain. Some historians believe it started when New Year's Day switched from March 25 to January 1. Those who did not recognize the change were regarded as foolish and given silly gifts as a joke.

In France, April 1 is called "Fish Day" because the population of young fish in the water begins increasing around this time. These youthful animals seemed more gullible than the rest, and were easily caught. Perhaps people "hooked" by a prank appeared similarly foolish.

Another possible source for this celebration is the Roman *Veneralia*, a holiday for Venus. On this day, women washed images of the Goddess and adorned her with precious gems. All activities on this day ensured easy births, joy, beauty, and happy relationships. If this is the source of April Fool's, one might suspect that it is because love tends to make even the wisest among us do foolish things!

Whatever the source, the art of fooling is taken to its pinnacle on this day, along with certain predictions about the weather. If the winds are blowing, it is a good sign for hay and corn. If it's chilly, the next fall harvest will be plentiful. And of course, we all know that "April showers bring May flowers."

For your own celebrations, let the youth have their fun with you today. Enjoy harmless jokes and rejoice in the sounds of laughter.

Autumn Equinox (approximately September 22)

The word *equinox* means "equal night." It is named after the Roman Goddess Nox, whose domain is darkness. Almost all celebrations on this day mark the changing seasons and shifting light. After the equinox, increasingly shorter days will foreshadow the coming of winter.

The Celts also indicated this moment of balance in their holiday Mabon, which honored the Fairy Queen Mab. The activities of faerie folk elevate during "in between" times, when the veil between worlds grows thin.

In Japan the holiday is called Higan, which means "other shore." The sun sets due west in this region now, which is where the Buddhist heaven lies. With the line between this world and the next so drawn, this becomes a date to remember and pray for the dead.

Egyptians celebrated the equinox with their holiday "Staves of the Sun." With the solar disk growing fainter, they believed it needed extra support in the sky; thus, staves would be lifted toward the heavens during this observance. They also played a special game in which they would ritually lose, and then uncover an image of a bull (the Sun God, Osiris). This portrayed the eternal power of light.

Magically, this is an excellent day to focus on personal balance. If you have neglected your health or rest, take time to refill those inner wells.

Birthday of the Moon (September 15)

Today the Chinese worship the moon as the ultimate representation of the *yin* or feminine principle. As the story goes, the Emperor Ming Wong walked through a garden with his priest. While conversing, the Emperor asked what the moon was made from, so the priest magically took him there. Upon their return to earth, Ming Wong played on his flute and tossed gold coins to the people below because of his joy. When asked the next day where the music and gold had come from, he replied that the wonders had occurred because it had been the moon's birthday.

It is traditional on this holiday to have lanterns burning all night (in fire-safe containers) along with white paper lanterns that look like full moons when lit. Families bake moon-shaped cakes to delight children and adults alike. Cassia wood incense, the scent of immortality, is burned while people take fruits of the harvest to rooftops to bask in moonlight. This brings good health and blessings.

If you would like to follow this folkway, your "harvest" can be represented by any easily stored food, such as potatoes, noodles, and rice. If a rooftop isn't available, how about the top of your car or a table in the back yard?

Another fun activity, which the children of China enjoy, is watching for falling "flowers" from the sky (meteors). The traditional interpretation was if a young girl saw one many children were in her future; if a young man saw one prosperity was his.

Bridget's Day/Groundhog Day/Candlemas (February 2)

The daughter of an Irish chieftain, Bridget lived beneath a great oak at Kildare. Bridget gave her life to caring for baby animals, specifically woodland creatures. She was worshiped as a triple Goddess in Celtic regions and was credited with many sacred wells which produced healing waters.

Candlemas is dedicated to rooting out any darkness in our lives. In Germany, people watched to see if hibernating animals came out of their lairs on this day. If they did and saw the sunshine, it foretold forty more days of winter. This activity translated into Groundhog Day, brought to America by German immigrants.

In the magic circle, candles can be left to burn themselves out (in fire-safe containers) to symbolize the power to the sun. Take time to meditate on the dark shadows in your life, then scare them with glowing candlelight! Also, extend special care toward the animals you cherish by way of blessings and special foods.

Carnival (date varies)

Just prior to the Lenten season, carnivals occur in various cultures as a time of revelry. The best example is Mardi Gras in New Orleans. Mardi Gras means "fat Tuesday," because it is traditional to eat meat and fatty foods before Ash Wednesday, which is observed with fasting. Similarly, the word *carnival* comes from two words, *carne vale*, meaning "farewell to the flesh," agains a reference to not eating meat.

Day of the Dryads (August 1-3)

Dryads are demi-deities, mystical creatures of nature which hold power over specific plants or water sources. These deities were celebrated in Macedonia. During the three-day celebration, no vine was to be cut and no washing done. Anyone attempting to do so invited mishap from the drymiais (dryads). If you needed to bathe, the only way to protect yourself was to carry iron.

Since summer months are perfect for outings, consider holding your own dryad celebration during this period. Take any children

in your life on a faerie hunt, looking for mushroom rings and fairy herbs. Leave small cakes for the fey and enjoy being outdoors!

Dervish Dancing Fesitival (early December)

In early December, time is set aside in Turkey specifically for dervish dancing. Dervishes are members of a Sufi whose participants attain altered states of awareness through ecstatic dance. The basic belief is that religious devotion, mirrored by bodily expression (dance), brings the individual into union with God.

The dervish's method for gathering divine knowledge and inspiration compare with those of early Israelite prophets. During and after the dancing, the dervishes perform divinations for those gathered.

Earth Day (April 22)

Earth Day began in 1970 as a version of Arbor Day with a more contempoary general ecological focus. This is a perfect opportunity to plant seedlings in a nearby park, coordinate recycling efforts, have litter patrols, and share ingenious, effective ways to help the Earth with your friends and neighbors.

Easter (date varies)

Easter is the traditional Christian holiday held each spring to celebrate the resurrection of Jesus Christ. There are many old customs that stem from this holiday. The Easter parade dates back to Constantine the Great, who ordered the people to bedeck themselves in lavish colors and clothes to commemorate the resurrection of Jesus Christ. Hot cross buns come to us from the Anglo-Saxon tradition of Esotre, named after that fruitful goddess. If you would like to make these yourself, almost any biscuit recipe will do, with a little flavored icing, but here is one version to try:

Hot Cross Buns

4 cups flour	⅓ cup sugar
2 pkgs active yeast	½ cup oil
¾ tsp. salt (optional)	3 eggs
½ tsp. ginger	1 egg white
½ tsp. cinnamon	⅓ cup currants or raisins
¾ cup milk	

Place flour, yeast, salt, ginger and cinnamon in a large bowl. Warm the oil, milk and sugar over low flame, then add to the dry ingredients along with your eggs. Beat these on low for ½ minute, then 3 minutes on high. Hand stir in your currants and/or raisins, sprinkling on just enough flour to shape the dough into a large ball. Place in a warm area and let rise for 1½ hours.

Punch down the ball and fashion into buns. Place these on a greased baking sheet. Allow to rise again for 45 minutes. You may either cut an equidistant cross in each at this time or decorate them later using confectionery sugar frosting. Brush the top of each bun with a mixture of egg white and butter. Then, bake at 375 degrees for 15 minutes.

The Easter egg has a very long heritage, originating in Persia more than five thousand years ago, where they used colored eggs as a celebration of spring and a memento of good wishes. The Greeks continued the tradition, later adding the symbolism of fertility. In ancient times, eggs were sometimes left in tombs as a charm to aid rebirth, or given to children to keep them healthy.

The most common form of dyed eggs comes to us from the Ukraine where many of the symbols placed on the egg were to encourage prosperity and healing, or were of natural elements such as the sun and water. These decorative items still make a lovely addition to any magical space or home during the Easter season. Eggs can be used any time of year to encourage fruitfulness.

Homemade egg dyes can be prepared from many natural materials, including onion skins, carrot tops, blueberries, zinnias, elderberry, goldenrod, dogwood, and pokeberries. Colors are created by soaking the plant or fruit in warm water to distill the juice, then adding a bit of vinegar to get the color to set on the egg.

Easter rabbits have also been popular in many cultures, including those of Japan and China, where the rabbit is associated with the moon. Since the full moon is the symbol of fruitfulness, the rabbit delivers eggs and is a sign of fertility. More than likely, this had much to do with the animal's uncanny ability to reproduce prolifically.

It is said that the sun dances for joy on this day, and those who cannot see this know that the devil stands between them and the sun.

In Yugoslavia, branches are blessed on Easter day and taken home to be used throughout the year as a protection from storms. If a severe storm is coming, they affix the branch to the housetop and burn it at the ends to turn the wrathful winds away.

At home, you might consider a similar technique for protection, but please use caution. High winds can carry sparks and do more damage than good if you're not judicious.

Start by picking a small branch of maple or oak, both of which are usually easy to find. The first is chosen for its five-pointed leaf as an emblem of magic, the second for its strength and resilience. If a bad storm is predicted, or if you happen to be having a particularly turbulent time in household relationships, take the blessed branch to a safe area outside (such as a dirt mound or sandbox) and light one end of it, setting the other in ground. Let it burn while you do your own personal protection ritual.

It is interesting to note that the actions of setting or waving fire probably date back to the time when a flame was used to drive away unwanted predators. In this scenario, it was quite literally the instrument of safeguarding the self and family.

Festival of Diana and Hecate (August 13)

During this holiday, women throughout Rome visited the temples of Diana or Hecate. There they gave thanks for answered prayers, and entreated the Goddesses for a bountiful harvest. In Christian times this celebration became the Assumption of Mary.

This festival truly commemorates the harvest, through awareness of the Full Circle (life-death-rebirth), for Diana is the youthful Goddess and Hecate is the Crone. If you choose to follow this tradition, decorate your altar with apples, moonstone, almond, and hazel for Diana, and garlic and poppies for Hecate. Consider the cycles in your own life and how to honor them.

Festival of Isis (July 19)

This festival was observed in Rome until A.D. 4. by the cult's followers. Its timing corresponded with the Nile's annual flood cycle. This water, rich in nutrients for the land, was regarded as the greatest blessing of Isis.

Isis was the most complete Goddess in history. She was characterized as a loyal wife, compassionate mother, great healer, and the life of Egypt itself. If Isis is in your pantheon, remember her today. Fill your cauldron or goblet with water until it overflows to bring abundance to your life.

Green Plays (date varies)

In New Guinea, early animistic tribal cultures celebrated spring's arrival in costume. They would dress in foliage, including leaves, flowers, roots, and bark adhered with mud. The purpose of this activity was twofold. First, it honored and appeased the plant spirits. Second, they hoped to encourage an abundant harvest using imitative magic.

Green plays could be a lot of fun for the children in our lives. Let them pick out the plant(s) they wish to portray and make costumes from painted cardboard, material scraps, etc. Once bedecked, they could sit in a circle around the sacred space to honor spring.

Hallows Eve (October 31)

This is the night when spirits and faeries are free to roam our physical realm, but if you happen to be afraid of such creatures, simply wear red and you will scare them away. The Welsh believe that at midnight on this night a ghost sits on every stile. There are also common sightings throughout Wales and Scotland this night of the ghostly apparitions known as the white lady and a black sow.

This was the most popular time of the year for attempts at divination by such techniques as apple bobbing and nut roasting. A boy who won the apple bob was certain that a girl loved him truly. A candle might be burned at church to foretell the next year. If it burned brightly, it meant success, while irregular flames portended trouble.

In some rural areas, it was customary to place five sheaves of grain, representing hope, ring, money, charcoal and thread, on the barn door. Then, the farmer would bring in a sleepy hen and allow it to walk nearby

until it chose a sheaf to peck at. If it chose "hope," the following year would be full of opportunity. A "ring" meant marriage, "money" was wealth, "charcoal" portended financial struggles, and thread was an indication of hard work to come. A more urban approach might be to place objects on a wall, named symbolically, then blindfold the members of your group, spin them around, and let them choose their futures!

This is the night when faerie folk hold their grand anniversary, so many people put out little treats to keep their friends amused with something other than mischief.

Many magicians consider this a New Year's celebration by the old Celtic calendar. It is a time when the veil between worlds is thin, and ancestors should be honored. In Ireland and Egypt, this was done by lighting a candle to welcome their presence.

Since there are so many people practicing occult arts this night, be sure to purify and protect your sacred space before beginning any work.

Healthful Holidays

People of various cultures regarded certain dates throughout the years as more healthful than others. Two notable examples are Hilaria in Rome (March 25), and Smell the Breeze Day in Egypt (March 27). In the first, laughter and joyful outbursts were encouraged in order to bring renewed health and well-being. In the second, outings were specially planned to ensure the participants of vitality throughout the year. These are two good days to focus on your own health, get a little extra rest, and eat well.

Leap Year's Day (February 29)

This is the day when it is considered proper for women to propose to men. With this in mind, it is also a good day to celebrate the Goddess and women's mysteries. This type of celebration should not be limited to women. Men can enjoy and benefit greatly from such a celebration, discovering many of their own *yin*, or feminine, aspects in the process.

The form of the ritual work may vary according to your particular Path. Wear white or pale-blue robes, adding similarly colored candles, decorations, and flowers to honor the Goddess throughout the sacred space. Activities can include, but are not be limited to: full-moon guided meditation and visualizations for creativity and insight; birthing canals made from the elder women's legs for everyone to pass through into new knowledge; and Goddess name chants. These help build a greater appreciation for that portion of your sexuality.

May Day/Beltane (May 1)

May Day began with the Roman festival *Floralia,* when the people gathered flowers dedicated to the Goddess Flora. Popular activities came to include fire leaping for luck, and purification of cattle by passing them through the smoke of Beltane fires (Scotland). Thus, Beltane is a good time to do specific magic to bless your pets.

Since this was a favorite time for magic rites, there was also a flurry of activity produced to protect against stray enchantments. These projects included burning gorse hedges, wearing rowan crosses and, in Scotland, gathering rowan and woodbine to ward off witches.

There is a long-standing belief that dew collected on this

morning, and applied to the skin will enhance beauty and take away freckles. It was also a popular pastime to get up early on May Day and skim a wealthy neighbor's well, thus stealing his luck and fortune for the coming year.

May Day activities from the Maypole to flower baskets have remained basically unchanged even among the nonmagical community. It is still a time to rejoice as the world is reborn, to dance with the land, and perhaps snitch a glass of water from your neighbors tap, pouring half of it back into their sink to share the wealth instead of steal it!

Midsummer's Eve (June 21)

This is the longest day of the year. From this point onward the season was judged dangerous because the strength of the sun was starting to wane. To this day, many herbs used for magical rites are harvested on Midsummer's Eve, and a hazel wand obtained on this date was thought to lead the lucky owner to hidden treasure.

In some versions of this celebration, a hen's egg might be broken and used for scrying. If a woman walked unclad through her garden on Midsummer's Eve, she was guaranteed fertility.

One interesting custom among some European cultures is for the children to scoop up the dust laying before the altar at the end of Midsummer rites. This dust is kept under their pillows in the belief that it will help them learn to read. We could keep to this tradition in a slightly cleaner manner by having a bowl of rich potting soil at the base of our altars. At the end of the Midsummer festival, all people who wished to empower their educational pursuits could take a pinch to carry home with them.

Finally, sowing hemp seeds or leaving bread and ale out beneath the moon on Midsummer's Eve are excellent charms for romance.

Midwinter Festivals (date varies)

At many midwinter celebrations in the British Isles, there is a special-game played. A silver ball is set in motion at 10:30 A.M. between two goals which are a mile apart. From this time until sunset, the ball is not allowed to touch the ground. Symbolically, this game is believed to help the sun on its journey back to the height of the sky.

Trying to recreate this activity might be a little difficult indoors, so an alternative for winter rituals would be to affix a gold colored volleyball to a line and pole (perhaps the same pole used for May Day) and allow the children of the coven to play "keep it up" while the rest of the group performs increasingly fast chants to strengthen the sun. One such verse might be something like:

Golden sun, star of light
return again, into your height...
yellow sphere, the bane of night
we call you now, give darkness flight!

New Year's Day (date varies)

New Year's celebrations probably began with the Romans as a festival day for revelry. In France, it was known as the Feast of Fools. In both instances, gifts were presented to the gods to ensure a prosperous new year.

In Portugal, it is believed you should pay all your bills on this day to ensure they will be met for the entire year. The Pennsylvania Dutch believe if New Year's Day is sunny, they will have plenty of fish and fowl to sustain them.

Dalmatians think anyone who is drunk on New Year's Day will be in that state all year round. In Romania, it is assumed that farm animals talk this day, but that it is unlucky to hear them. In England, the first water drawn from the well is called the cream and will stay fresh all year. Finally, in Wales, all the hens are given a share of the fruit in the house to ensure that they will continue to lay for the next twelve months.

While the dates for New Year's celebrations vary among different cultures, the theme behind them is universal. It is a time to release the old, welcome the new, and hopefully get a new lease on good fate.

Open your windows New Year's Day to let in good luck.

Passover (date varies)

Passover generally falls in late March. It celebrates the liberation of the Israelite nation from its bondage to Egypt. In its earliest stages, Passover was observed by sacrificing a lamb to God in thankfulness. Later, this was replaced with the Seder, a narrative feast with prayers, blessings and rhymes.

Matzoth (unleavened bread) is eaten because Moses and his people had to leave in such haste that bread did not have time to rise. Bitter herbs are consumed to remind everyone of their victory over hardship.

Additionally, a special blend of apples, nuts, wine, sugar, and cinnamon is prepared to emblemize the bricks made by the Israelites in Egypt.

For the contemporary practitioner, this holiday is a time of reflection. Consider the things you are grateful for. Enact spells and rituals to liberate you from any form of bondage (ie, an addiction, a bad habit, etc.).

The traditional food mentioned above equates to the following associations as part of your celebration:

> Matzoth—expedient movement and decision-making.
>
> Bitter herbs—success, victory, overcoming harship, protection.
>
> Apple brick—strong foundations, hard work which is eventually rewarded.

Rosh Hashana (early October; date varies)

Rosh Hashana marks the Jewish New Year. There is a story in Jewish tradition about how, on this day, God checks the account of every person in a great book. As part of the holiday ritual, a nine-day period of contemplation and repentance is undertaken with the hope that, when God's book is closed, some sins will be forgiven.

This ritual can be translated to magical circles by tending your Book of Shadows, if it has been neglected. Also, take a moment to consider if you are using your magical knowledge with wisdom and love.

Sacred Well Celebrations (various dates in May)

During the month of May, sacred well celebrations take place throughout England. These owe part of their origins to the Roman festival of *Fortunaillia* (Rome, May 26), where all the water gods of the empire were appeased.

For both observances, the holy wells (those wells with indwelling, beneficent spirits) throughout the region were adorned with garlands. With proper appeasement, a petitioner could get aid from the well spirit. Offerings appropriate to requesting help included grain, flowers, and gold. This last sacrifice led to our modern tradition of tossing a coin in water and making a wish.

Twelfth Night (January 6)

In Syria, bathing on this night ensures beauty, and brushing your hair at midnight aids its shine and growth. In other lands it is traditional to shake wheat, oil, and wine to increase supplies in remembrance of the way the Magi expanded Joseph and Mary's ability to care for Jesus.

In Romania, priests give out blessed hemp and basil to be tied to fishnets, which ensures a favorable catch.

On your own altar, place a bit of rice or basil as a request to the Great Spirit to keep you from wanting in the months ahead.

St. Valentine's Day (February 14)

St. Valentine's Day grew out of the Roman festival *Lupercalia* when hundreds of young Romans would draw from various types of lots to determine the name of their lover-to-be. There is a long-standing belief that birds and animals choose their mates on this day.

St. Valentine's Day is dedicated to the patron saint of love, who died on February 14. St. Valentine himself is claimed to have owned a cherubic ring. An interesting point of information is that the lace we see on many older Valentine cards derives its name from a Latin word meaning "to snare," which is somehow appropriate to the season (see Chapter 16: Knots).

In England, a young man wishing to know if he will happily marry his present beloved carries a bachelor's button flower in his pocket all day. If it is still alive by nightfall, his love is likewise as strong.

This is the best day to work magic pertaining to romantic love, as long as you remember not to become manipulative. No one caught in a magical web of love unwillingly will ever make you truly happy (see Chapter 25: Relationships).

Yule/Winter Solstice (Dec. 21)

In many lands, fires are lit on Yule, the longest night of the year, to help give fortitude to the returning sun. In Baltic regions you do not cross a strange threshold on Yule day; it is bad luck. Corn is scattered near the door of the house for sustenance, and ashes of the Yule log are given to the fruit trees to increase their yield.

A child born on Yule, according to English tradition, has the ability to see ghosts.

Known as *Sacaea* to the Mesopotamians and the Festival of Kronos in Greece, winter solstice observances are held by every culture in the world. In Norse regions, valkyries searched for heroic souls at this time to carry to Valhalla. In Celtic lands, the druids were busy harvesting the sacred mistletoe for future rites and sacrificing a boar's head to Frigga. This last custom found its way into England's King Henry VIII's court as an annual Christmas feast, and almost certainly had some influence on the custom of Christmas ham!

Modern Christmas observances have many Pagan origins. For example, the Christmas tree comes from the worship of Thor and tree veneration. Holly and ivy, both potent herbs, were used to protect from baneful spirits. Candles and fires were originally lit to empower the sun on its journey back into the sky for spring.

Yule comes from a Northern European term, *jol*. The feast known as *Jolnir* took place around December 25 as a celebration honoring Odin. As the chief among Norse Gods, Odin loved good drink. Beers were offered to him during this celebration. Over the years this translated into Christmas beers, frequently mentioned in medieval law, brewed just for this occasion.

In old Russia it was traditional to toss grain upon the doorways where you caroled. This kept the household from wanting through the remainder of winter. Romanians bless the trees of the orchard with sweetened bread dough to bring bountiful harvests. Serbians (Yugoslavia) cover the Yule log with wheat while it burns to bring many farm animals to the family. In Germany, the weekday that Yule falls on is an omen of coming weather. Tuesday means a blustery winter, rainy summers and a bad time for brewers.

For modern practitioners, Yule is the winter solstice, a time to welcome the sun back from its slumber and exchange tokens of joy with friends. Some people decorate live trees to honor the spirits of nature, using bread bits, cranberries, and other edibles for the birds. If you wish to get a tree, consider buying a live one which you can return to the earth as your gift to Gaia. Share a little food with those in need and by all means hang a little mistletoe to add a flair of romance to the season. It is an excellent time for celebrating kinship and family.

15 KITCHEN AND HOUSEHOLD LORE

*Most men appear never to have considered what a house is, and
are actually needlessly poor all their lives because they think they
ought to have one as their neighbors.*
♦ Henry David Thoreau, *Walden* ♦

THE FOLKLORE of the kitchen influenced the traditions for the
entire house. This room was the center of family activity. A
newborn's cradle was placed here because it was the warmest
room in the house. Before the advent of modern heating and
other technological conveniences, school lessons were taught at the
table; food and herbal medicines prepared; ironing, mending, and a
myriad of other important functions took place in this one room.

Most kitchen and household lore is familiar to us because our grand-
mothers still use it. This familiarity makes kitchen magic one of the simplest and most accessible types of folk traditions, tha can easily blend
into any form of magic you practice

When society was predominantly agrarian, women frequently took
care of both inside and outside chores while their husbands tended the
fields. Because of this, a fair portion of household enchantments were
considered "woman's magic," the home being her territory and responsibility. This, however, should by no means preclude men from trying
their hands at it as well. I think any individual who feels they need a gen-
tler balance to the daily grind will find kitchen magic quite a relief.

The key to successful kitchen magic is to remember the terms frugality, resourcefulness, and common sense, all of which our ancestors lived by. Even the simplest cooking endeavor can be made magical by adding a spell, chant, incantation, blessed herb etc. (see "Canning" for an example.)

Kitchen magic, while not necessarily disregarding moon signs and "proper" tools, tends to forego regalia and/or timing in favor of meeting immediate needs or questions. The kitchen witch looks around the home, recognizes necessities, and then meets them magically by using the items at hand. By way of illustration, a woman baking bread who also has a nagging question on her mind might intuitively toss a little flour on her damp counter and see what images develop to answer that concern. No history books report this particular form of inventive divination, born out of the materials of the moment, but it certainly works.

Accidents

An old wives' tale indicates that aloe vera kept in the home prevents accidents. This reputation probably derived from the desert plant's healing quality: aloe has long been the most popular homecure for many minor burns and cuts.

If you do not have a green thumb, don't worry; aloe is a hearty plant and thrives in most homes. To use aloe, break off one of the green shoots and squeeze the juice on the affected area. Aloe juice and gel are available at most health food stores. For magic, aloe is a component in healing and protective spells.

Apron

Putting your apron on backwards portends good luck. If you are having a day filled with particularly annoying nuisances, you can reverse your apron to change your luck. If you turn your apron by the New Moon, you should also make a wish.

While not all witches today cling to this bit of clothing as our ancestors did, something else you use consistently might be substituted; for instance, turning your favorite ring around, or a pair of socks inside-out.

Ashes

Ashes from the kitchen hearth (which today might be from your fire-place or even a barbecue) were added to charms and spells for fertile fields and love. Wood ash is best if you plan to use it in your garden as a blessing. This offers the additional benefit of fertilizing your soil.

For love spells, sprinkle the ashes from your hearth on the path or road (rather like bread crumbs) right up to your door so that love may follow you home.

Baking

It is always best to bake bread, or any foods that need to rise, when the moon is waxing. Apply this rule of thumb to any magical preparation where you are bringing positive energy into play. The idea behind this superstition is that as the moon "grows," so will the power of your magic (or food preparation).

Bread

It is bad luck to throw away or burn bread. Food scraps are almost always best given to the animals. In some instances, an offering of bread was left for plants when one of their flowers or leaves has been taken for magical use. This was considered a way of thanking the spirit of the plant for its generosity.

I have always really enjoyed the traditions associated with bread. It is broken and shared as a sign of kinship and hospitality in a large number of cultures. As such, we have the saying, "let us break bread together." With this in mind, it would be appropriate to use bread in any ritual where personal relationships are being celebrated. In this context it is also easy to understand why burning bread was a sign of ill fortune, for this ruined the object of sharing.

I also sincerely appreciate the idea of giving the leftovers (such as stale bread) to the animals and plants as a way of living in greater reciprocity with nature. While the plant may not be able to acknowledge the token, the bread doubles as a small offering to the Great Spirit for all the earthly wonders we have been given.

Brewing

Brews will be tastiest if made during the last two quarters of the moon, and when the moon is in a fruitful sign (see Chapter 5: Celestial Objects).

If you would like to try this yourself, one of my favorite home-brews is currant wine. It makes a very refreshing ritual beverage during summer months, and the recipe is easier than you might expect.

Begin by taking two quarts of currants fresh off the bush and cleaning them of any dirt or leaves. Mash the berries gently and place them in a large, non-aluminum pot. To the currants add three-quarters gallon of water, three pounds of sugar, a sliced orange, and one one-inch piece of bruised ginger root. Warm this slowly. When the sugar dissolves and the taste of the currants is strong in the water, turn off your flame and cool to lukewarm.

While you are waiting, take one level tablespoon of active bread or wine yeast and suspend it in one-quarter cup of warm water. Set this aside. Strain the fruit juice so it is free of pulp, then add the yeast when the temperature of the juice is lukewarm.

Cover the entire pot carefully with a clean, thick towel (this keeps dust out) and leave it in a semi-warm area for seven days. You will hear it fizzing or bubbling actively. Once the week is past, pour the wine into a sterilized glass gallon bottle. Affix a balloon to the top of the bottle, using a rubber band to secure it in place (this allows the release of fermentation pressure). After about four weeks, test the wine for taste. It should be lightly sweet and bubbly, and may be drunk at this time. You should also be able to cork the bottle now without it popping out from the pressure. If you prefer a drier wine, allow it to ferment for two more weeks and test again. Then return the wine to the stove and bring to a low boil covered.

This kills the yeast and allows you to age the wine from one to two years with truly remarkable results.

Brooms

The most commonly used kitchen "appliance" and a necessity in most homes, the broom had hundreds of superstitions grow around it.

It was considered lucky to find one in your new home. You should never sweep towards a door in a new domicile lest you sweep out the good luck. And old brooms were never just thrown out, but either burned on the hearth fire or respectfully disposed in some other manner, lest the hearth spirits become angered.

Because the broom was an emblem of domesticity, fertility, and womanhood, superstitions about it extended into relationships. In England, joinings or separations were sometimes marked by jumping over a broom handle before village elders . Something similar might be fun to try for a handfasting.

The magical home is not totally complete without a broom, even if only decorative.

Building Materials

It is considered bad luck to use wood brought down by lightning to build a home or barn. To do so is thought to attract another such storm. On the other hand, some people think just the opposite is true, because "lightning never strikes twice."

For magic, branches brought down by a storm make wonderful air or fire wands and staffs for casting the circle, or for use as a competent walking stick! You can clean out the knots with a small hand knife, place stones of your choice within, add a hand-grip, and decorate to your heart's content.

Butter and Jam

An old charm states that if your butter or jam does not set properly, continue to work them while naming the eldest people in your community.

Something about the longevity of these individuals is thought to magically correct the problem.

Another charm frequently used if butter wouldn't come was to toss a little salt on the churn to drive away any malignant spirit.

Canning

Like brewing, canning is recommended during the third and fourth quarter of the moon. Jams and jellies are best prepared when the moon is in Aquarius, Taurus, and Scorpio.

The idea of canning may date back as far as Hermes and the prevalent use of witch bottles for protection. Hundreds of sealed bottles have been found buried in the ground throughout Europe with an image or symbol for Hermes stamped upon them; hence the term hermetic seal.

One of the marvelous things about canning is not only the money it can save you, but also the fact many of the herbs used for seasoning can be employed for their magical effect. In jam or jelly, cinnamon is for prosperity, cloves for friendship and ginger for health. In pickling, dill is for strength and blessings and garlic for protection.

Please be careful, however. Not all herbs recommended for magical use can be consumed safely. Except for those items you use regularly in cooking, always check a reliable herb book for proportions and toxicity.

Cats

Cats have been respected in the home for their ability to keep it free of rodents (see Chapter 2: Animals and Insects). An interesting superstition is that three-colored cats in the home act as protection against fire. If you happen to be allergic to this animal, perhaps you can make a sachet out of tricolored cloth and stuff it with catnip instead!

Charm Wands

A charm wand is a type of glass wand that is filled with tiny colored seeds and hung on the wall of a house near the entryway. This was done in the belief that any evil spirit which entered would be forced to count all the seeds by dark, leaving them no idle time to create trouble in the home.

To make a charm wand of your own, go to a pharmaceutical supply store and get a test tube with a stopper, or use another clear recycled container. Fill it with little seeds. Fennel might be a good choice, since it is considered a protective herb. Tie the top with ribbon, bless it at your altar, and hang it near your door.

Chicken Soup

Chicken soup as a cureall may date back to the time when chickens and roosters were used frequently for disease transference (see Chapter 2: Animals and Insects). For the latter, the creature was buried near the afflicted person's bed or placed in the center of a crossroad with clippings of the individual's hair and nails to effect a cure.

Most people still agree that a bowl of chicken soup is a good recommendation when one is feeling under the weather, especially for colds. While canned soup will suffice, nothing tastes as wonderful as homemade. Bless the ingredients of your homemade soup to infuse it with purification, health, protection, and renewed energy.

Coins

A silver coin buried under the doorstep of your home brings prosperity and good fortune. If you live in an apartment, try placing it at the bottom of a decorative planter or glued securely to your doormat instead.

Eggs

These ancient symbols of fertility were also sometimes used to avert and/or cure illness. For this, an egg was hung around the neck to absorb the sickness usually for a duration of three days. It could then be broken (thus shattering the illness) or buried. This might still be a good approach, along with regular medical treatment, to try yourself. If you can't hang the egg around your neck, sit with it and visualize all your sickness leaving your body like a dark cloud and pouring into the egg. Then break or bury the egg, releasing the sickness to the earth.

Bring eggs into the home by day to keep them fresh longer and bring fruitfulness. If one should accidentally break on the floor it portends good news soon to follow.

Fireplace

The kitchen fire was by far the most important in the house. For hundreds of years it was considered terrible luck to allow this hearth-flame to go out. If for some reason it did, every method was used to try to rekindle it without the aid of an external flame.

If you would like to continue this tradition as a way of honoring the God/dess and blessing your home, trying keeping an oil lamp or well-protected candle that can be replaced before it goes out. Anoint your candle or add a few drops of scented oil to your lamp for more specific effects (use patchouli for prosperity, for example). If you choose a candle, I suggest investing in an enclosed container to safely house the taper without its having to be supervised.

Any indoor hearth with a flue can be used for a unique form of country magic. Write one wish on a piece of paper and toss it into the fire. If the paper is sucked up the chimney, it is a sign that your wish will come true. If you do not have a fireplace, you can take a handful of bread crumbs and hold it tightly while making a wish. Sprinkle a little on self-lighting charcoal, then release it to the winds to give movement to your desire. The crumbs are then enjoyed by the birds, who transport the energy of your magic even further!

Glassware

Accidentally making a glass ring means someone is drowning. Touch the glass quickly and stop the ringing to ensure that help arrives quickly.

Harmony

A bunch of fresh coriander tied with a ribbon (blue is preferred as the color of tranquillity) and hung in the kitchen will bring harmony to the home.

Hearth Gods and Goddesses

In the Far East, the Gods of the home and hearth receive special honors. On November 8 in Japan, they hold the Festival of the Kitchen Goddess. This day commemorates *Irori Kami*, or *Daidokoro Kami* the Goddess of the hearth and kitchen. She represents all the people who provide food for the tables.

Similarly, on January 20, the Feast of the Kitchen God begins in China. Taking place just before the end of the Chinese year, the Feast of the Kitchen God celebrates the robust caretaker of the family's virtue. The image of Tsao Wang is always round and smiling. He carefully watches the family, then, on the twenty-third night of the twelfth moon, he returns to heaven and reports on their actions.

For this observance, all household members gather in the kitchen. They lay out cakes, sweets, meat, and vegetables as offerings. In some regions, molasses is dabbed on the God's mouth so that only "sweet" messages will be conveyed to the great jade emperor.

Here is one special activity for this celebration you may wish to try: go to an image of your Hearth God or Goddess and ask a secret question. Whisper your query into the God's ear then firmly clasp your hands over both your ears. Next, go outside and listen. Since the Kitchen God is wise and helpful, the first sentence you hear clearly is your answer.

Hot Cross Buns

This is an old Anglo-Saxon tradition that began as a celebration of Easter. Special cakes were made with solar crosses on them at this time of the year, some of which were kept around the house as amulets for prosperity and health (for recipe, see Chapter 14: Holidays).

For a longer lasting version, make a clay or salt-dough bun, appropriately decorated, and hang it in your window. The basic recipe for salt dough is one cup of salt, two cups of flour, and one cup of water mixed together thoroughly. Let this sit for seven to ten minutes before forming. Once your shape(s) is created, bake in the oven at 325 degrees until hard. Paint according to the token's magical application.

Lily

In China, dried lily petals are burned to honor and send supplications to the kitchen god. As such, it is an appropriate flower to keep in your pantry, or to use as part of an incense to help empower kitchen-related magic.

New Homes

Breton folklore says that a house is not safe to live in until someone has died there. When the doorstep is first laid, the *Ankou* (or figure of death) waits there for the first person to cross. The only way to dislodge him is by leaving an offering of a fertilized egg. This may also be one of the reasons for the custom of carrying someone over a threshold; it was a means of protecting them.

A modern alternative to this protective rite is to place some freshly cut flowers or a bit of grain at the door of your new home the day before you move in. This welcomes beneficent spirits.

Passing Food

From the days when our ancestors worshiped the sun as the source of life and warmth, food has been passed clockwise to ensure health and continued good fortune. We also see this tradition in magical circles, where most dances and movements are done clockwise.

Pins

A pin found or accidently dropped in the home was for a long time looked upon as an omen or sign. Long pins found in the kitchen indicated travel, for example. If the head is facing towards you, it will be a pleasant vacation.

Prosperity

Legend has it that finding a cricket in your new home brings prosperity. If you haven't moved lately, or don't plan to, an alternative suggestion is to keep alfalfa in your cupboard to prevent poverty and hunger.

Protection

Hundreds of methods were devised throughout history to protect the home and family from disease, spells, and any other unwanted fate. Most of these can still be used with very little modification. Just add a personal prayer, or chant, for example, to more specifically direct the energy for you and your family.

Take a fresh sprig of fennel from your herb garden and use it to sprinkle water around your home for protection.

Hang white sachets of rosemary and garlic in any area where you feel extra security is needed. To secure your entire plot of land, sprinkle iron filings into the soil, moving clockwise, then cover them with the earth. This particular measure is most effective against any unwanted faerie visitors.

In England, witch bottles were popular during the 1600 and 1700s as protection for the home. They were handblown glass bottles filled with glass, urine, and other repulsive substance and buried near the house in the conviction that no evil magic could breach such a barrier. If made from a mirror, the glass reflected any malignant energy back to the sender.

In England's Yorkshire County, another unusual protective item could be found in the home. Known as a witch post, it was made of oak and rowan, marked with a St. Andrew's cross, and placed near the hearth bearing a crooked sixpence in the center as a powerful charm against magic.

Salt

One of the most precious commodities known to early man because of its preservative and cleansing abilities, salt is a treasure and symbol of friendship.

Any salt spilled at the table must quickly be tossed over the left shoulder to keep away malignant spirits who wait there to tempt you. Legend has it that this is how Satan tempted Judas (a story derived from DaVinci's painting, *The Last Supper*, where the salt spilled on the table points to Judas).

Finns have a myth of the God Ukko who flung a spark of heavenly flame into the sea and made salt. The Aztecs had a salt goddess, and in the Old Testament there is discussion of a covenant by salt that was a means of binding an oath.

In many lands, salt is the symbol of brotherhood. An Arabic way of describing such a relationship is to say "there is salt between us." In this region to accept an offer of salt at someone's home means two things. First, the host is promising protection and hospitality. Second, the guests promises to reciprocate this by not overstaying their welcome.

Today, salt is used to represent the Earth element on our altars. It can help cleanse or protect the sacred space by if it is sprinkled in a circle.

Silverware

The knife was originally a utility dagger used for everything from eating to protecting oneself. In the days of feudal lords, the dagger was placed on the plate to show good intentions. Any time two knives accidentally crossed, it was a sign of an argument, so they were separated immediately. To this day such implements are treated with respect.

When the fork came into use, the crossing of a knife and fork emblemized hostility. Hosts therefore carefully laid out the two implements so they weren't touching. We still see this evidenced in proper place settings where the knife and fork are placed on opposite sides of the plate.

This idea can be effective when trying to bridge the gap in a relationship where anger has taken root. For example, between members of a coven each person could lay his or her athame on the table before a rite as a show of peaceful purpose.

If someone gives you a knife or sharp implement as a gift, always give them a coin in return so that friendship is not cut between you. Lay a knife under your doormat to keep out any baneful magic and place a knife beneath a mattress or pillow to decrease pain.

If a spoon is dropped in the kitchen it means you will soon have a woman guest, a fork indicates a man, and a knife a child.

Wine

Often associated with Dionysus, wine is widely considered a symbol of resurrection. In ancient Greek burial sites, the ashes of a person were kept in a wine jug for just such a reason. Interestingly, many of the ingredients of alcoholic drinks (grains and fruits) are associated with long life and knowledge. One story of Dionysus recounts how he was held captive on Naxos' pirate ship. At one point in the story, he tossed his cup into the water, changing the sea into wine. The feast of Dionysus is held in spring because this is the time of rebirth. Therefore, the wine present at our rituals is a symbol of new life, transformation, fruitfulness, and insight.

Various types of wine are, to this day, considered good for the health. Dandelion wine is suggested for indigestion, elderberry and currant for colds, and raspberry for throat infections.

16 KNOTS

A subtle chain of countless rings,
the next unto the farthest brings
the eye reads omens where it goes.
♦ Ralph W. Emerson, *Nature* ♦

KNOTS SERVED as one of the earliest mnemonic devices in history. Herodotus (400 B.C.), recounts their use in his historical essays. In one account, he tells us of the Persian King Darius commanding a trusted soldier to guard the bridge at the River Ister. There were sixty knots in a rope handed to that guard, who was to untie a knot each day. Should the king not return when all the knots were undone, the guard could take the ship for his own and leave.

Sometimes travelers left knots for family members to show when they could be expected home. In East Africa, for example, a man gave his wife a string with eleven knots assuring her that, when the last knot was loosened, he would be home. A similar system was used in India where knotted strings acted as festival invitations. The recipient of one of these string invitations would untie one knot each day. When the last knot was reached, it was time to go to the celebration.

Knots also provided a way to record dates and numbers. Among the Yakima in the Washington area, knots show the number of lunar cycles required for proper mourning. The abacus owes its existence to knot mathematics, and Incan astrologers kept track of solstices, equinoxes, declinations, and so on through a complex system of weavings.

Among some societies, knots were used to help in the recounting of oral history How someone could tell the difference between one knot and another to indicate what came next in their story must be left to conjecture, however. Some theories maintain that small particulars added to the knot, unnoticed by the untrained observer, aided recollection. These changes might have been twists, colors, a leaf, the technique of tying, or even the size.

The Hebrews eventually adapted knots into a functional alphabetical system and writing. This is part of the reason why the Hebrew language is so numerical in construction. To this day, the boxes that hold Hebrew scriptures are bound with knots shaped like the letters *daleth* and *yod*. Additionally, Jewish holy garments frequently have blue and white threads tied in double knots of five. In this one example we see how superstitions can affect a culture's present traditions.

The importance of knots for magic comes from their ability to simultaneously function as a tool and a strong symbol. The most common traditional knot magic centered on disease, sex, spirits, and weather. Fastening the knot bound the desired element or sickness; releasing the knot would free it. Undoing a knot and leaving the cord in the wilderness was also the only accepted means of dissolving knot magic.

Even Pliny the Elder, a great herbalist and healer, recommended certain variations of knot magic to heal difficult ailments. Incantations or other components were added during the tying process. Then the knots were blown or spit upon to give them increased potency, thus endowing the cord with spiritual essence. Since this is a fairly straightforward procedure, the modern practitioner can certainly create similar rituals to aid his or her magic, especially for any activity that lends itself well to knot symbolism.

Amulets

Linguistic studies indicate that some of mankind's earliest amulets may have been knots (see *Quipus and Witch's Knots* in bibliography). In Russia the word for *magician* translates into "knot tier," and likewise the Hebrew word means "one who ties magic knots." The word *amulet* in several languages is related to the English word *knot*. For example, in

Aramaic literature, the amulet is called *qami'a* which originally meant knot, then later meant something attached by
knots. Magic charms are still called "knot tying" in Indonesia today.

In Egypt, several of the hieroglyphs that look like string
or cord have protective significance to them. The *ankh*,
meaning "life," is probably the best known. Egyptians in their
art frequently carved double ropes around the names of their
leaders, presumably to protect them. Another Egyptian emblem looking like a three-quarter folded cloth or string means fitness or health.

Cords and knots were used as amulets in other countries as well. In
Japan, women made body bands for their husbands and sons going to
war. They felt these would protect them from wounds. In other cultures,
small necklaces of knots are hung around a child's neck or wrist to help
keep them safe.

Numerology was also an important factor in cord amulets and their
ability to work. Three, seven ,and multiples of seven are the most popular
figures used. A Babylonian headache cure instructs the healer to use a
triple cord tied twice with seven knots while using a specific incantation. In
Rumania, lumbago was treated by using nine knots laid across the patient
and left there for three days.

Back Pain

In Rumania, a long cord laid along the spine is tied into nine knots. As
the cord is tied, the healer recites, "I do not bind the knot, but the pain."
He or she then places the knotted cord in a pitcher of water until it can
be thrown into a rushing stream. It is never taken to a well for fear someone else might internalize the same trouble by drinking soon thereafter. If
running water was not available, it was considered acceptable to bind the
cord to a tree, toss the cord away from you, or bury it (see Chapter: 13
Health and Medicine).

Children

In Scandinavia, the pet name *Knut* (knot) is given to the last child born
to parents who desire no more children. This is thought to prevent
future conception. In Australia, a knotted willow branch was loosed to
help bring improved milk flow to a nursing mother. In other countries,

all knots in a home were undone, and all buttons
unbuttoned, and doors, opened to help bring a
smooth delivery to a laboring woman (see Chapter 24: Pregnancy and Children).

A lovely idea for a couple expecting
their first child is to tie a small knot in one
supple branch of a young tree and
plant it nearby. Because the tiny
boughs are flexible, they will not be
harmed by a carefully tied loose
knot. This becomes a symbol which
shares the strength of the tree with
the baby and helps produce an
ardent appreciation of nature. Should
the tree ever become sickly, however,
it is best to loose this branch so that
the empathic connection is severed. If
the tree grows well, the child can loose the knot at an appropriate
moment in his or her adulthood, akin to cutting the apron strings.

Colored Cords

Cords of every kind, but especially woolen ones, have long been
employed towards magical ends (with or without knots). Red is usually
the color of blood and life, black indicates sickness or death, and white
is healing and protection (see Chapter 6: Color).

In Assyrian lore, if white wool is bound to the bed and black wool
bound to the left hand, you are fully protected against even the most powerful magic. Similar customs appear in the Hebrides Islands located off the
northwest coast of Scotland, where black cords with knots are used; in
Macedonia, red and white cords are applied.

Today in several magical traditions, red, white, and black cord are
tied together (sometimes with beads) and worn as a belt to symbolize the
triple goddess.

Curative Knots

The symbolism of binding becomes most important when speaking of
curative knots. A Babylonian prescription from 8 B.C. instructs that one
should tie knots in the plaited bark of a tree and add an incantation to

heal sickness. The implication of this and similar writings is that the evil which caused the illness is bound securely by the knots. This would also explain why many curative knots are thrown away, buried, or burned after the healer finishes with them.

In England, for example, the ague, or fever and chills, was cured by tying the left hand to an apple tree with tricolored yarn. The patient then slipped his or her hand out of the knot and left for home without looking back. To stare was a way of accepting their sickness back.

Today, it is best to use the symbolism of the knot in conjunction with other medically sound advice. If you have a cold, for example, tie seven knots near your chest or throat (for wholeness and completion) on a small piece of natural fiber cord. As each is secured, focus on your sickness being taken into that spot. Then, bury the cord and continue your regular treatments (see Chapter 13: Health and Medicine).

Fishnets

Fishnets figured greatly in knot lore, most likely because of the vast number of knots they contain. In China, a pregnant woman was surrounded by just such a net to keep her and the child safe. This type of superstition extended itself to the hanging of nets near any cattle pen, sometimes over crops, or near the door of a house so negative influences (or a thief, for that matter) would be tangled within.

In Russia, a fishnet was tossed over newly-married couples to bind them together and protect the union. Sometimes, it was placed only over the bride to keep her safe until the ceremony. Later, this combined with some ancient customs in Israel and Australia of wearing knotted cords and headbands at weddings. This old custom carried over to the modern tradition of the bride wearing a veil (see the entry Love Knots in this chapter).

Thus in modern magic, a fishnet would make a marvelous wall, ceiling or altar decoration for protection and unity. Alternatively, Native American dream catchers made in a net-like fashion and hung over beds help bring peaceful and/or visionary dreams. One version of a Victorian dream catcher can be found in Chapter 3: Birds. Another magical use of this symbol would be to procure a bit of fishnet and adorn it with items of personal significance. Bless all the items and the net for discernment and intuition, then suspend it over or near your bed for much the same effect.

Fruitfulness

In Rome, a woman would wear a Herculean knot in her girdle when she arrived at her husband's home. This knot stayed tied until the husband removed it in the couple's bedroom, thus ensuring fertility.

Hercules was worshipped in Rome as a protector, and much veneration was given to this form of square knot in art as well. It was believed an excellent aid to bearing children and for curing sickness. The only odd variation is that this knot often appeared in sets of four instead of seven or three. Conjecture has it that this was because a square knot has four sides, but the actual reason has been lost in antiquity.

For modern magic, the Herculean knot can be applied for protection, strength, endurance, and health and to bring fruitfulness to any endeavor.

Gardening

Go to your prospective garden plot with a long blade of grass. Next, close your eyes and listen for the call of a favored bird, a chirping that sounds happy. At this moment, tie a knot in the blade of grass, binding within it the vision of a productive harvest, and place it gently in the earth. In Indonesia, this practice is believed to bring fruitful, strong crops of any kind.

Keep insects at bay by dipping some cord in tincture of pennyroyal and chamomile. Place it on your garden fence, knotting it every few feet. This is an example of some practical knot magic combined with herbal know-how. The herbs act as natural bug repellents, to which you add the strong symbolism of the knotted cord to protect your handiwork (see Chapter 12: Gardening and Farming).

Handkerchief

Tying a knot in your personal handkerchief while thinking
of an item will help you remember it. It will also ward
against evil.

A friend of mine makes beautiful Goddess images by
simply knotting a large handkerchief in creative ways. If
you would like to make one, consider the things you
want to remember and visualize white-light energy as
being bound into the image as you are tying it. Then
hang it in an appropriate spot in your home.

Headaches

Ancient Babylonian and Assyrian cuneiform tablets dating to 8 B.C. show
knot magic being used to cure headaches and other sicknesses. For
headaches in particular, they instruct us to take a piece of cedar with a
triple cord hanging from it and tie seven knots twice while speaking an
incantation. Then, bind this string around your head. An alternative version has a wise woman spin black and white cord together. This is
touched to the head, then thrown in rushing water. The Musquakie wear
magically-prepared headbands for the same cure.

Hemorrhoids

In Punjab (Northern India) the cure for this uncomfortable problem is to
tie a cotton thread of five colors around your big toe at night and wear
it for two weeks, making sure the duration ends on a Tuesday. The cord
is then either buried, burned, or tossed in running water. This particular
theme for the symbolic destruction of sickness is seen repeatedly in folk
medicine (see Chapter 13: Health and Medicine).

Ligaturae

A special type of knot magic, known mostly in Scotland and popular
through the Age of Enlightenment (eighteenth century), was created to
render a young man impotent. A more likely explanation for its renown
would be that a young man could blame the workings of a knot discovered later in or nearby his home for any sexual failure. Even so, these
knots were feared and were often bought at a high price by worried par-

ents or someone wishing to embarrass a foe. Even through the late 1700s, it was considered a terrible crime to make such a knot. Anyone who did was subject to death.

Love Knots

The poet Virgil in the *Eighth Eclogue* portrays the efforts of a young Roman woman to gain love by using a wax image, or poppet, woolen cord, and charmed knots. Such efforts were not unusual in the hopes of realizing enduring love. In Iranian weddings, the couples' wrists are bound by a woolen cloth tied into a double knot. Raw yarn from this cloth is then wound seven times into a ball of yarn. Such symbolism in various cultures may be the seed for calling marriage "tying the knot."

In Sweden there are distinct differences between love, friendship, and betrothal knots. The love knot is the common fisherman's knot. The betrothal knot, in whatever form it took, is probably the earliest representation of our modern engagement ring. Instead of being placed on the finger, though, it was tied to the wrist or ankle.

During the Middle Ages, knots were used to witness any contract, not just marital ones. Eventually this led to the legal term *notador,* which meant "knot tier" or "knot observor," more currently known as a "notary," which refers to one who attests the validity of a contractual obligation. With such a background, knots are very serviceable in magic pertaining to commitment, love, and trust.

One type of love knot is made with a tender willow branch, tied by the waxing moon, with some type of incantation appropriate to your desire. Hide this branch until the relationship or situation blossoms. Then, return the branch to the land with thankfulness. Substitute a pussy willow if no willow wood is available (see Chapter 25: Relationships).

I do caution careful consideration with any love magic. Remember you are working in a gray area that also pertains to another's will and desires. Be thoughtful of your true motivations for any such spell or rite, perhaps leaving the actual result of the magic in wiser hands: those of the God/dess.

Sacred Knots

When they reach eight years of age, Brahman youths are taken into an initiation ceremony where a cord of three strands is wrapped three times around the waist. Upon marrying, this must be changed to six strands to reflect the new status. Similar commencements are done in many Eastern cultures with only minor variations.

Certain religious orders continue to use knot symbolism to this day. In Slavic monasteries, nuns and priests are given a knotted cord when they take their final vows. Franciscan monks wear a knotted rope that hangs from their waist to the floor. Ritual magicians use the "measure." This is a type of cord used as a pledge of trust between the novice and the coven, and is a sign of their new connection to the whole (see Chapter 18: Magic and the Supernatural).

Sickness

The Apache have a sacred cord called *izze-kloth* that is believed to heal the sick. Similar holy relics and knotted cords were used around the world even until recent times. In Malaysia as late as 1899, natives sought to cure their children of smallpox with knots. The infected children were sent out on a boat with knotted strings tied into their hair. Then the knots were undone and retied to the boat to keep the illness bound securely there so it would not spread (see Chapter 13: Health and Medicine).

Efforts like this were also used in ancient Egypt where the *ukad*, a woolen cord with seven charmed knots, was used to treat colds and fever, primarily in children.

Sin Knots

In Mexico, sin knots are tied as part of a special ritual during a pilgrimage. At this time, all sins are confessed in front of the other participants, tied into knots and burned on the sacred Grandfather fire. This purifies the participants' hearts before taking offerings to their Gods.

This particular procedure would be excellent to reenact before an initiation or during a change of leadership in a coven. In the former, the initiate preparing for a new spiritual path would be given the opportunity to begin again. In the latter, it would allow the leader to enter his or her position feeling free of old burdens and thus better able to focus on the energy of the future.

Slip Knots

Found among the paintings, rings, and carvings of Minoans, the slip knot was of great magical value, for with a small tug it disappeared. Usually this type of knot is worn around the neck to bring luck, but the Malaysians have an alternative approach and employ it to trap sickness. When the medicine man feels the spirit of the illness is trapped within the knot, it is pulled to make both vanish. With this in mind, slip knots would be very suited to any banishing magic, and especially potent when combined with a waning moon.

Snakebite

Among the original inhabitants of Ceylon, the Veddas, the cure for snakebite was to utter a charm (which inevitably varied according to the healer) and tie string made from human hair around the limb just above the wound. This idea might be reapplied to magically ease itching from various insect bites today.

Spirits

While we do not usually think of people being as possessed by spirits and demons today, this was how many of our ancestors explained mental illness and other serious maladies. Knots were again employed to rid these possessed people of evil spirits (see Chapter 13: Health and Medicine).

The best evidence we have of this comes from a mummy on display at the Metropolitan Museum of Art. This mummy, from 1000 B.C., has seven strings tied around her throat, fourteen around the wrists, and twenty-one around the ankles, which were to banish the spirits that had made her body ill.

In Scotland, black-and-white thread was wound around the limbs of animals or people believed to be touched by evil, to bind the spirits and make them leave the body. While these types of efforts might not have actually helped the individual, they certainly didn't hurt them. Such actions served to give family members some vestige of hope to cling to.

In much the same manner, use black-and-white cords today for any protective magic to mark the edge of our magical circles, or to bind the outside of containers for our magical tools as a symbol of safety from unwanted energies.

Virgin Knots

At many Irish and Scottish wedding ceremonies, the groom presents himself to the Priest/ess to have his virgin knot untied. The bride does not do this until after the ceremony, at which time she changes and unties all knots placed in her accouterments symbolizing the couple's freedom to unite as man and wife.

An alternative to this, if a handfasting is followed by the Great Rite, might be to allow the bride and groom to undo each other's knots.

Warts

Folk medicine instructs that if you have warts you wish to be rid of, take a string and make one knot in it for each wart. Touch the knot to the wart, and then toss it over your shoulder into a pond or hole where it can quickly decompose. As it does, your warts will disappear (see Chapter 13: Health and Medicine).

Wind/Rain Knots

In Shakespeare's day, the village witch would sell wind knots to sailors and mariners. It was believed that the wind could be imprisoned in the string or handkerchief, and then cautiously released as needed. In the home, knots to inhibit or bring wind and rain were often left hanging under the eaves for easy access. You may do likewise in your home, preparing the knotted cord on a waxing moon and pouring a bit of water onto each knot. Thus, when the knot is undone, you release the moisture.

Homer's *Odyssey* gives us clues about some wind-knot lore. In one story, Aeolus, king of the winds, gives

Ulysses a zephyr bag. Within the satchel, the west wind has been bound by a silver cord. Similar stories occur later in Egypt, Syria, and finally in Europe in the Middle Ages.

Wind knot magic was most popular in Finland and Lapland, where witches made strings of three knitted knots for sailing merchants. The first knot when released would bring a mild breeze. The second one would bear a stronger gust, and the third would produce a devastating tempest. Norse mythology recounts similar tales, showing that these old magicians were not unaware of responsible magic. The third knot was not really meant to be used, but if someone got greedy, the storm that followed would certainly act as a not-so-gentle reprimand (see Chapter 30: Weather Lore).

17 LUCK

*Time is never turning; secret fates guide
our states both in mirth and mourning.*
♦ Thomas Champion, *What if a Day* ♦

SUPERSTITIONS DESIGNED to bring more good or ward off bad luck are the common element through the world's folk beliefs. Throughout time, people have looked to the world around them for a vestige of promise and opportunity when all else seemed dismal. They prayed that the things they interpreted as harbingers of good were true. The hope such occurrences inspired was far more important than anything else.

Ash Leaves

For extra good fortune, a Victorian superstition instructs that you pick an ash leaf while saying, "Leaf of ash, I do thee pluck, hoping thus to meet good luck." Then carry the ash leaf with you (see Chapter 29: Trees, Bushes, Woods).

Autumn Leaves

Catching a falling autumn leaf before it reaches the ground means good fortune. The number of leaves you capture symbolizes the number of happy months to follow.

In magic, use the autumn leaf for any magic pertaining to lasting joy. When obtained as described here, it is also a charm against winter colds, and would be a thoughtful additive to any gift sachets during the winter months.

Bes

In Egypt, this dwarfish God of Luck was carved out of various stones and worn to bring favor on its owner (see Chapter 1: Amulets and Talismans).

Bridges

It is unlucky to be the first person over a new bridge, or to speak beneath one, most likely due to accidents that occur in these sites. In mythology, bridges generally symbolize points of transition. This symbol can be carried into modern magical practice, especially for visualizations aimed at personal transformation.

For such a visualization, see yourself at a bridge, labeled on each side according to the circumstances. When you get up the courage to cross, stop at the other side and either cut the ropes or burn the bridge behind you.

Business Profits

It was common for frontier traders to set aside the first coin they made in a day, being sure not to give it as change to ensure continued good sales. This tradition evolved into the modern practice of saving and framing the first dollar of profit for luck.

Magically, you can continue this heritage in much the same manner if you have a business or job you cherish. Retain your first check stub, sales receipt or other memorabilia. If you are a craftsperson, keep a bit of your first jar of paint, spool of thread, modeling clay, or whatever material you use. Carry this with you to ensure that your efforts are well received.

Buttons

A button fastened in the wrong place by accident is a sign of good fortune. In this manner, a button makes a good magical charm
for dealing with security and serendipity.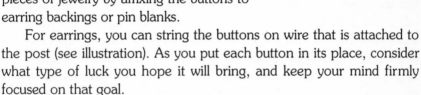

One fun project for children and adults
alike is to create button charms by collecting
unusual, antique, or personally meaningful
buttons and laying them out in a collage-
type design. These trinkets can be as
large or small as you desire and can
also be made into quite attractive
pieces of jewelry by affixing the buttons to
earring backings or pin blanks.

For earrings, you can string the buttons on wire that is attached to
the post (see illustration). As you put each button in its place, consider
what type of luck you hope it will bring, and keep your mind firmly
focused on that goal.

Cards

If someone was having bad luck at cards, turning the chair around three
times or placing a handkerchief upon it would end the streak. The best
seat to take at any game is one that faces the door, and if you have to
move, it is said that you should always do so clockwise.

This idea can be used any time you feel you need a change in luck.
Turn a belt around, or turn socks inside-out, or wear a T-shirt backwards
to likewise turn bad fortune away.

Cleaning

Most country folk would be certain all their housework was done on the
night of December 31 so they wouldn't accidentally sweep out good fortune with the new year. Because of this, December 31 would be a relevant day to consider doing cleansing magic for your home. If you don't
want to do in anything extravagant, just straighten up, light white candles, and burn sage or cedar, both of which are excellent purifiers. This
way, you will enter the new year with a spiritually clean living space.

Clocks

All clocks in your home should be set or wound right after midnight on New Year's Day to ensure luck and timeliness for the coming year.

If you have a winding clock in your home, it can be used at any time in any spells for motivation and alertness. For the latter, the actual alarm should be sounded at a prearranged moment during the spell to symbolically awaken your senses.

Coal

Where homes were heated by coal, to find a piece on the road was fortunate. It was then to be taken into the home and kept by the hearth to ensure warmth and prosperity. Interestingly enough, it was once regarded as a very thoughtful gesture to give someone a piece of coal at Yule.

With this in mind, it might not hurt your personal fortuity to keep a piece of unlit charcoal in your brazier upon the altar as a symbol of sustenance and comfort. Another practical alternative is to leave a piece in your refrigerator to safeguard your food while keeping nasty odors away.

Corn Dollies

At the turn of the century, it was considered good luck to affix corn dollies to both ends of your roof to act as guardians (see Chapter 12: Gardening and Farming).

If you are going to create a corn caretaker for outdoors, I suggest using a sturdy waterproofing solution on the exterior of the husks to give it greater longevity.

Days

The ancient Babylonians possessed detailed lists of lucky and unlucky days. In these records, the lucky days were equivalent to modern Monday, Wednesday, Thursday, and Sunday. Besides using the days of the week, Babylonians also predicted their fortunes by the hour or segment of the day as follows (again using modern equivalents): Monday was the moon's day and a time for peace or joy. The hours of 1 to 3 P.M. were considered most fortuitous. Wednesday was associated with Mercury and success in business, being most blessed between 10 P.M. to midnight.

Thursday was affiliated with Jupiter and the time between 9 and 10:30 A.M. gave courage to those who needed it. Sunday was a day of rest from labor and was most lucky during the hours of 3 to 4:30 P.M.

The unlucky days, Tuesday, Friday, and Sunday, were thought to bring quarrels, misplaced passion, and danger, respectively. They too had their most unfortunate hours: 3 to 4:30 P.M., 10 to 12 A.M., and 9 to 10 A.M., respectively.

A slightly different version of these folkways is found in Arabic lands, where Sunday is considered a beneficial time for building or planting, Monday for business and travel, Tuesday for slaughtering cattle, Thursday for any negotiations, and Friday for marriage. Wednesday is considered a day of trouble and Saturday a time when frauds are perpetrated.

Any of these associations may be used in choosing a day and time for a specific spell or ritual. For example, if you plan to travel and follow the Arabic system, a safety spell should be performed on Monday. If it were a business trip, according to the Babylonian technique, Wednesday would be best.

Four-Leaf Clover

The four-leaf clover is one of the most easily recognized symbols of good luck. However, its ancient use was as an amulet protecting and inspiring love. According to legend, three sisters, Faith, Hope, and Charity, came over the seas. Wherever they walked, clover bloomed beneath their feet. During their travels, another being, Love, joined them. In honor of this sorority, certain clovers added a fourth petal.

If you happen across a four-leaf clover, carry it as a lucky charm, or use it in any spell to inspire and refresh love.

Good Luck Day

January 2 was considered a lucky day in Macedonia. First thing in the morning, water was drawn from the village fountain and splashed gently on the courtyard steps so that the coming year would be as peaceful as the libation. It was also sprinkled on the people as a protective agent against witches. In your own home on January 2, consider asperging the entire living space with spring water to bring harmony and protection for the coming year.

The Japanese have several special holidays on which good fortune flourishes. These include:

February 3 or 4: Bean Throwing Day. In temples and shrines throughout various localities, people scatter beans on the ground with shouts of, "Fortune in—the devil out!" At the same time, lanterns are brought to the Kasuga Shrine in Nara to be lit. Families dedicate each lantern to a loved one and inscribe it with wishes for that individual. The glow of the lantern is symbolic of hope: belief that the Gods will see and answer that prayer. When all the lanterns are lit, those in attendance say, "May we have a good year," then turn toward their homes.

November 24: Tori-No-Ichi. This is a festival where participants carry decorated bamboo rakes to gather in their luck. The emblems on this rake are all traditional good-luck charms.

October 19: Bettara-Ichi. Held near the shrine of Ebisu, a Japanese luck god, the streets fill with people buying and selling charms for good fortune on this day. The favorite tokens by far are sticky pickled radishes strung on rope. These "capture" fortuity for anyone carrying them. The positive energy can not escape the gluey surface.

Gorgon

In Greece, the face of a gorgon or another ugly creature was worn on a necklace for luck and to keep harm at bay. These types of faces can be easily formed in clay if you would like to make any for your own use.

Hands

The hand, humanity's most essential tool, has long been venerated for many mystical powers (see Chapter 4: Body Divination). In talismanic form, the open hand with outstretched fingers is considered lucky and a protection against the evil eye. It is also considered an appropriate sign of friendship and sealed promises.

One of the most beautiful and functional means of using your hands in magic is in sign language. Sign can be easily changed and adopted as a secret vernacular for cloistered groups. With this you can portray the goals of your magic in both movement and word. Another option would be to try pantomime.

Horseshoe

The use of the horseshoe as a charm may have originated because its shape is similar to a crescent moon, which was sacred to the worship of Isis. Because of this, the horseshoe could be used in rituals in Her honor. In similar fashion, rites where Odin or Epona are called as God and Goddess aspects can include a horseshoe, the horse being sacred to both deities. Most people believe that you must mount a horseshoe with the open end up so that the luck will not run out of it.

Norse cultures considered the horseshoe as lucky, but they had to be found, not absconded with from an unsuspecting smithy, to have any power. One theory holds that because horseshoes were made of iron, they were sacred to Thor, and, therefore, finding one was a sign of His favor. With this in mind, a horseshoe is appropriate in any spell or ritual where Thor is invoked.

There are two different schools of thought regarding the best way to hang a horseshoe. Some hang it open side up to catch blessings. Others place it open side down, so luck can pour out on those passing beneath.

Keys

Keys were used in Greece and Rome as a symbol of Janus, the gate-keeper of heaven. As such they were considered lucky, bringing foresight and good judgment to the bearer. The modern version of this is to carry a specially blessed key any time you feel the need for improved discernment and concise decision-making. Uniquely crafted keys can often be obtained in hardware stores (ask the key maker), junk shops, and wherever second-hand hardware is sold.

Pins

Pins, when found, should always be gathered and kept; you never know when you will need them. A pin discovered pointing away from you portends a friendly visitor from that direction. In earlier days, pins would be used in poppet magic against an enemy, so to leave a pin where your nemesis could find it was ill luck indeed (see Chapter 15: Kitchen and Household Lore).

The modern magician can use pins for any magic dealing with connections, or travel (especially that of a friend).

Rusty Nails

To discover a rusty nail on the road was a sign of good luck, mostly because they were made of iron (see Chapter 7: Crystals, Gems and Metals). This nail should be taken home and concealed or carried to turn away the evil eye.

Since a rusty nail might be considered a little risky to keep around from a health perspective (except as part of a witch bottle), a piece of clean iron could act as a modern substitute to convey fortuity.

Shoes

Throwing a shoe when anyone sets out on a journey was a traditional means of wishing luck in England well into the seventeenth century. We see this continued today when shoes are tied to the back of newlyweds' cars. This symbolism may prove useful for love, luck, and travel spells today. In all instances, the shoes should be tossed in the intended direction of movement.

Umbrellas

By 1880, the first superstitions regarding umbrellas were developing, mainly because of the increasing use of the practical and pretty object. In the 1890s, cavalrymen in Maine carried-cream colored parasols as part of their kit, and even the British army allowed their officers to have them in Africa and Asia to help prevent sunstroke.

A symbolic language developed with the umbrella that was an aid to many romantic Victorian scenes. To assure himself of a date, or at least company on the road home, many young men might ask to carry a lady's umbrella! To decisively snap open an umbrella was a show of disapproval to a too-forward suitor. The most common superstition regarding the umbrella, however, is that it is unlucky to open one indoors, and that if you carry one with you, it won't rain.

Umbrellas make a lovely and sometimes useful addition to a spring circle, especially if held outdoors. It is a good focus for magic pertaining to weather and romance. If using the umbrella for the latter, consider opening it to open the way for love, or closing it to signify a quiet, peaceful end to a relationship.

18 MAGIC AND THE SUPERNATURAL

We whisper the words by the warmth of the hearth-light
which touches the shadows with gold,
cloaked ever in magic, reclaiming the night
and dancing to pan pipes of old.
♦ Marian ♦

THE SUPERNATURAL—from coincidence to verified psychic phenomena—has been been a part of human culture for millennia. Much of what we now know as part of our everyday lives once would have been considered demonic—such as gunpowder, for example. How else could man produce such a thunderous noise and deadly explosion? Surely it must be a mischievous spirit.

How could man begin to explain the seemingly inexplicable? Why did some people appear to possess superhuman abilities and insight? What was the strange magic produced by a small portion of the population to heal, aid in birthing, and increase crops? Was it a gift of the Gods?

To those who employed such talents with care, the answer was an emphatic "yes." Some civilizations respected their special talents. Others shunned and despised them. Many wise people died for the generous use of their gifts. Fortunately, many more lived for the same reason.

Common people were used to the old ways, and if need be would seek them out in secret.

In this section we will not only explore superstitions surrounding magic and the paranormal, but also associated lore about witchcraft. This includes information about how many of the images and tools for the Craft developed from ancient sources.

Aura

Auras are like sheets of energy surrounding every human being, and all living things. They appear to a psychic like a cloud of light infused with color. Some people believe that the shining light Moses spoke of in the Old Testament, and that of St. Paul's vision are Biblical examples of visible auras.

It is interesting to note that the halo often depicted around Saints' heads is called an *aureola*. Other cultures depict this energy similarly, as shown clearly by temple drawings of holy persons in India, Japan, Egypt, Greece, Mexico, and Peru. Paracelsus in the sixteenth century described it this way: "the vital force is not enclosed in man, but radiates round him like a luminous sphere."

Black Dog

Spectral animals haunt the British Isles; one example is a black dog that is part spirit and part faerie. It often spooks people on dark, gloomy nights, but will leave you alone if you do not attempt to harm it. Goethe adapted this story by having Mephistopheles appear to Faust as a black poodle.

A black dog is sometimes regarded as a witch's familiar (see Chapter 2: Animals and Insects). English rural superstitions believe that seeing one portends a relative's death. A black dog still haunts Newgate prison, thought to be the spirit of a thirteenth-century scholar wrongfully accused of witchcraft.

If a black dog appears in your dreams, regard it as a gentle warning that a wrongful allegation may be coming your way.

Blood

Blood sacrifices occurred on the altars of many ancient faiths, including those of the Israelites, Romans, Greeks, and Druids. Because blood is the life force, people believed such offerings would gain divine recognition and action. This is also probably why people believed that bloodstains from a murder could not be washed away but remained as a sign of the crime (note Lady MacBeth). Today, the term "blood feud" is a remnant of these beliefs, describing disputes between families over a murder.

Between the years A.D. 1500 and 1850, people believed you could take away a witch's power by scratching her upper face and drawing blood. In an English ballad written in 1579, "The Scratching of Witches", this was called "scoring above the breath" (referring to the nose). This would place the mark near the third eye, with the potential of literally draining away psychic power with each drop.

During the Middle Ages people used blood to mark contracts, usually with a thumbprint. This folkway changed slightly over the years to become the mark of a special pact between two people, or blood brothers.

Most contemporary magical traditions do not use blood (human or otherwise) as part of their rites because of the Wiccan rede "harm none." On occasion, an individual may choose to prick his or her finger to produce a small drop for marking magical tools or as a component of other very personal spells. As long as such action is done with proper care (please sterilize the pin first) and motivated by positive intentions, it is acceptable. However, if anyone ever tries to coerce you into giving your precious life essence away for any reason, think twice before saying "yes." This is something that definitely should be led by your own inner voice and sense of propriety.

Bones

A potent ingredient in old charms was a bit of bone. In some areas people used bones and corpses to determine the innocence or guilt of those accused of crime. For example, in *Henry VI* by Shakespeare we read, "O gentlemen, see, see! Dead Henry's wounds open their congealed mouths and bleed afresh!" This occurs when the Duke of Gloucester disrupts the funeral. Another example is in *Daemonologie* by James I (1597) where the author states that a skeleton touched by its murderer will bleed as if crying out for revenge.

The most popular use for human bone was in sleep potions, because sleep was regarded for many years as a kind of death. The Western tradition of mourning for three days after a death originated hundreds of years ago, when people knew nothing of comatose conditions and were waiting to see if the dead person might "wake up."

Another prevalent use for bones (usually those of animals) was in divination. In China, soothsayers and priests searched the cracked bones remaining from offerings for meanings (see Chapter 2: Animals and Insects). We see this type of custom continued today on Thanksgiving with the breaking of the wishbone. Two people pull either and make a wish. After it breaks, the person holding the largest piece of bone will have his or her wish come true. For those of you who eat meat, add a wishbone to your altar any time you are doing magic for personal goals, ambitions, or preparing incense to aid slumber. If you do not eat meat, ask a friend to save the wishbone for you.

Broom

The broom of Wiccan circles was originally a bundle of herbs known as "broom" because, more than likely, this is what the first cleansing items for the home were made from. During these years, a broom propped up outside a woman's home signaled it was a house of prostitution.

The broom is an ancient token of womanhood in its fullness. One interesting custom from Madagascar has the women of the area dancing with a broom while their men are at battle to figuratively "sweep" their enemies from the earth. This tradition is very similar to that of other cultural groups who sweep luck into the house and negative energy out during festival days. In this respect, a specially decorated and blessed broom would be a very useful tool for cleansing the sacred space and casting a magic circle (see Chapter 15: Kitchen and Household Lore)!

Bruja

Bruja, Puerto Rican witches, frequently burn charcoal, seeds, and incense on Fridays to make special magical potions for sale. In the same tradition, try working on Friday any time you are creating magical potions for someone else.

Candles

A light in the darkness has always been a symbol of hope and protection. During the Middle Ages, candles were placed near beds to protect the occupants. Unfortunately, they seemed to provide just the opposite results, ending in hundreds of conflagrations. There is evidence to suggest that Jewish custom had a type of divination by candles. Pope John XXII condemned the practice in the early 1300s.

It is a popular custom in magic today to use colored candles in the sacred space according to the goals of the working (see Chapter 6: Color). Most commonly, the white candle is the symbol of the Goddess; red or orange for fire; yellow air; blue or green water; and brown or black for earth. The number, type, and position of the candles present at any ritual can also change depending on the season, your tradition, and personal preference.

Cauldron

Cauldrons, cups, horns, wells, and other similar containers for water play important roles in legends from every part of the world. The Norse teach us of the horn of plenty; the Celts have the Grail; the story of the cauldron of Cerridwin comes predominantly from Wales; and the Irish speak of the cauldron of Dagda (the "good God"), which would feed any kind soul.

What all of these types of folktales have in common is a magical container purported to heal or feed many. Frequently, only the pure of heart can partake of the powerful item without dire repercussions. The implied conviction was that a powerful beneficent spirit had created this immense positive force, which should not be corrupted under any circumstances.

This probably influenced the belief in sacred wells (see Chapter 26: Sacred Sites) and other holy water sources. There is no doubt it had an influence on Christianity, most notably the search for the Cup of Christ. Although this object is frequently called the Grail, it is probably not the same cup as appears in pre-Christian Scottish, Irish, and Welsh lore.

Most modern magical practitioners have some type of cauldron or cup to represent the element of water, the direction of west, and the ever moving wheel of life. Traditional cauldrons have three legs, presumably to reflect the threefold natures of both humanity and the God/dess.

Circle

Circles are significant religious symbols throughout the world, probably representing its most basic cycles and the womb. Throughout Europe there are numerous stone circles where ancient rites were held. Carvings of circles appear in every culture, and beautiful circular Celtic knot-work dominates illuminated manuscripts.

In one fifteenth-century manuscript, a picture of a magical circle carried and used for protection included pictorial representations of a sword, ring, oil vessel, scepter and the inscription *AGLA,* standing for a Hebrew phrase meaning "Thou art mighty forever, O Lord." To be effective, the maker of the circle had to be certain that its outer border was unbroken, and thus contained the potent energy.

In later years, a magical circle drawn on the floor was thought to pertain to the necromancer's art. Such individuals required vast amounts of protection from the spirits they summoned. Again, the boundary of the circle, inscribed with runes or secret symbols, created an atmosphere of safety.

Today, this idea continues in that modern witches usually gather in circles, prepare a sacred space that takes this shape, and use spells, chants, and/or symbols as a means of protecting sacred powers. While many do not actually draw lines on the floor, there are very definitive spiritual lines of force drawn by athame, salt, water, wand, or any number of other magical implements while invoking the watchtowers—the four main sources of natural energy: earth, air, fire and water. These elements are ascribed to the directions of north, east, south, and west, respectively.

Crystal Balls

Polished surfaces of all kinds, but especially beryl, became scrying tools for the ancients. An Orphic poem entitled *Lithica* describes a black, round magic sphere. Arabic author Haly Abou Gefar wrote of a golden ball used by the magi to aid hypnotic trance states and arouse visions.

Other accounts of crystal balls include that of Helenus, a Trojan seer, who fasted and enacted specific rituals with his sphere to foresee the downfall of Troy. Agrippa also wrote about these objects in the sixteenth century, saying that the character and quality of a crystal was paramount to its effectiveness. He recommended round ones of clarity, and about the size of an orange. He also felt they worked best when fit into an ivory or ebony pedestal.

Ibn Kaldoun, a very astute writer born in Persia in the 1300s, noted that while certain dark and light spots in the stone might help the visionary sense, it is not so much a physical as it is a spiritual kind of seeing. This is probably why many of the stands and cloths for crystal balls were elaborate, inscribed with all manner of protective magical sigils and words, including the names of angelic beings.

In the Highlands of Scotland, the proper regalia for royalty is topped with a crystal globe and the mace is crowned with beryl sphere. According to natives, magical use of these stones began with the druids. They were called simply "stones of power."

Today, the most popular scrying stone is quartz because of its clarity, variety, and durability (see Chapter 7: Crystals, Gems, and Metals).

Cunning Folk

Probably one of the oldest terms for witches, the name applied to those purported to practice white magic. As late as A.D. 1800, almost every town in England had at least one of these people who spent their time locating thieves, curing disease, and performing various divinatory functions. They were usually adept herbalists, who had learned their arts from elders of their families. The tradition of handing down knowledge of the Wise Craft may be the basis for the belief in magic being characteristic in certain family lines.

Curse

The belief that words or items have the power to injure a person is the essence of a curse's power. Those spoken by a priest, mage, or parent are twice feared because of the respect these individuals command. The most potent curse is one sealed with blood.

Most individuals involved in white magic prefer not to use curses for many reasons. Not the least of these is the "threefold-law": whatever energy is sent out out returns three times. It is akin to the Christian "golden rule:" do unto others as you would have them do unto you. While there might be certain extreme instances that call for a curse, it is not entered into lightly or without firm conviction of necessity.

Demon

While most people thought of demons as malignant spirits, the original Greek word *daemon* means "supernatural being." The Catholic Church influenced the shift in emphasis by associating pagan gods and spirits with the devil.

Common assumptions about demons included that air demons brought tempests, water demons caused flood, and mental illness was considered demonic possession of a person.

Doppelgänger

A ghostly double or counterpart of a person, the doppelgänger was believed to appear to an individual a few days before his or her death, or be seen by a loved one at the moment of death. The wraith could take many forms and was also sometimes known as a fetch. Such creatures would warn of impending problems by changing their form and giving visual clues.

In Scandinavia, they are known as *fylgja*, and are regarded as a kind of protector. Eventually, this belief translated into what we know as guardian angels. Modern magicians interpret the *fylgja* as a spirit guide.

Dowsing

A dowser searches for water or precious substances by using a divining rod, often made from a forked branch of hazel wood. Known as "water witching" during the Victorian era in the United States, dowsing first gained popularity in the Middle Ages. German miners brought the craft to England in the fifteenth century, and then to the United States when they emigrated there.

The *Critical History of the Divining Rod* by LeBrun in 1733, shows the proper way to hold the rod as firmly in both hands with the palms pointing downward. In this configuration, the dowsing rod acts like a compass' needle guiding the dowser to the goal (see Chapter 10: The Elements).

Contemporary students of sacred geometry still use metal and wood dowsing rods to discern the location of lay lines and other natural centers of energy.

Envoutement

Appearing in old French magical transcripts, *envoutement* refers to wax figures used for enacting spells. These figures were the forerunners to stuffed dolls (or poppets) and were created for specific magical intentions. To work properly, the figure had to be formed as closely as possible to the person it represented, and even had to carry a bit of that individual's clothing or hair. If wax was not available, the alternatives offered were that of mud from two sides of a river, or a paper drawing properly named.

This is a perfect example of sympathetic magic. In all cases the *envoutement* was given the same treatment wished for the individual, as a chant, spell, or invocation was pronounced over it. For example, if the person had eye trouble, a healing salve might be applied to the waxen eye of the *envoutement*. If shingles were to be healed, a little wax might be peeled away in the appropriate area to elicit results.

Similar magical approaches are used today in Santería. In contemporary Wicca, a stuffed poppet is sometimes used.

Evil Eye

For some reason, the evil eye became one of the most commonly feared magical abilities in the world. It was widely believed that some individuals had the capacity to blight other people, cattle, and so on, with a mere glance. This particular ability was thought doubly harmful to children. With this in mind, the contemporary phrase, "if looks could kill," takes on a whole new meaning.

The reason for this may have been partially rooted in the assumption that the eyes are the windows of the soul and that they are also one of the most emotionally expressive parts of the human body. The evil eye may also have helped explain many seemingly baffling plagues. To already superstitious minds, these mysterious illnesses had roots in the spiritual world. These evil looks were easy to blame for the illnesses.

The lengths to which individuals went to protect themselves from this magic were bountiful. Amulets of all kinds (see Chapter 1: Amulets and Talismans) were devised to ensure safety of the self, children, home, and farm animals. Many of these amulets can easily be adapted for contemporary practice.

Familiars

Many divine beings hid in the form of animals. Hecate chose that of a cat until Zeus banished the hideous creature. Through her magic Hecate became a patron Goddess for witches and familiars (see Chapter 2: Animals and Insects).

Cats were the most predominant familiar because of their glowing eyes. Any woman with a black cat was often suspected of witchcraft just by association. Today, familiars are regarded as special animal helpers and friends whose insight strengthens magic.

Ghosts

The idea of life after death is known in virtually every culture. Where beliefs differ is in what happens to the soul after it leaves the body. In some instances, usually those of violent or untimely deaths, the spirit of the individual is thought to be trapped in a kind of limbo, and thus a ghostly apparition stays in that area.

A southern United States superstition says to keep a ghost from following you, toss the hair from a black cat over your should, saying "Scat, scat, turn to a bat." This little incantation is believed to literally turn the ghost into a bat, thus nullifying its power. Today people still report ghost sightings. Two notable examples are the phantom hitchhikers all over the United States, and Lincoln's Funeral train.

Grimoire

Grimoires are the secret texts of European magic, with topics including divination, spells, and herbs. The grimoire may have obtained its name from the Norse *grima*, which means "specter," or from *grammarye*, an Old English word for magic.

One of the more famous grimoires, the *Grimoirum Verum* appeared in 1517. It took its material from the *Lesser Key of Solomon* (*Lemegeton*), and discussed the hierarchy of spirits.

The grimoire has been translated into the modern "Book of Shadows," which contains personal or group methods of practical magic. These collections are sometimes passed to students, family members, or close friends.

Healing Gifts

In England, Scotland, and France, the prevalent belief was that those of royal descent could heal with a touch. According to English history, Edward III performed a number of cures. This practice probably originated from with the idea of divine right, where God determines rulership and the king is sanctioned by that power.

The gift of healing is something for which one may have to have a predisposition. When Moses knew his death was coming, he prayed to God to send a suitable successor (Numbers 27:18, 20). To instill the divine gift in this successor, the laying on of hands had to occur (see Chapter 4: Body Divination). Sometimes healers also presented their successors with a token of power (such as their books). On the European continent, this token usually passed from man to man or woman to woman. A few cultures suggested it should change sex with each generation, but this idea was not often followed.

Within our modern magical communities, there are many who work within this tradition, employing everything from herbs to crystals, or just their hands (see Chapter 13: Health and Medicine).

Hermetic Texts

These books, dated to about A.D. 3, contain six sections of information on the education of priests, temple rituals, medicine, geography, astrology, hymns, and guidance for kings. While modern historians believe the texts represent a collective effort, the ancients attributed it to Hermes, the inventor of writing. Hermes Trismegistus was also equated with the Egyptian Thoth, God of Wisdom.

The actual authorship of these books is not as important as how they approached magic. Metaphysical studies are seen as a science of the mind. If we can reclaim this outlook today, it will help change the connotations of magic to something positive, practical, and life-affirming.

Hikuli

In Mexico, the *hikuli* is a sacred cactus used in certain magical rites. As part of the Mexican mourning rite (see Chapter 8: Dance), the cactus is first soaked in fresh water. Next, the water is sprinkled over the mourners to protect them from any angry spirits. This is similar to the asperging of sacred space to cleanse it of negativity.

Other large, home-grown cacti might function similarly for your fire rites, the cactus being a plant which grows vibrantly in the blazing desert. Its spiny exterior gives protection from any negative elements lurking about.

Image Magic

Image magic uses another person or object to represent its actual subject. An example is the *envoutement* described earlier. Another illustration is the belief that one could kill a person just by leaving his or her image under the eaves of one's home during a storm. Here, the likeness would be completely drenched in water. If the magic worked correctly, the affected individual might subsequently catch a deadly cold, or perhaps drown accidentally.

This last illustration is one I hope no one actually tries, except toward more positive ends, such as washing away a negative habit.

Iron

The magnetic properties of iron, and its use in forging, contributed to the mystique of this metal. In Deuteronomy 27:5, God commands the Israelites not to use any iron upon their altars, nor was any tool of iron used in the building of King Solomon's temple (I Kings 6:7). Similarly, iron should not be used to cut magical herbs as it mars their potency (see Chapter 7: Crystals, Gems, and Metals).

In Scotland, iron spikes placed crosswise on the dead will keep angry or restless ghosts from wandering. In Israel, midwives and healers waved iron knives above newborn children to protect them from evil. In Ireland, an iron bar across a barrel of beer is said to keep the brew from souring.

Pliny the Elder recommended iron nails above one's threshold to protect the home. This particular counsel may have given rise to the use of iron horseshoes above the doorway.

Lituus

A *lituus* was a special wooden staff used as the sign of a Roman augur. It could not have any knots in it, due to the belief that the augur must be free to perform his observations. A knot in the staff would bind the magic (see Chapter 16: Knots).

With this in mind, the Celtic form of divination by wands known as "wittan wands," takes on new meaning. Here, smooth pieces of wood are read and interpreted depending on the patterns they form after being thrown to the ground. This particular practice may have had its roots with the Roman *lituus.*

You can make your own set of wooden divination tools simply by marking twenty-one equally sized, smooth sticks, etched or painted with traditional runes (or other symbols of personal meaning) and casting them in similar fashion. There are hundreds of individual adaptations which can be made with attached feathers, crystals, etc. Just remember to mark down the meaning of each stick you create, and how they affect each other, then enjoy your handiwork.

Magic

The term *magic* comes from the Greek *mageria*, which described the science/religion created by the priests of Zoroastrianism (the magi) in Persia. They were students of omens, dreams, and astrology and were seekers of profound wisdom. Their founder, Zoroaster (whose name means "keeper of old camels or goats"), became so well-known in Chaldea that during the Persian empire (sixth century B.C.) the term *Chaldean* meant "wizard."

To the magi, the principles of magic were both divine and natural. No sign or opportunity for enlightenment was overlooked. They attempted to explain the mysteries of the universe and define their own role in it.

The New Age movement today is not really much different. Those who participate, like the ancient magi, seek to find guidance and truth from the natural world in an attempt to comprehend God/dess. The spirit of discovery and the yearning to understand still dwell within us. Through that spirit (with a little bit of study) we can reconnect with the wisdom of the ages, bring to it a bit of our own discernment, and then create truly remarkable magic for the future.

Measures

In many covens, it was traditional to take a specific measurement of when an individual undergoing initiation. While the exact technique of taking the measure varied according to group, the idea was that this item was kept by the priest or priestess as a sign of trust. It is considered a direct link to that individual. Because of this bond, should they ever place their coven members in danger or betrayed that trust, it could then be used to direct magic against them. In more modern traditions, the measure is not always kept, and it is rarely employed for bane.

Offerings

One of the best ways to thank the Gods and Goddesses and/or win their favor was to give them appropriate gifts or offerings. The earliest form of offering was frequently animal sacrifice, because animals were the most valuable thing most people had to give. Some early manuscripts indicate the animal world did not always take this position of honor. Breads, cheese, nails, salt, barley, flour, and even milk and honey were sometimes substituted, depending on the situation and the severity of need.

Today, many of the latter items mentioned are best dispersed to the natural world, not only as offerings of thanks to the Divine, but also a gifts to the earth's creatures. In this way you have an opportunity to give back a little of your bounty without wastefulness.

Pentagram

The pentagram appears frequently in Sumerian pottery designs, and was connected with amulets pertaining to good health. It is also seen in early manuscripts of the Cabbalah, and may have actually been an early version of Solomon's Seal.

Certain Japanese sects sometimes use the five-pointed star to represent five elements, the fifth being spirit, or the void.

Power

Superstition has it that a male magician's power resides in his hair. This has ties to the ancient Jewish story of Samson, and the myth that hair continues to grow even after death. This particular folk belief was so strong in certain areas of the world that cutting hair and beards was considered an effective way to discourage any magical pursuits in young men.

There is similar lore about female witches that says her magic is more potent when she creates it with her hair down.

This may be tried by anyone with long enough hair. Otherwise, if you want to add direction or more personal power to any significant spells for yourself, use a small clipping of hair, best taken close to the root for maximum vitality (see Chapter 22: Personal Care).

Protection

Protection against magic has taken many forms throughout history. Some of the methods include spitting, and planting elder or bay trees near your door.

A charm against sorcery from circa A.D. 1470 distinctly indicates a strong Christian influence. It begins by calling upon the power of Christ as a type of medicine to cure enchantment, and then adds other mixed symbols of the Virgin Mary (who basically replaced the Goddess image for many Pagans in the early Catholic Church) and the Hebrew *AGLA*. This charm was written in entirety and was meant to be carried at all times.

In England, a calf's liver imbedded with pins and hidden in the chimney was thought to be a very effective amulet against black magic, and in New Mexico burning red peppercorns on Friday will stop any witchcraft directed at you. Carrying or wearing jet and sapphire is an alternative means of warding against spells and incantations.

Rituals

The text of a mid-nineteenth-century treatise on magic by French occultist Eliphas Levi indicates that specific days of the week were best for certain ritual work.

For those who may wish to try adding the significance of these days to the timing of their own rites, they are as follows: Sunday was a time to work with the "light." Magic combined with the effects of gold and chrysolite was especially effective. Monday was for divination and the greater mysteries, while wearing yellow robes and pearls. Tuesday was for justified wrath, donning the color of red and using iron or amethyst in one's work. Wednesday was best for science and any magic pertaining to the mind, the preferred color being green, and silver or agate being used as spell components. Thursday was for religious ritual and/or politics while dressed in purple and wielding tin or emeralds. Friday was for love, wearing blue robes and using turquoise. Finally, Saturday was a time for mourning or bringing death to old ways, putting on brownish colors, and utilizing lead or onyx as part of the rite.

Salt

Salt was valuable to the ancients, being the main preservative for foods. Soldiers of the Roman Empire were paid in salt, which is where the phrase "worth their salt" comes from.

The Sky God Ukko in Finland made salt by throwing fire into the sea. The ancient Aztecs have a salt Goddess named Huixtocihuatl. In the Old Testament, a covenant of salt is mentioned as a binding trust. This has similarities to the Teutonic custom of sealing an oath after dipping ones finger in salt. Additionally, in Arabia, the bond of salt between host and guest is a sacred confidence. It means the host will protect the guest and the guest will not overstay the welcome.

In Thailand, women used to wash daily with salt to protect themselves from harm, specifically malevolent magic. In Morocco, people carry salt after dark to keep ghosts at bay, and in the United States, salt kept near the hearth protects the home from spirits (see Chapter 15: Kitchen and Household Lore).

Secrecy

The idea that magical knowledge should be carefully guarded is very old, but most characteristic of the Renaissance mages. There was a strong belief that this power could not be trusted to the common folk, and students should be chosen with great care. Part of the reasoning was to protect the aura of mystery which the magical arts created. Even deeper than this, however, was the feeling that the more commonplace magical information became, the less potent its results would be, as if there were a limited amount of energy to be disbursed through the pool of practitioners.

In keeping with this kind of thinking, many cryptic languages and sigils were created for the Book of Secrets where a mage kept his insights. This may have been the first version of the modern Wiccan Book of Shadows for magical rites, theory, etc. Some of these languages, such as Enochian, not only protected the magic user and aided the craft, but eventually helped establish whole traditions.

Today there is a diversity of opinion on the subject of secrecy. High and ritual magicians preserve the mysteries of their craft by using a system of initiation and degrees. Folk magicians, however, tend to be more open with their practices in the hopes of educating the world about Wiccan/Pagan ideals. Both approaches have merit. You do not want to give a loaded gun to a child, but you also want them to be able to recognize a gun when they see one. Which course of action you take is up to you. Simply remember in the process that you are responsible for what you teach and share with others as truth.

Standing Stones

Also known as megaliths and dolmens, standing stone structures appear throughout Europe as an enigmatic reminder of ancient rites and beliefs.

Dolmens are still created by many today in conjunction with magical gardens and/or to prepare ritual circles. For this, rocks native to the area are most often used and are set out either in a circle or as inspiration dictates. These stones then act as a boundary between world and not-world. They also guide and protect the magical energy created within that space.

Tattoos

The tattoo has a very long history. Some Egyptian mummies had tattoos, each with a social or magical function. In Tahiti, people believed the Gods taught tattooing to the people. Here, they adopted it as an initiation rite and primitive form of writing (see Chapter 4: Body Divination).

The magical aspects of tattooing probably originated because the process draws blood (see the entry for "Blood" in this chapter). Some people so revere the tradition that it is dishonorable to die without a mark. In northwest India, for example, the Great Lord will toss you out of heaven if your body appears without tatoos.

Australians place patterns on their upper arms to protect themselves from boomerang attacks. In Burma, women use tatoos on their lips to secure love, and in Bengal tatoos cure various maladies, depending on their placement.

Vampires

Stories of vampires appear in literature throughout the world. The Slavonic/Balkan regions bear a higher proportion of vampire legends than anywhere else. In Russia, the name *upuir* means "to drink." In Greece, Vampires were called *broncolaia*. In all instances, these creatures were considered neither dead nor alive. They had little tolerance for sunlight (which could kill them), and needed fresh blood for nourishment. The only means to kill a vampire was to drive a wooden stake through the heart, or destroy the body during the day.

In recent years, scientists have discovered a disease which may have given rise to the stories of vampirism. This sickness causes the afflicted person to become very light-sensitive and pale, and sometimes even have a craving for blood because of iron deficiency.

Werewolf

In Anglo-Saxon, *wer-wulf* meant "man-wolf." Stories of lycanthropy reached their height around the sixteenth and seventeenth centuries. This particular creature owes it origins to the days when witches were thought to frequently take the form of animals. Their shapeshifting was believed to take place at night. If the person was hurt while in animal form, they would continue to bear the wound come daybreak.

Not all instances of change were voluntary, according to superstition. If an afflicted person happened to walk over a wolf path, or drink from a haunted stream, the wolf nature could get the best of them and cause them to change. Thus we see today the popular werewolf finding its form change during the full moon; this moon phase having long been associated with powerful magic.

19 MIRRORS

*What do I say—a mirror of my heart
are not thy waters sweeping, dark and strong?*
♦ Lord Byron, *Stanzas to Poe* ♦

THE EARLIEST version of a mirror was probably the clear surface of a well or other water source. Later, polished stones, the metal of a sword, or small pieces of brass were used by those who could afford the workmanship. Whatever the form, the individual reflection has been approached with great trepidation, and mirrors with the feeling that they could reveal or capture the spirit.

If a person looked into a mirror and saw no reflection, it was considered a terrible sign. The lack of likeness meant that the soul had left and death was soon to come. This particular belief later gave rise to the superstition that a vampire had no reflection because it was "un-dead" and had no soul (see Chapter 18: Magic and the Supernatural).

Mirrors have strong connections with the moon and, therefore, the Goddess. The almost eerie silver light cast by the moon, reflecting off the waters, became associated with mirrors and magical-mirror creation. Stones and crystals aligned with the moon, such as rock crystal or polished silver, have been heralded as the best materials for making this divinatory device.

Mirrors figure predominantly in the stories of many cultures. One of the best-known mirrors in folklore is from the fairy tale "Snow White." The villain (a sorceress) looks into a mirror asking, "mirror, mirror on the wall, who's the fairest of them all?" This is perhaps the most famous line from all the Grimm's tales. There is also the Greek myth of Narcissus who was so infatuated with his own reflection that he languished away and died. Similarly, Dionysus became so mesmerized by his image in a mirror that he could not move. Each of these stories, in one way or another, is a gentle moral lesson that advises against overt concern with outer appearance.

Breakage

The idea that breaking a mirror causes bad luck comes from the belief that one's reflection was really one's soul. To injure such a powerful thing would naturally portend difficulties. The only way to rid yourself of this bad luck was to sweep up every remnant of the mirror and throw it in a river rushing away from you, thus carrying the misfortune with it.

This practice is not only bad for the environment, but also dangerous. A contemporary alternative for this is to use the pieces in a witch bottle (see Chapter 15: Kitchen and Household Lore) so that any negative energy may be captured within and returned to its source through the mirror's reflective power.

Cabbalist Mirror

Cabbalists used seven mirrors inscribed with planetary names. Each mirror was of an appropriate metal and could only be consulted on the day of its ruling planet. For example, the moon (or water) mirror would be made of silver and consulted on Monday. Sunday was a gold mirror; Tuesday, of iron; Wednesday, mercury; Thursday, tin; Friday, copper; and Saturday, lead.

You can make a similar set for yourself, consulting each mirror with questions appropriate only to that metal/planet; for example, the water or moon mirror would be consulted for queries pertaining to the intuition or healing (see Chapter 7: Crystals, Gems, and Metals).

Consecration

Folklore of the sixteenth century said that the only way to consecrate a scrying mirror was to work during the hours of Mars (the first, eighth, fifteenth or twenty-second hour of Tuesday). The mirror must be properly paid for first, then buried in a grave for three weeks before spirits are called to inhabit the glass. The alternative to this was to set the mirror in the baptismal water of a firstborn son for three weeks, and then pour the water out over a grave while reading from the book of Revelation. After all this, the mirror was finally charged by the user so that nothing under heaven would be hidden from the scryer's eye.

The form you choose for blessing your own magic mirror is up to you. However, the timing given above might improve results.

Covering or Turning Mirrors

Until about a hundred years ago, when someone was sick, or just after the death of a loved one, it was traditional in both England and the United States to cover all the mirrors in the house. In the first instance, it was so that the sickly spirit would not be tempted to enter another body through this revealer of the soul. In the second case, it was so that other people would not get carried off by the soul of the departed.

Similar ideas pertain to turning mirrors. In some cultures, turning a mirror away from you will help reflect away any negativity, while in the Orient, this acts like a doorway for a spirit to enter. Depending on your viewpoint, bless a mirror in your home and have them turned appropriately for protection. During a ritual for shielding your home, symbolically cover the mirrors within to keep any unwanted influences away from your sacred space.

Divination

One interesting type of divination by mirrors comes from ancient Greece. A specially selected mirror was placed on the head of a blindfolded child, who for some reason was believed to receive signs in this manner. The ancient Hebrews may have used the surface of liquid in a cup as a type of scrying mirror as indicated in Genesis 44:1-5.

Magic mirrors continue to be used for divination today. In most instances, certain types
of patterns within the glass presage events
or a generalized atmosphere. White clouds
appearing are favorable; violet ones portend joy; red is an indication of danger;
yellow, playfulness, and energy; purple,
matters of the mind or spiritual study;
green, growth or maturation; and blue,
tranquillity, solitude, and relaxation.

The direction of movement in these visions is also considered important. Upwards indicates an affirmative answer; downward, negative, and
to the right, interest on the part of the spirit guides for that mirror. Some
people more adept at scrying may actually see images appear, especially
in past-life readings where one's reflection transforms to reveal the former self.

When the clouds just seem to move in a circle, this is an indication
that a more specific question is required or that an accurate answer is
unavailable at that time. In complicated matters, the divination mirror
cannot always give a response due to the limitations of time, space,
freewill, etc.

Earth Mirror

A German manuscript dated from A.D. 1650 describes the making of an
Earth or World Mirror by placing a mirrored glass two inches above a
board upon which questions were written. At this point the diviner
placed three grains of salt on his tongue, prayed, made a sacred sign
(sometimes the cross), and breathed on the mirror three times while
reciting an invocation for knowledge (which had Christian overtones).

The description of this process is similar to other divinatory techniques for this era, except that Hebrew names for God and angels were
sometimes substituted. During this period, it would not be uncommon to
find a church which kept a scrying mirror on the same side of the altar
as its gospel, in the belief that this Divine gift was best used by a servant
of God.

Construction of the mirror can be attempted today by substituting
appropriate invocations to your guiding God or Goddess, and following
much the same procedure.

Healing Mirrors

In India, a silver basin filled with water is held beneath the full moon while an afflicted individual stares into it. Afterwards, the water is drunk to help bring about the healing.

This method might still be used in matters of physical or mental rehabilitation. I would recommend the light of a waning crescent moon to accentuate the symbolism of diminishing difficulties. This water could be further empowered by adding ingestible herbs known for their soothing effects, such as lavender, fennel, and garlic, before placing it beneath the moon. Strain this to make it more palatable.

Mirrors as the Face of Gods

Certain Native Mexican tribes regard mirrors as the face of the Gods. To look into a mirror brings power and allows the Gods see into our hearts, especially when used by a shaman.

This belief is very similar to an old story about someone who was given the book of all knowledge only to discover that it had but one page—a mirror. Both of these stories serve to remind us that, while spiritual teachers are wonderful, ultimately our greatest lessons will be found in our own lives and hearts.

Moon Mirrors

Moon mirrors are designed to foretell how long it will be before you meet a mate. This scrying is often done on Yule.

Begin with a mirror and silk handkerchief and go to a nearby pond, lake, or stream. Sit with your back to the water and hold the mirror so it reflects both the actual moon and the moon's image in the water. Next place the handkerchief on your face and count the number of moons seen. If there are only two, it will be more than a year before a serious relationship comes. If there are more than two, each moon equals one month.

You may also use this mirror for any question which requires a specific time frame as a response.

Operating Magic Mirrors

Many people perceive blue or black magic mirrors as the best for scrying. Frequently, the mirror is placed on a dark cloth during a waxing moon for improved results. Candles are also added, providing flickering reflections for the scryer to focus on. Some scryers have been known to sleep with their mirror or other visionary tool to ensure an empathic link.

When the mirror is a polished blade, it is recommended that it be bathed in mugwort before scrying. This herb is associated with the moon and the intuitive senses.

The best advice for the novice scryer is to relax and not to expect anything specific. Find a comfortable chair and set up the mirror (or reflective stone or blade) so it is easily seen. Do not look directly at the reflection, but at its edges, so that you see not only the mirror but also the candle, table, etc. Continue this gaze. You will probably feel a little weary after a few minutes, but breathe deeply and try to continue looking. As you do, you may notice wisps of light or color forming on the surface of the mirror, or the reflection of the candle flame changing oddly. This is the first sign that you are scrying correctly.

Again, do not try to see anything specific, but keep your question clearly in mind. Watch for images, symbols, and colors and make note of them all; you can worry about specific interpretations later. Most of the time these readings, unless done for someone else, are personal in nature, and the symbols appearing should make sense to you. If not, check a dream interpretation book or similar text for probable meanings.

Don't be disappointed if you don't succeed immediately. Scrying and divination take a refined form of concentration that are not mastered overnight. Keep practicing, and maintain a log of your progress and experiences to refer to later.

Protective Mirrors

In the Greek myth of Perseus, he was able to avert the stare of the Medusa by using a polished shield to capture her reflection, thereby averting the danger it presented. For the magical home, this might effectively translate into having a small mirror as part of your altar or medicine shield. Pieces of polished metal hanging from lines near a window can reflect protective light to all areas of your house with every breeze.

Scrying Mirrors

According to a sixteenth-century text, the best scrying mirror is made from glass or stone, and then anointed with olive oil to consecrate it for use. The olive oil serves to give the surface of the object a hazy effect that makes scrying a little easier. To the olive oil, add other lunar herbs or those associated with divination, such as chamomile, rosemary, camphor, ground ivy, or distort, to increase the overall effect. To prepare this, warm your olive oil and add the desired herbs. Place the mixture in the light of a full moon for three nights, each time warming the preparation first. The  use of the full moon is to improve the intuitive sense. Finally, strain the oil and apply as desired. This concoction is also an excellent anointing oil for any divinatory efforts.

Tezcatlipoca

In Mexico there is a long-standing belief that the god Tezcatlipoca, had a magic mirror in which he could see everything happening in the world at the same time. This deity's name translates into "shining mirror," and the looking glass was said to be made out of obsidian. Many similar glasses are still made in Mexico today.

With this in mind, a polished obsidian may be added to your medicine pouch or personal staff to improve universal understandings and perspectives.

Water Mirror

The oldest form of magic mirror was a vessel filled with clear water drawn from a well or river, or a handful of ink held in the hollow of the left hand. These two surfaces would be gazed at until all ripples ceased and an image appeared.

Weather Mirrors

In France, mirrors were once used to chase away sudden storms or hail in the belief that, since mirrors reverse a person's image, they can also reverse natural influences and luck (see Chapter 30: Weather Lore).

With this in mind, get a small hand mirror and keep it with you. When things seem to get disrupted, turn the mirror to reflect the negative energy away from you.

20 MISCELLANEOUS

Hear the voice of the bard, who present, past and future sees!
♦ William Blake, *Songs of Experience* ♦

RESEARCHING THIS book turned out to be a much bigger task than I had originally expected. There is a wealth of books exploring folkways, but none reach a more profound level than saying approximately where they developed and why. How this affected various cultures seems to be a study left to anthropologists.

While perusing various tomes, I found some superstitions with magical potential that I wanted to share, but couldn't quite find a "niche" for within this book. So, this chapter serves as the catchall for those folkways.

Apple Seeds

Placing apple seeds on your eyelids could forecast your travel plans. This was accomplished by placing one apple seed on each eyelid, one representing home and the other travel. After blinking, whichever seed stayed on the lid longer told whether a long trip was coming within the next year. If the seed representing home remained in place, so would you.

As a magical application, use an apple seed as a charm anytime you wish safe, fortunate travel. Please use caution if trying the above divination as the seed could injure your eye.

Buttons

The first person you meet on New Year's Day or Halloween can give you a peek at your future if you count the number of buttons they are wearing. One button is luck; two are happiness; three portend a new vehicle; four, an alternative mode of transportation; five, new clothing; six, accessories; seven, a new dog; eight, a new cat; nine, an unexpected letter; ten, pleasure; eleven, extreme joy; and, finally, twelve buttons tell of a treasure soon to be discovered (see Chapter 17: Luck).

This superstition might be extended to using specific numbers of buttons as spell components, special buttons being chosen to adorn your ritual garb, or unique old buttons as an inexpensive addition to a medicine bag.

Departure

When you leave on a journey, it is considered bad luck to turn back for any reason. If you must return to the house, walk in backward to retrieve what you need. This idea comes from the old story of Sodom and its destruction and is strongly connected to other superstitions associated with turning around an item to change fortune. For the magic circle, this might translate into dismissing the quarters by walking backward.

Another interesting bit of lore on the same subject has to do with a guest's departure. Here, you are instructed never to clean the guest's room before an hour has passed after his or her departure, lest you sweep your friendship away with the dust. It was also generally considered poor manners to perform such chores while a guest was still in the house. An extension of this idea might be to use a broom to sweep inward in a sacred space to inspire kinship or, when a member is leaving permanently, to sweep outward as a way to break the ties cleanly.

Ear Piercing

This fashionable trend started as a means to chastise the ear for indiscretion in hearing secrets it was not meant to hear. The injured body part was then consoled with a jewel as a reminder of the lesson. Thus today, an earring can become a an emblem of protection against gossip or to ensure greater privacy.

Land Deeds

In olden days, the seller of land was supposed give the buyer a bit of wood or earth as a symbol of the land's exchange. While they signed the deed, they had to look directly at it, to be able to attest that they had witnessed the signature. Today, this metaphor could be employed for any ritual of land blessing, to aid the smooth purchase of a new home, or to assist with moving transitions.

Left Side

Long associated with evil, in heraldry left is called "sinister," which may have encouraged some of the superstitions associated with this side. The Anglo-Saxon word lyft, which gives us our modern English derivative, translates to mean "worthless" or "meek"; again, not a wonderful association. It may be because of this root word that for many years lefthanded individuals were regarded cautiously, as possibly being imbalanced.

We continue to call those who choose to practice Dark Arts in magic as "walking the left-hand path."

Life Index

The condition of this item, which is left behind by a loved one before a long journey, is said to be directly linked with how your friend or mate fares while away. One specific item often used was a blade. If the dagger remained shining, all was well. If it dulled, there was trouble brewing, and if it began to rust, it was a sign that sickness or misfortune had struck.

With the advent of the telephone and other communication devices, the use of such measures have waned. However, the emblems could still be applied for safe travel spells. In this case, the person going abroad would prepare a piece of silver or other token to be tended by those remaining behind. Each day after they leave, it would be the duty of those at home to clean and care for the token so that their loved ones would receive the same care and loving attention while they travel.

Lockerby Penny

This penny, a unique item owned by an English family and used to cure many illnesses in animals, was actually a round silver piece the size of a half crown. When a local farmer was having difficulty, the coin was immersed in water and turned; then the water was given to the ailing creature (see Chapter 15: Kitchen and Household Lore and Chapter 27: The Sea).

The actual whereabouts of this coin is no longer known. However, another blessed silver coin might be substituted in ritual drinks for pets who are not feeling well.

Photographs

Many people, especially those of tribal nations, have a definite hesitancy or outright fear of having their picture taken. The feeling is that in some manner the photograph is not just paper, but a part of the soul. So, taking a picture is thought to steal a part of someone's essential spirit. In American tradition it has also been considered bad luck to tear up or burn a photo of someone still living. This will bring them troubles.

This type of superstition can be used effectively in sympathetic magic for friends and family who live far away. When you want to send them special energy, bring their picture into the sacred space. If they are ill, anoint the edges of the photo with a healing salve. If they need money, shower the picture with various coins and bills.

Pilgrimages

There is a belief in Mexico that, if a specific pilgrimage is not made every year to honor the great ancestors in the land of the Ancient Ones, then the world itself will cease to move.

In actuality, this pilgrimage is also an annual harvest festival for peyote, known as the "footprint of the magical deer." Peyote is regarded among these people as a sacred root and is used for various rituals in the year to come.

In the same manner, I think the idea of an annual festival to honor the magical teachers who have come before us is really a lovely one. For this, each participant could share eulogies or stories about those individuals (well known or not) who have made an important spiritual impact on their lives. The entire ritual would be aimed at returning sacred energies to these people by way of well-deserved thanks.

Shadow

As with mirrors, the shadow was widely thought to be directly linked to the spirit. Consequently, to step on someone's shadow was believed to do them direct harm. If you felt someone was possessed, you might secretly measure their shadow, write the measurement on a slip of paper and bury it to confine the malicious spirit within.

Statues

In Greece, if you whispered a question to the statue of Hermes in a temple, then put your fingers in your ears, the first chance phrase you heard upon leaving was your answer. While I would not consider this a tried and true method, you could experiment with your own God/dess image to see whether the technique is applicable to other figures.

Tea Leaves

If strewn in front of your living space, they are said to keep away evil. However, tea leaves are more commonly used for divination, where the querist swirls the cup three times with only a little liquid left in it, then turns the cup to see what patterns emerge. These patterns closely resemble those in dream interpretation or charms, the configuration closest to the reader being the soonest to materialize in reality. This process may or may not be done with a specific question in mind. Without the inquiry, the reading will be generalized to an overview of present, past, and future circumstances.

Theater

Any fresh flowers, real food and drink, etc. are frequently considered ill luck at the theater because of the use of props. Likewise, no whistling was allowed on sets. Sometimes the last line of a play is not spoken until dress rehearsal. This last bit of theater lore might work well in a ritual setting, leaving the final invocation or salute out of any practice until the actual working.

Visiting Friends

When going to a friend's new home, it is appropriate to take a small gift to appease the Hearth God. This token can include fresh bread, grains, or anything else which reminds you of a warm, welcoming fireside. This tradition is a throwback to the days when an actual foundation sacrifice was made beneath a building. Also, never place wood on their fire without asking, lest the Hearth God feel insulted by your presumption.

Today, this practice can be maintained for oneself as well. Whenever you move to a new location, take a bit of kitchen spice and burn it on your stove or in the fire to bid welcome to the spirit of the dwelling.

21 NUMBERS

*The first monad is the Eternal God, the second Eternity
the third the paradigm or pattern of the universe.*
♦ Proclus ♦

THE STUDY of numerology is very old, showing evidence of practice in ancient Egypt, Greece, Rome, and Arabia. The Hebrews based their language on a system of twenty-two letters with numeric and mystical correspondences. To those who practice Cabbalism, each letter is one of the building blocks of the universe and a key to understanding God. A book called *Sefer Yetsirah*, written between A.D. 200 and 600, expounded on this belief. Later, the *Key of Solomon* continued the tradition.

The numbers that appear most frequently in superstition and folklore are three, four, seven, and thirteen, three and seven being particularly fortunate. A child born in the seventh month of the year had a better chance of living than one born in the eighth, for example.

In medieval Europe, numbers were important to folk healing. In the course of disease treatment, the fourth, seventh, and ninth days were critical. Pliny the Elder recommended twenty-one centipedes mingled with honey for asthma, the number twenty-one being fortuitous. In Rome, a sty was prodded nine times with barley to affect a cure, nine being the number of dominance and manifestation (see Chapter 15: Health and Medicine).

Numerology also played a role in early forms of divination and other magic. In a text by Jabir Ibn Hayyan, an Arab Sufi, the author recounts a method of discovering whether a sick person will recover. This information was reprinted in Latin in the twelfth century. Here, the name of the healer and the messenger bearing the news were numerologically combined. If the sum was an odd number, the person would recover; if even, death was portended.

In 529 B.C., Pythagoreans formed a secret society about which only traces of information remain today. There is reason to think that they believed in reincarnation and the mystical nature of numbers. The best-known instance of someone using the Pythagorean system of numerology for a prophecy was Cagliostro in his prediction of Louis XIV's death in the French Revolution. A source from that time indicates he translated the king's and queen's names into ancient Persian, then worked out the numerical value for his reading. His prediction came true in 1793. Unfortunately, because of Cagliostro's reputation for black sorcery, few believed this was by chance; most thought that Cagliostro had helped bring about the king's demise through magic.

Pythagoreans felt that self-divisible numbers, or those only divisible by one, were the most potent. In Babylonia, certain numbers were reserved for the Gods: 60, for Anu; 50, Bel; 40, Ea; and 15, Ishtar; just to name a few. Throughout historical texts the numbers 3, 4, 5, 7, 10, 12, 40, 70, and 100 appear predominantly for magical purposes. The number three, is by far the most consistently seen and frequently used.

Numbers were featured in magic either as prescribed repetitions, quantities, dates, times, or actual counts of individuals or items to be included in observances. This remains unchanged today, with the numbers chosen being appropriate to the working. For example, if you are working toward an improved personal balance of your masculine and feminine attributes, the numbers one and two (or three, as a combination) might figure strongly into your spell by way of candles exhibited, or number of times you reiterate the spell.

One

One represents unity, the sun, nature, and birth, comprising all things. In the Arabic alphabet, one is the number of God. In Egypt, one was ascribed to the great Sun God Ra. One is most often deemed a masculine number.

The Babylonians considered one an unlucky number, and interestingly enough drawing the ace (or one) of spades in a card deck is considered an ill omen. One is the number of creation and the beginning. It is a solitary figure, full of authority and leadership.

Magical applications: unity, sun magic, singularity of mind, wholeness, reaching accord.

Two

Two represents duality, balance, the waxing moon, awareness of others, the power of two good hands and eyes. Two was once considered the origin of evil because it brought duality and an insurrection against the unity of one.

Despite this negative connotation, Christian ministers use two fingers for blessing, and certain Egyptian amulets had the form of two digits to indicate the twofold nature of their country. Two is considered feminine in nature. Two is the number of culture, truth, beauty, and consciousness. An appreciation of intellect, cooperation, and enthusiasm is found in two. It is the number of friendship and love.

Magical applications: balance, blessing any handcrafts, appreciation of other people.

Three

Three stands for the ancient Goddess and the threefold nature of humanity, as well as the three dimensions that the human eye can perceive. Spells or prayers were often repeated in multiples of three to honor all of these. When dice were used for divination, throwing three of the same number was considered very fortunate (especially if the number was a multiple of three).

Most cultures regard three as a fortunate number, symbolic of the beginning, middle, and end, triune God/desses, and universal aspects. Examples of this include the Egyptian gods Anu, Ea, Bel; the Babylonian model of the universe comprised of, Heaven, Earth, and the Underworld; the Greek legends of the three fates; and the three magi of Christian tradition.

The followers of Plato felt there were three great principles: matter, idea, and god. Three virtues are spoken of in order to make a marriage successful, those of justice, prudence, and fortitude. Dream authorities claim that any dream which recurs three times will come true, and we still speak of how the number three "is a charm."

Finally, Apollo sat on a tripod of truth, which may be why the number three is considered masculine. Three brings enlightenment, precision, and sympathetic energies to bear. When this number appears frequently, it either warns of too much self-sacrifice or a moment of illumination soon to come.

Magical application: truth, symmetry, unity of purpose in a group, representations of the God/dess.

Four

Four represents the elements, directions, and winds, the four great festivals of the wheel of the year, and boundaries. In Egypt and Babylonia, it is the representation of completeness.

In the Cabbala, the great holy name of God (YHWH) has four letters. Such is the case in several other languages as well, including the Greek God Zeus, the French *Dieu*, Latin *Deus*, Italian *Idio*, and Sanskrit *Deva*. It is the number of awakenings and security. If you have asked a question and the answer is four, it can means true friends, good ideas, and fellowship are on the horizon.

Magical applications: celebrations of time, overcoming limitations, a focus on goals, fruitfulness, and maturity.

Five

Five is a fortunate and sacred number. In the Islamic worlds, it is customary to pray five times a day. The Hebrews had five men to a household, many altars were constructed in measurements of five cubits, and the Pentacle of the Templars (an early Solomon's seal) was a five-pointed emblem for protection (see Chapter 18: Magic and the Supernatural). It is also considered a powerful charm against the evil eye.

Five tapers were burned in traditional Roman marriage ceremonies, and Islam teaches that everyone has five sacred duties: prayer, fasting, purification, giving of alms, and pilgrimage. The negative aspects of this number are uncertainty and doubt. When five appears in your life, you may find yourself restless and moody or disagreeable for no apparent reason. Check to see if you are being true to yourself.

Magical applications: humanity, versatility, astuteness, the senses, pentagram (unity of the elements with self), sacred responsibilities, and five vowels for meditational toning.

Six

Six is a perfect digit. The Star of David, love, and fertility are expressed through the number six. It took God six days to create the world in the Old Testament. So revered was this number in Egypt that they had a festival in its honor.

Part of the wonder of the number six may come from the fact that many crystals naturally take the hexagonal form. Double triangles were considered a ward against evil, as evidenced by the Seal of Solomon, or the Star of David today. Also a number of temptations and excess, if it is yours you may not always be understood by others. Accept your failures, learn from them, and begin to take control of your life. This change will lead to success.

Magical applications: protection, devotion, productivity, finishing projects.

Seven

The number seven represents the number of the spirit and of the power centers. There are seven days in a week, and in one phase of the moon. It is often used in spell work, especially with knots.

In Middle Eastern cultures, there are believed to be seven heavens, seven seas, and seven great seals. It is considered a mystical number by cultures from the Assyrians to the Celts. Please note that there are seven great wonders of the world, seven deadly sins, seven spiritual gifts noted in the Bible, seven colors of the rainbow, etc. In the Middle Ages, this symbolism was used by the Church altar decorations of seven precious stones (crystal for vitality, a blue stone for discernment, a green stone for versatility, topaz for a keen mind, agate for grace, garnet for worship, and amethyst for supplication).

Pythagoreans admired the number seven as the highest single-digit prime number which was divisible only by itself and one. There are seven notes to a musical scale, allowing for the harmony of the universe. Seven is a spiritual number that indicates wisdom and growth on a metaphysical level. If it is yours, your understanding of life and universal truths is about to deepen, and new friends may enter your circle.

Magical applications: diversity, synchronicity, any work focusing on chakras or moon phases, spiritual insight.

Eight

Eight represents power, the eight solar holidays and the turning wheel. The number eight seems to have been especially venerated by the Egyptians, who felt it was the number of rebirth. Because of this, there were always eight people present in sacred processions to the Nile.

There is also evidence that it was important to the Hebrews, who wait eight days before circumcising a child and use the measurement of eight cubits for temple foundations. Representative of justice and positive change, eight is a magnetic figure of independence. If eight turns up in a reading for you, make sure all your current dealings are forthright and candid.

Magical applications: sun magic, increased energy, authority, personal abilities or attributes, drastic change.

Nine

Nine is completeness. An important factor in many divinations and folk cures (such as how often certain techniques are repeated), it also is represented by three times three.

There are nine muses and nine orders of angels in the Bible. Cats have nine lives, and Shakespeare's witches repeat their spells nine times.

Romans held a special market day every ninth day. Certain mystical traditions in the East have nine degrees before attainment of mastery, and many ancient magicians drew their sacred circles in nine-foot diameters for protection. Nine brings renewed energy in the psychic realm, if you have had a "gut" feeling, go with it!

Magical applications: this is the number of universal law, our connection to others, service, and compassion.

Ten

Comprehensiveness and absoluteness are embodied in the number ten. There are ten commandments. David's harp had ten strings. In Cabbalism, ten represents a change in conditions, specifically the spiritual aspects of one's life. Ten is ruled by the planet Uranus.

Magical applications: thorough studies or efforts (and the energy to follow them through), matters of spiritual law, following your inner voice.

Eleven

In terms of dreams, it is considered a bad omen. However, certain multiples of eleven (namely thirty-three) are much better fortune. To the Cabbalist, this is an emotional, psychic figure, ruled by Neptune.

Twelve

In Babylonia, twelve was considered bad luck. Yet the zodiac has twelve houses, there are twelve months in the year, and a day has twelve hours. Hercules performed twelve labors in Greek mythology, there were twelve sons of Jacob, twelve tribes of Israel and twelve kinds of fruit on the Tree of Life. In Cabbalistic practice, twelve is the number of the philosophers' stone and twelve represents the deeper human emotions and self-sacrifice. It is ruled by Pisces.

Magical applications: purification, durability, fruitfulness.

Thirteen

The number of the Goddess, thirteen also represents the number of lunar months in the year.

Most superstitions state that thirteen at a dinner party is asking for trouble. Thirteen and a half pence was the price paid the hangman at Tyburn (the half penny being for the rope). Yet, thirteen is also the number of a baker's dozen, which when received is lucky indeed! This is the number of pioneers, military leaders, and people of great daring or courage. It represents a new cycle.

Magical Application: patience, devotion, conviction, and perseverance.

Twenty-one

A multiple of two other important numbers, three and seven, this was the number of wholeness and magnificence. Thus, the twenty-one-gun salute given at certain ceremonies today is a reflection of this belief. A number of power and authority, if you were born on the twenty-first expect recognition for work well done. This number is ruled by the sun, and is an emblem of opportunity.

Magical applications: remembrances, homage

Forty

A number which frequently appears in the Bible at times of cleansing, most notably in the story of Noah. It is quite likely because of this that the length of most quarantines in early years were forty days.

Magical applications: purification, hermitage, solitude.

Birth Path Numbers

Transform the month, date, and year of your birth into numbers. For example, October 10, 1960, would equal $10+10+1+9+6+0 = 36$. This is a double digit number, so add the figures together again ($3+6 = 9$.) Use this number with the following correspondences, adapted from Zolar, to discern general trends of fate in your life:

1—Strange experiences await you. You are a constructive person with strong convictions.

2—You may tend to repeat cycles at regular intervals. If you have trouble with self-control, cultivating that attribute will bring success.

3—This number portends financial stability, travel, and a bit of good fortune.

4—Good friends, strong professional alliances, and success are your future.

5—You have a strong personality, which will be needed to handle the odd circumstances that continually arise in your life.

6—Be careful of your actions and personal health. Rashness may be your undoing, so learn to think ahead and put foundations under your dreams.

7—Almost anything you undertake with certainty can be accomplished.

8—You are ambitious, driven, adventuresome, and very active. If temperamental, take care, because this can become a serious problem.

9—Travel, unique experiences, and a love of the arts is in this number.

Please remember that these are tendencies only, meant for amusement. You always have the ability to determine your future.

Cabbalistic Numbers

Cabbalists (Hebrew mages) believed deeply in the power of numbers and words. Some numbers not listed previously have special meaning in Cabbalistic numerology. They are (adapted from Zolar):

14—Ruled by Taurus. Materialism, determination, and stubborn will, like the bull itself.

15—Ruled by Saturn. Filled with mental activity, especially ideas that are logical or that have solid foundations.

16—The number of deep, abiding passions, sixteen is ruled by fiery Mars. Many inventors and explorers are born on the sixteenth.

17—A number of faith and charity, seventeen is ruled by Gemini. If this number begins to pervade your life, intuition will bring you success.

18—Associated with the sign of Cancer, this is an explosive number that portends arguments or deception. However, it can also be the number of a good mystery.

19—A lucky number ruled by Leo. The golden color of this animal brings happy times and good humor. Self-esteem and personal recognition are soon to develop.

20—Connected to the moon, this number is also connected to change. This is a number of fate's movements.

22—A weak figure that brings separation and material failure. If you have been vain or puffed up, now is the time to reconsider spiritual values.

Colors

Every color was thought to be strongly attuned to a specific number, which coincidentally is also its order in the spectrum. Thus red is 1, orange is 2, yellow is 3, green is 4, blue is 5, indigo is 6 and violet is 7. Red was considered to double also for the number 8, and orange for the number 9 (the sequence simply starting again).

These representations may be added to the colors of candles used, altar cloths, ritual robes and other decorations in the sacred space. For example, instead of reciting a spell to help you overcome a bad habit eight times, substitute a red robe or candle to accentuate change.

Destiny Numbers

Transform your name into numbers as follows:

1	2	3	4	5	6	7	8	9
A	B	C	D	E	F	G	H	I
J	K	L	M	N	O	P	Q	R
S	T	U	V	W	X	Y	Z	

Add those figures together. If the figure is double-digited, add those two numbers together (see "Birth Path"). This final number is added with your birth path number. It shows other subtle undercurrents to your destiny as follows as adapted from Zolar:

1—Success comes through your own constructive ideas and efforts. This indicates a self-made person.

2—Life alternates a lot on you, but your friends help see you through the tough times. Keep your eyes open for a profitable possibility.

3—Victory! Your ambitions begin to bear fruit.

4—A number of honor. Your profession or personal convictions will bring you notoriety.

5—Take care with your own safety; don't trust strangers. Develop a greater sense of others' motivations.

6—This can be the number of drifters, so if you tend to have your head in the clouds, it's time to find an anchor.

7—Prominence and adventure await you.

8—Financial difficulties, but they can be overcome.

9—A versatile, multi-talented person is found in this number.

11—Big undertakings, many interests. You have the ability to create your own wealth.

22—Avoid any questionable dealings and don't let your emotions control you.

Lucky Numbers

According to Zolar, your may find your lucky number by counting the number of letters in your first and last names, and then adding that figure together. For example, Mary Smith would be 4 + 5 = 9. Therefore 9 is one of Mary's lucky numbers.

Another method is to combine the values of the day and month in which you were born. If born on February 21, for example, the numbers would be 2, and 21, or 2+2+1 = 5.

Monthly Numbers

Add your destiny number to the number of any month and year. If your destiny number is 6, for example, add this to the current month (say, February, or 2) and year (1994). This equals 6+2+1+9+9+4 = 31 = 4. This number shows the general disposition of this month for you as follows:

1—A good month to start new projects. Write any overdue letters and focus on positive communications.

2—A month to expect the unexpected. Be careful with your health and avoid arguments.

3—Take a trip, make a desired change in your life, clear up financial matters, and watch for opportunity to knock.

4—Complete any unfinished tasks and make efforts to realize your goals. Your personal judgement is excellent right now.

5—Be careful with everything right now. Carelessness, awkward moments, or loss of focus could bring bad luck.

6—Take initiative. Effort will be met for effort. There might be minor delays of a scheduled event.

7—A month for results. Trust your gut instincts. An excellent month for visiting, looking for a new job, and investment.

8—Transformation. You feel courageous and enthusiastic. Focus on material matters but don't rush blindly into new situations. Take your time and test the waters.

9—Opportunity presents itself, bringing hope and encouragement.

11—Lots to do but little time. Take care not to overextend yourself. Remaining steadfast to your convictions will bring forward movement toward a goal.

22—Don't blindly accept advice. Avoid extravagant spending and rash ideas. Keep your temper and emotions in check.

22 PERSONAL CARE

> *'Tis the Divinity that stirs within us.*
> ♦ Joseph Addison, *Cato* ♦

JUDAISM BUILT a code of sanitation into its religion. Throughout the Old Testament there are instructions for washing. These directions pertained to rituals that ensured one could go before the Almighty without blemish. They also speak of how to properly wash after caring for plague victims (Lev. 13:54, 14:8). In this manner, local religious leaders were not only keepers of the holy word, but also became the guardians of hygiene.

The ancient Roman Empire was far ahead of many civilizations in ways to keep its cities and citizens clean and healthy. They had paved roads, aqueducts, sewage disposal, and public baths. Unfortunately, when this mighty civilization fell, so did these advancements.

It was the Arabs and other Eastern cultures who preserved the art of personal care, the Japanese most notably following strict bathing routines even when these were unheard of in Europe.

Religion, medicine, and personal care remained interconnected well into the 1600s. For example, a healer in Cornish regions may have prayed to Christ while gathering club moss for a medical kit. A Scottish wizard by the name of John MacWilliam used the phrase, "God restore you to health" when performing healing magic. One Scottish cure recommended using the names of God and Mary in a prayer/incantation to cure sores. While at first this intermixing may seem odd, we must remember that Christianity grew up in a Pagan world. For hundreds of years, there were no clearly defined lines.

In terms of magic, transforming a simple personal folkway into something with an extra spark is only a matter of your attitude while preparing it. Focus on the goals of your preparation; use visualization, incantation, song, or chants to enhance the healthful effects. As with folk medicine, keep caution and common sense as your most important guidelines.

Acne

Wash three times daily with tincture of dandelion and chamomile. Another technique is to take one teaspoon each of borage flower tips, ash leaves, mugwort, and sage and boil them for forty-five minutes in a quart of water. Place this liquid in a bowl and steam your face for at least five minutes, repeating once a day for three weeks.

An Irish alternative is to steep bean pods in wine and vinegar for a week, and then rinse your face with this daily.

Bathing

The bathtub did not really find its way into American culture until the early 1900s. Rumors that frequent bathing was dangerous during a woman's menstrual cycle, bad for one's health, and bad for  linen prevented general acceptance of the bathtub and found itself commonplace only among the wealthy for many years. It is believed if you bathe in myrtle on April 1 it will bring you great beauty and fortune.

The bathtub can be used today (especially larger ones) for relaxation meditations, ritual baths, and cleansing efforts.

Birthplace

In your later years, it is said to increase longevity if you make a pilgrimage to your place of birth. If this is not possible, try holding a special ritual using a picture of your hometown as a focus and send it special energy for continued prosperity and blessing.

Breath Rinse

A rinse of marshmallow leaves, red wine, agrimony, oak bark, comfrey, sage, chamomile, mint leaves, and a pinch of salt may be used daily. Simmer one tablespoon of each herb in three cups of red wine over a low heat for forty-five minutes. Strain and use (but do not swallow). This mixture is said to relieve bleeding gums as well.

Dandruff

A rinse one teaspoon each of camphor, lavender, bay, sage, one capful alcohol, and rosemary steeped in two cups of water for two hours, then bottled, will help rid you of dandruff. Apply each time you shampoo.

Deodorants

Any of the following herbs in finely-powdered form act as a natural deterrent to perspiration: orange peel, lemon peel, orris root, chamomile, marigold, comfrey, lavender, and sage.

Depression

Clover mixed with mallow, chamomile flowers, and milk in a bath soothes despondency.

Ears

Ringing in your right ear portends good news soon to follow. Buzzing means people are secretly talking about you.

Facials

Some of the best facials today come to us from folk-techniques. Most predominantly recommended was a mixture of oatmeal, ground almonds, and a bit of orange peel. Other ingredients included were buttermilk, elderflower water, and rosewater.

Freckles

Dry mustard and lemon juice applied for four successive nights will get rid of freckles. May dew gathered on Beltane helps, also.

Another option is to take an egg white and beat it until stiff. Continue beating and add one cup of water, the juice of one lemon, and a third of an ounce of powdered sugar. Apply this mixture to your freckles before bed, rinsing each morning.

The Scottish aid for freckles is to wash in buttermilk that has been steeped with silverweed for nine days. Buttermilk figures into various other folk remedies as well, probably acting as a mild bleach.

Hair

The ancient Assyrians and Egyptians adored rich, long hair. Flowing locks were predominantly displayed in many art forms. This inspired romantic feelings about hair in general.

In Asia, hair was valued so highly it was used as currency. Hebrew women regarded hair as crowning glory. In the Middle Ages it was commonly held that having a bit of someone's hair gave you power over them (see Chapter 18: Magic and the Supernatural).

Many religious orders used a change in hairstyles to mark the transition into sacred offices. Monastic orders frequently shaved their heads, or left only one braided gathering. Many nuns still wear habits that at least partially covering their hair. In all cases, the covering or loss of hair seems to cut the ties to the more "material" world.

To rid yourself of gray hair, wash with grapevine root, eat potato peels (England), or rinse your hair with potato water on a regular basis.

To promote hair growth, it is best to have your locks cut during the moon signs of Pisces, Cancer, or Scorpio and when the moon is waxing to full. For luck, trim it on the new moon. To inhibit growth, cut during the waning quarters. Hair falling out in larger than usual amounts was often interpreted as a sign of illness.

Honey

One of the most useful item for skin care, recommended even by Hippocrates, honey is said to be good for skin softening, scratches, blisters, and even as a base for a facial mask.

Itching

If your nose itches, expect a kiss; your right shoulder, a legacy; your stomach, a dinner invitation; and if your lips itch, someone is gossiping about you.

Lip Care

An old folk remedy for chapped lips was to make an ointment of red clovers, violets, and sage. Boil one-third cup of each of the flowers in three cups of water over a low heat for about forty-five minutes. Strain off the liquid and repeat the process twice more. Allow the remaining juice to cook down until a syrup forms. Apply as needed.

Another balm is made with one cup almond oil, once ounce of beeswax, two teaspoons of honey and one teaspoon of rose or vanilla extract for flavor. Mix all of these ingredients over low heat until well blended, then store for use.

Nails

If you cut your nails on Monday it is said to help bring you news; on Tuesday, new clothes; Wednesday, health; Thursday, wealth; Friday, knowledge; and Saturday, travel. Use these nail clippings in spells for similar goals.

Shoes

It is considered very unlucky to put your shoes on the wrong feet. When Augustus Caesar did this, he soon thereafter lost his life to an assassin. The easiest way to avert this is to lay them out properly on the floor.

Shoes and socks should always be donned right foot first. This tradition dates back to the Roman Empire when it was done to appease a deity thought to have charge over the right side of the body.

If you feel your luck has been running sour lately, make an effort to follow this folkway for five days (the number of fortune in many lands), or an alternate number of personal significance.

Skin Cleanser and Softener

In Turkey, ripe avocado is applied and left for a while then rinsed with rosewater to thoroughly clean the skin.

In Hawaii, coconut and almond oils massaged into the skin in an upwards direction is recommended to get rid of wrinkles. For very oily skin, take a cup of violets and steep them in warm, fresh milk overnight. Next, soak a washcloth in hot water, wring it out, and saturate it in the milk solution, applying it to areas of your skin which get greasy.

Sleeplessness

Anise, chamomile, parsley, valerian, clover, lavender, woodruff, dill, and/or a verbena tea are believed by folk healers to aid in bringing restful sleep.

As an interesting sidenote, in ancient times grave dust, ashes from a funeral pyre, or any portions of a dead body were considered potent aids to sleep magic (see Chapter 2: Animals and Insects).

Warts

A medieval herbalist, Sir Kenelm Digby, recommends washing your hands by waning moonlight to rid yourself of warts. In this instance the symbolism of the shrinking moon is thought to empower the action (see Chapter 13: Health and Medicine and Chapter 16: Knots).

An alternative is burying a piece of potato touched to the skin. Or take a strand of your hair and tie knots in it, one for each wart. This needs to be thrown away to affect a cure.

Washing

One should not wash out of the same basin as another. It will bring an argument. This particular superstition also helped to promote cleanliness and decrease the spread of disease.

23 PLANTS

Nature is not fixed, but fluid. Spirit alters, molds, makes it.
♦ Ralph W. Emerson, *Nature* ♦

MANY CULTURES, from Native American to Far Eastern, believed all things in nature contained spirits. Eating a plant or drinking its juice brought the positive aspects of its spirit to the human flesh. A prime example of this is the fact that, to this day, drinking alcohol is called imbibing in "spirits." This expression derived from the conviction that drunken people were possessed by the spirit of the fermented fruit.

Almost every plant in the world has been tried for the treatment of disease (see Chapter 13: Health and Medicine). Some of the remedies proved to have amazing merit and continue to be used today. Usually symbolic aspects of the plant were used to decide what its best application would be. Cold, moist plants were recommended against fever; a liver-shaped leaf might be prescribed to cure a liver ailment.

Alongside plants that heal, another less pleasant pastime grew—the development of poisons. By the Middle Ages, creating unique poisons had become an art, encouraged by certain power-hungry, wealthy lords.

The most well-known herbalist of the Middle Ages was Galen, who lived around A.D 150. He developed a therapy made up primarily of vegetable ingredients. This treatment became known as the Galenic system, and was popular from the Middle Ages through the Renaissance.

Like many other herbalists to follow, such as Culpepper and Parkinson, Galen recommended harvesting plants before sunrise for maximum benefit. The healers also suggested gathering tree bark from the most potent spot on the left side of the tree, where it greets the morning sun.

Much lore involving herbs and other plants has resurfaced with the growing interest in the environment and natural healing. Many fabulous books by authors such as Scott Cunningham, Jude Williams, and the Reverend Paul Beyerl provide opportunities to explore plant use for health, beauty, cooking, and magic. This section is not meant to repeat their foundational work, but hopefully shows some of the lore's historical roots, while adding some practical knowledge for modern practice.

Aphrodisiacs

While a wide variety of plants are thought to bolster romance, two rather interesting ones come to us through Greek and Egyptian superstition. Both cultures considered radishes and asparagus aphrodisiacs, the latter being especially potent if grown with basil, an herb of fidelity, and parsley. So, if you are planning to do some magic to strengthen the bonds between you and your love, consider serving these during a candlelit dinner for two.

Agrimony

In the home or garden, agrimony helps to detect the presence of witches and keeps evil at bay. A sprig under your pillow brings sweet dreams. In the kitchen, agrimony flowers can be made into a delightful tea (one handful to a pint of water), or added to home-brewed beer.

Basil

In India, basil is dedicated to the God Vishnu and given to the dead to help ensure their safe passage to the afterlife. The scent of fresh basil is believed to promote sympathy between people, and can be used for this in forgiveness rituals. It was also frequently used as an herb of faithfulness, and might be a good ingredient in an incense for dedication between people or to a cause.

Carnation

One of the most popular flowers for the kitchen garden, the carnation appeared frequently in beverages and foods of the Middle Ages. In the language of flowers, carnations represent pride and beauty. Their name is a derivative of the word "coronation," because they were used in so many festivals. With this in mind, add dried carnations to incense for leadership, commemoration, and self-esteem.

Carrots

Old-time farmers pluck and eat carrots to help keep their eyesight keen. This root has long been nibbled for its medicinal and health value. Since it is high in vitamins, try a small sip of carrot juice before magic pertaining to the development of your personal visionary skills or for improving health.

Chrysanthemum

Eastern peoples have cultivated the chrysanthemum for two thousand years. On the ninth day of the ninth moon, Chinese people drink Chrysanthemum wine to insure long life. An old Chinese superstition states that eating chrysanthemum increases longevity. With this in mind, a gift of these flowers to an ill friend would be a thoughtful gesture.

The Japanese also observe the chrysanthemum festival. In ancient times, the shogun met with all his feudal lords on this date. Now it is simply celebrated with competitive flower shows. The Japanese flag is actually a depiction of a chrysanthemum with sixteen petals around a disk.

Writing in 1904, Maurice Maeterlinck claimed that these flowers were a favorite meeting place for faerie folk. Thus, this flower may be added to any mixture that encouraged friendship with the fey (see Chapter 11: Faeries).

Clover

A four-leaf clover is always considered lucky (see Chapter 17: Luck), not only because of its rarity, but also because clover was a favored green for cattle feed. When farming was the center of every community, having well-fed cattle meant food for many, and enough money for long winter months.

For the four-leaf clover to be most potent, it is best picked during a new moon, between the hours of noon and 3 p.m. on a bright, sunny day. Any form of clover can be employed for magic pertaining to luck and providence, or if you wish to see faeries.

In the pantry, clover flower makes a lovely tasting honey-like syrup. Add three cups of sugar to two-thirds cup of water, twenty clover flowers, and a dash of alum, and boil until clear. Strain and store in an air-tight container. In Scotland, the seeds and petals are favored for breads.

Cohosh

This herb was thought to heal relationships, especially when sprinkled liberally near the bed. It is also an appropriate herb to burn in incense pertaining to resolutions and peaceful communication.

Coriander

Considered to ensure immortality by the Chinese, this herb eventually became very popular in perfumery. Use coriander in rituals where you wish to gain more a universal perspective or to celebrate a loved one who has passed over.

Daisy

There is an old saying that tells us if you put one foot on seven daisies at the same time, you know that summer is here to stay. This might be related to the fact that the name daisy comes from an Anglo-Saxon word meaning "day's eye." This flower opens with the first rays of the sun and closes at nightfall, thus to find so many is surely an indication of

bright, fair weather. In much the same manner, using the
daisy for magic pertaining to clear skies is quite suitable
along with any rites that honor the sun and its cycles.

The daisy was a favored ingredient in salads in the
fifteenth century. It gathered a hundred or more folk
names, including banewood, bennest, bruisewort, cat
posy, gowam, measure of love, and silver penny.

Dandelion

If you rub your skin with dandelion juice, no home can refuse you hospitality. It is also believed that if you blow on dandelion seeds and all go
to the winds, you will soon get your wish.

Dandelions were sometimes equated with ancient oracles in the
language of flowers. If you are doing divinatory work, you can prepare
a dandelion salad, soup, or even sandwich beforehand to encourage
this energy. Be sure to wash the greens well before eating and avoid taking the leaves from lawns that have been sprayed with chemicals.

Dock

Nettles and docks often grow together; if one is stung by a nettle, the
juice of the dock will ease the sting.

A good farmer never buys land without docks growing on it because
this bush is thought to thrive only in rich soil. This is a good plant to
include in any ritual to bless your home or land.

Fennel

If you place a bit of fennel in a keyhole, it is said to keep ghosts away.
Fennel was one of nine sacred herbs believed in medieval times to cure
the nine causes of disease, such as Displeasure of the Dead, an offended
spirit, or the wrath of a powerful enemy.

Fennel was placed in doorways on Midsummer's Eve to turn away
evil spirits, and is still considered a good ingredient for protection and
healing work.

Fern

The seed of a fern is so small it is almost invisible to the naked eye.
Because of this, this kernel when carried brings invisibility. Carry one
whenever you are feeling too visible in a particular situation. The male

fern was used to create the Luck Hand, a rather unique and durable charm for healing, protection, and luck. According to Culpeper, the male fern is shorter than the female and also has larger leaves. Female ferns also have more divided and dented leaves. The process is fairly easy to follow. On Midsummer's Eve, dig up a fern with its roots. Cut away all but five leaves (which will make it appear like an old, withered hand). Place it next to your bonfire (or fireplace) and let it smoke and harden there.

Flouromancy

Plants have inspired several divination techniques including the I Ching, a system that derived from the yarrow plant. Several very interesting systems also appeared during the Victorian era in the United States.

One of these says to look in your garden and gather a bouquet for yourself. While you pick, contemplate a specific question. Return to the house with your flowers in hand and refer to a list of flower symbolism (such as was given in *A Victorian Grimoire,* Llewellyn, 1992 and *Victorian Flower Oracle*, Llewellyn, 1994). Randomly pull out one flower at a time, making notes of which are picked and in what order. When finished, you can review the "reading" and see what the blossoms disclose.

A more intricate rendering was invented in 1847 by Thomas Miller. For this, you need to have pansies. Pick a single petal from one without looking. The number of lines in the petal then determine the actual reading (see Chapter 21: Numbers).

Floral superstitions pertaining to the seasons and days of the week were also popular, even in 1900. If you happen to find the first flower of spring on a Monday, it means good luck for the season. If on a Tuesday, your greatest attempts will thrive; on Wednesday, it portends marriage; Thursday, a warning of small earnings; Friday, prosperity; Saturday, misadventure; and if on Sunday, is excellent luck for many weeks to come.

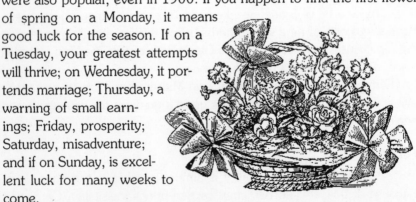

It was exceptionally good luck to wear the blossom associated with your birth month. January is snowdrop; February is the violet; March is the daffodil; April is the primrose; May is the white lily; June the wild Rose; and July the carnation. Come August white heather appears, September is the Michaelmas daisy, October rosemary, November chrysanthemum, and, finally, in December ivy is worn.

Any or all of these affiliations can be used in conjunction with your seasonal celebrations by way of decorations or additions to ritual incense.

Garlic

Garlic comes to us from Asia. It was distributed daily to the workers at Cheops to give them strength and protection for their sacred tasks. In Sweden, people sometimes place garlic around the necks of livestock to protect them from trolls.

Garlic continues to be an herb favored for its virtues of psychic shielding, improving blood circulation, and increasing vitality.

Geranium

Ancient lore claims that the geranium was born when the prophet Mohammed's shirt was hung upon a mallow plant to dry in the sun. In this respect, it is a good flower for enhancing solar magic, especially for transformation.

Hawthorn

In Rome, a twig of hawthorn was attached to the cradle of a newborn for the child's protection. In the time of the Crusades, a knight offered his lady a bit of hawthorn tied with pink ribbon for safekeeping, which token ensured that he would live and return to her. The Bible says Jesus' crown of thorns was made of hawthorn.

During the fourteenth century and later, hawthorn flowers slowly moved into the diet through jellies and syrups. The syrup is prepared in a similar manner to most conserves, except that the flower petals are strained out after boiling.

Heather

If you want great beauty, folklore says to bathe in heather water once a year by the light of a full moon. In gypsy lore, a sprig of white heather carried with you helps bring luck wherever you go.

In Scotland, an ale was made by Picts which honeyed the heather flowers into a dulcet beer. The drink was said to be so wonderful that the preparers would die if necessary to protect the process of consecration. Unfortunately, that recipe was indeed lost during various invasions. Even so, heather flowers can still be used in brewing ritual wines, especially for good fortune, bravery, and excellence.

Lavender

Often burned in the Greek temples, lavender is a traditional midsummer incense. An early custom was to wear sprigs of lavender stuffed in a hat to protect oneself from getting head-colds. The sight and smell of lavender flowers will ease sadness.

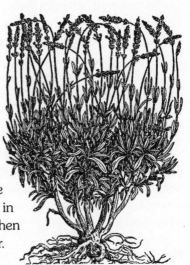

To make a tea of lavender (very refreshing iced on hot summer days), take one pint of water and a half-ounce of lavender flowers. Steep the flowers in warm water until they turn translucent, then strain. Mint may also be added for flavor.

Lily

There is an ancient Shinto festival still celebrated in Japan on June 17, which strives to drive away the rainy season using lilies. Known as the Cleansing Lily, it begins with the collection of lily stalks from a nearby mountain. These are taken to the temple and blessed by seven women in white robes. The following morning, the priest lays a bouquet of the flowers on the altar while seven maidens dance with flowers waving in the air. The celebration ends with the attendees walking the streets with tiger lilies to bring fresh air.

This particular flower also participates in a variety of other religiously-based observances. Chinese families rub their stove with lilies before making offerings to the kitchen god. In Muslim lands, yellow water lilies are used in a wine known as *nufu*. As they drink of this, it is traditional to raise the glass and say, "In the name of Allah, may it benefit thee."

Lotus

In the Orient, the lotus is sacred to the Goddess Lakshmi, patroness of beauty and luck. This flower gives anyone who carries it Her protection and good fortune. In Egypt, the lotus was considered to be a symbol of Isis's purity and is an excellent scent to anoint yourself with in rituals honoring Her.

Mandrake Root

This member of the nightshade family is thought to shriek when pulled from the ground. In the Middle Ages, the root was a popular purgative, narcotic, and fertility aid used in the form of a poppet. The eleventh-century text *Lacnunga*, popular among the European folk cultures, also recommends mandrake for eye care, wounds, snakebite, earaches, gout, and baldness.

Sometimes known as the love apple, the mandrake resembles various human parts. In Baghdad, these roots sold as amulets to aid fertility and prosperity. In Europe, it was laid under the marriage bed to aid virility, and most people believed the best place to dig for mandrake was beneath the gallows.

Because of its deadly poison, mandrake is not used remedially anymore, but may be added to poppets or incense to promote fidelity and abundance. Please keep this root well out of the reach of children and pets!

Mistletoe

A symbol of immortality, mistletoes was a sacred plant to ancient Europeans. It was called the "plant that heals all ills" by the Druids. The priests would gather it ritually with a golden sickle and use it as a talisman to protect from evil. In Austria, mistletoe branches are placed in bedroom doorways to safeguard against nightmares.

The Teutons believed that carrying a sprig of mistletoe would make their warriors invincible, and in Scandinavia, when placed outside the home it is a sign of a hospitable welcome. In these countries, if two enemies happen to meet beneath the mistletoe, they must lay down their arms and fight no more that day.

I think it's time to hang a lot of mistletoe all over the world.

Mugwort

In a pillow, mugwort inspires prophetic dreams which is why it, with marjoram, rosemary, balsam and lavender, has become one of today's most favored herbs for making dream pillows. Mugwort is also recommended to promote passion and friendship. If placed in your shoe before a long journey, Mugwort will help keep you from tiring.

Mushrooms

In some Native American tribes, eating mushrooms was either forbidden or strictly controlled by the shaman. The reason for this was not so much superstition as practicality. There are many types of mushrooms, some of which are deadly.

So, for modern magic, the mushroom might best represent common sense and caution.

Onion

In Germany, it is traditional on New Year's Day to slice six onions in half, hollow them out, and fill them with salt. These are placed in the attic of the home (or the room closest to the sky) to predict the weather for the next twelve months. If the salt in the onion stays dry, it is an indication of an arid month (see Chapter Chapter 14: Holidays and Chapter 30: Weather Lore).

Because of its appearance, the onion was also applied in folk-cures for baldness, usually by rubbing its juice into the scalp.

Parsley

The Romans thought parsley caused sterility. During the Middle Ages pulling up parsley while speaking someone's name would bring death to that person. Fortunately, these beliefs halted when certain medicinal qualities were later discovered in the plant. A more positive application of the older belief would be to pull the parsley while speaking of habits you wish to "weed" out of your life.

Rose

Legend claims that Cleopatra covered her floor with rose petals when visited by Mark Anthony so their scent would secure his love. Long ago it was believed that all roses had once been white, until they were stained by Athena's blood when her foot caught on their thorns.

The Catholic rosary was frequently made from rose beads (see Chapter 1: Amulets and Talismans).

In Greece, June 4 was the festival of Rosalia, which honored the rose. Primarily people littered the temples of Aphrodite with rose petals while praying for love or beauty. Women bathed in rosewater to increase their attractiveness or burned rose incense to improve luck.

The rose is the most celebrated flower of all time. There are thousands of medicinal, culinary, and magical uses for it. In the kitchen, it is often added to sweets like jellies and candies.

For magic, the color of the rose is as important as the flower itself. White is for purity or cleansing, yellow for friendship, pink for passion, and red for romantic love.

Rosemary

The Romans considered this an herb that would bring peace after death, and joy during life. It also appeared in almost every ceremony in between. If a rosemary bush grows in your garden, it means a woman is the head of your house. This herb often is often used in bridal bouquets because of its purported ability to improve love and remembrance.

Rue

Milton claimed that rue was good for vision, both physical and spiritual. It is appropriate on the altar during any magic where you are seeking improved insight.

St. John's Wort

Take care not to step on this faerie weed lest you be carried off for a day by the wee folk. On the other hand, if you happen to pick some on Midsummer's Day, it will protect you from any of their mischievous antics.

Sweet-smelling Flowers

Sweet-smelling flowers were once considered the souls of the dead. From this came the modern custom of sending flower arrangements to a wake. Releasing sweet-smelling flower petals to the wind during a funeral rite is a lovely means to symbolically send the spirit of your loved one on his or her way.

Tomatoes

When tomatoes were first brought to Europe from the New World, they were considered poisonous. It wasn't until John Quincy Adams planted his garden full of this member of the nightshade family that adding them to the diet caught on.

Later, gardeners discovered that tomato leaves (or a tincture made from them) helps decrease insect infestation. It was around the same time that popular superstition held that tomatoes stimulated love.

Tulip

Persians use the tulip as a declaration of love. Turks have a feast of tulips. Francis Bacon believed that the opening and closing of this flower greeted the sun's arrival and mourned its departure. The tulip can be used in solar rituals, as well as magic related joinings, time, and transitions.

Valerian

There is some evidence in folklore that the Pied Piper of Hamlin may have used this plant to bring cats with him to drive away the mice of the village and thus ensure his success. It is also one of the most effective herbal sleep aids known.

24 PREGNANCY AND CHILDREN

Thy face is like thy Mothers, my fair child.
♦ Lord Byron, *Canto III* ♦

CHILDBIRTH IS much safer today than it was even a hundred years ago. Prior to the last two-thirds of the twentieth century, birth frequently took place at home under less than sanitary conditions, with little if any medication to ease the mother's pain. Additionally, women did not have the luxury of maternity leave, sometimes returning to their household and farming chores the next day. Childbirth was one of the leading causes of death for young women through the nineteenth century.

Beliefs about the process of pregnancy and childbirth, were inspired by the profound awe these wiggling life-forms caused. For many years the reproductive process remained a mystery. When a woman gave birth to another living being, it was truly a miracle. But considering disease, poor health standards, lack of proper sanitation, and limited medical knowledge, it was even a greater marvel if the child managed to live through its first three years.

In an effort to overcome the odds, produce an heir, and cope with many of those worrisome childhood difficulties, people would go to great lengths to insure the well-being of their children, both before and after birth. And, while our reasons for doing so are probably more sentimentally based today, there is no reason why some of these ideas can't be incorporated into fertility rites, blessing-ways, baby dedications, naming rituals, puberty observances, and other important moments.

Another important note is that some of these things should not be limited to just "natural" children. Adoptees can be made to feel more a part of the family when they are included in your beliefs and rites. For those people who don't have children, adapt some of the ideas in this chapter for your pets, or to stimulate your own inner child instead!

Ash Trees

Ash trees (or oak and cherry in Germany) were used in the blessing of newborns and as part of folk-healing rites for children. For this, a young ash tree was split and the child passed through the opening (a sign of new life). The tree was then swathed carefully back together. If the tree lived and prospered, so would the child.

A nicer alternative to this is to plant a baby tree in honor of the birth or adoption of a child. Mix some of the clippings of the baby's first hair with the soil so that, as the tree grows strong, so will the baby. If, however, you notice a severe decline in the tree's health, likewise check your child. Something may be happening which has eluded you. It might also be best at this time, should matters get worse, to dig the tree up to release the bond. This will symbolically break the roots of illness.

For pets, different plants or trees might be substituted. A puppy could be celebrated with a dogwood tree. Upon the arrival of a kitten, plant catnip.

Black Sheep

The term *black sheep* derives from the time when black bulls and sheep were part of necromantic practices, which were looked upon unfavorably by many. Later this term of disapproval was applied to naughty children.

Perhaps for magical homes, the notion of black sheep should be eliminated in favor of treating all children on as equal a basis as possible, allowing each to have his or her own unique potential. I mention this because magical parents are no less susceptible to moments of anger and harsh words than others.

Blessings

It is the custom in many cultures to bestow a blessing on a newborn child. In England, the baby's head is washed in gin to insure a lovely complexion. It is also given a taste of honey, butter, and cinder-water, respectively representing the sweetness of life, the product of labors, and a rich hearth. Sometimes little gifts are given to the child, such as matches and salt, so that its fires will never die and it will be protected.

The time-frames for such mini-rituals vary from area to area, depending on parental choice and the health of the child, but three months seems to be the most common time frame.

All of these customs can be adapted in some manner for your own baby blessing rites. For example, instead of cinder-water, give the child a bit of charcoal-filtered water. Honey and butter can be blended together in small amounts, placed on crackers, and served to guests to likewise grant them bounty.

Couvade

An interesting tradition comes to us from Ireland, where the father undergoes the same medical care during the mother's labor and delivery as if he were experiencing the same. It was believed that this would fool evil spirits and show the man's claim on the child. It was also considered a sign of a happy marriage.

Midwives claim that, if need be, they can even transfer the birth pains to him through this symbolism. Because of this, the men who follow this tradition tend to take better care of themselves during the pregnancy and have a greater respect for the process of birth itself.

Crystals

Besides those mentioned in Chapter 7: Crystals, Gems and Stones, a wide variety of stone lore has grown around pregnancy and delivery. Hyacinth amulets are said to bring safe births. Wearing jade or carnelian eases labor pains. Milkstone increases mother's milk. Any of these stones set into a necklace, charm, wand, or other portable item make a thoughtful gift for expectant women.

Another unusual stone, known as the eagle stone, came from Asia and was thought to protect both pregnancy and delivery. It was first worn around the neck as a charm, then fastened to the left thigh during delivery. Originally thought only obtainable from an eagle's nest, this was actually a brown form of lapis, and probably unobtainable today.

Fertility

In India, a woman wishing to conceive would remove her clothes and circle a sacred fig tree 108 times, wrapping it with cotton thread. In this way, the tree became a symbol of the protected womb. This resembles certain May Day activities, such as walking naked through a garden. The symbolism here can be applied to any project where you need improved productivity.

In this case, use a branch from an appropriate tree (see Chapter 29: Tree, Bushes, Woods) to represent your goal. For example, if you desire to cultivate improved leadership abilities, choose a bit of hazel. To this tie a cotton thread, which again should symbolize your desire by its color. For this specific illustration, a combination of gold and blue might be fitting.

Once you have secured the thread(s), concentrate on your objective and begin to wrap it around the branch. On each complete turn, speak some type of affirmative phrase to encourage the magical energy toward your goal and tie a knot there to bind the power. Repeat this however many times you feel necessary, but make sure this number is likewise emblematic of your intention (You might use eight repetitions in this example, for authority).

When finished, either keep this stick on your altar to further empower the spell or bury it in rich soil where it will remain undisturbed, allowing the magic to grow. If this spell is being used specifically for fertility, keep your charm beneath or beside the bed.

Many herbs, plants, and foods have long been used to aid fertility. Some did so because of their shape (a banana, for example). In other instances the belief seems to have no distinct roots. If you are trying to conceive, or even if you are simply working towards improved personal productivity, bless any of the following and add them into your diet in small quantities: carrots, cucumber, daffodils, figs, grapes, hawthorn, hazel, myrtle, oak, olives, peaches, pines, pomegranates, and rice. Non-edible items can be added to such things as incense and used as altar decorations.

Fever

Scottish witches used a wreath of woodbine to help cure children of severe fevers. They would wait for a waxing moon, then pass the child through the wreath, head to foot, three times. Following in this tradition, woodbine would be an appropriate herb for healing rituals, especially those pertaining to children and pets.

Fingernails

It was traditional not to cut a child's fingernails before his or her first birthday. The mother bit them off when they got long, then buried them under an ash tree for protection. Similar superstitions surrounded hair clippings as well. Hair and nails were thought to be used by wizards for curses (see Chapter 18: Magic and the Supernatural).

Actually, it is far safer to bite a child's nails, because their hands are so small. Bury the remnants in rich potting soil to help encourage the child's foundations and growth. Fingernails and hair can also be added to the home compost pile.

Frail Children

Scottish mothers wash children who are sick or frail in the dew collected from ash leaves to endow them with strength. Keeping this in mind, any item made for a child out of ash wood and kept near the crib can be used to encourage vitality.

Labor

In one Philippine tribe, when a woman goes into labor, the husband will disrobe and go to the rooftop with a sword. Below him, other friends of the family enact a battle to help ward off any evil spirits endangering a safe birth. More appropriate in hospitals today would simply be a protective circle of energy, prepared during private moments in the birthing room. To adapt this for an adoptee, your home could be smudged to cleanse it of any negative influence and sprinkled with a rosemary tincture before the child arrives at your home to promote lovely memories.

Carrying and wearing sard, emerald, or pumice stone is a long-standing charm for easy labor. To interpret this more metaphorically, carry any of these stones when your struggles are seemingly unbearable.

Placing a knife or scissors under your bed during delivery will cut the pain. If the baby is slow coming down the birth canal, open any doors, lids, etc., to help ease the way.

Legitimacy

In Arabia, one way to determine if a child was indeed legitimate was to have it crawl through an opening in a natural rock formation. If the child could crawl through without getting stuck, it was of proper birth.

It is also interesting to note that openings in trees and stones figure heavily in folk-healing methods. The symbolism of the womb cannot be overlooked. While I suspect such methods would not be used to determine legitimacy by the modern practitioner, the symbolism could be adopted by those who practice rebirthing as part of visualizations.

Miscarriage

A pregnant woman worried about miscarriage should, according to Anglo-Saxon tradition, walk over a grave three times. How she does this is up to her, but the subtle message being conveyed is victory over death. A less grisly approach might be to simply walk over a small, dead patch of grass.

Other protection for pregnant women comes to us through the ancient Hebrew culture, where prayers or spells were written in ink mixed with holy incense on parchment, doors, and walls, while small, semiprecious stones were tied to the woman's body. This endowed her with each stone's attribute.

This type of preparation for the birthing space has not been lost to magical midwives. The items which make the expectant parents feel at ease and secure are very important both spiritually and emotionally. Likewise, if this is being used for pets or adopted children, the little knick-knacks lend an air of familiarity, warmth, and welcome to the new life entering the home.

Moon

Children born during the full moon are thought to be larger and stronger than others. If a child is born during a waxing moon, the next sibling will be of the same sex; if waning, it will be the opposite sex.

A country belief says that if a woman goes into labor when the moon is shining, the baby is a boy.

These types of beliefs are fun from the aspect of seeing how often they prove themselves out. Since only the woman having a Caesarean section can plan the time of her labor, these superstitions are best applied to other forms of magic, for example, using the full moon to bring improved growth and strength to crops (see Chapter 12: Gardening and Farming).

Names

Many early cultures believed that names carried power, and that if someone knew your true name, they could gain control over you, your family, or your clan. These beliefs played definitive roles in the way parents named their children. For example, there are Jewish tenets that state it is bad fortune to name a child after an elderly person in your family because death might mistake the two. Some families even went so far as to name a sickly child after a household object in the hopes that death would be fooled.

Such folklore also carried over into medical treatment, where a sick child (or adult, for that matter) might receive a new name to mislead death into thinking it has come to the wrong person. An alternate version of this was to burn an individual's name and mix it with medicine to help a cure. This last idea is still quite useful in healing rites.

A Puritan custom was to name an infant after a particularly motivational moral value. This name inspired that trait in the child.

Prenatal Care

Historically, a woman's prenatal care was most often left in the hands of her midwife. During the late Middle Ages, midwives were licensed in some parts of Europe. These midwives often used superstition and folk magic, frequently making charms for the expectant mother.

Today, most states have legally recognized and licensed midwives who work according to standards that allow for a blending of ancient and modern knowledge. These individuals generally work closely with a specific hospital or medical group. For those of you who may wish to have a midwife present at the birth of your child, check with your local hospitals and medical referral lists for the area. Some Hospitals provide birthing rooms, which have a homier appearance and are generally a little more comfortable for all participants.

Protection

Rowan leaves and iron near a cradle will protect an infant from faeries and magic. Coral necklaces or blessed knotted cords are believed to ensure its safety.

In Greece, running around the newborn was a means of protection and purification. Similar customs existed in Rome, where a running dance was performed on the eighth day after birth for a girl, and ninth day for a boy. By this time people felt it was safe to celebrate the birth, the first week being most dangerous with regard to serious health problems. The running was a simple way of producing an empowered magical space.

A common custom in various areas of the world is to place a pinch of salt in the mouth of a newborn to insure its safety from evil spirits.

All of these techniques may be used as inspiration as your own Path dictates.

Standing Stones

Certain women, mostly of Cornish decent, were known to use these stones as places to thank the Goddess for a healthy delivery. Most frequently the placenta of the child was laid at the foot of the stone, but there may have been instances where other gifts were left (see Chapter 26: Sacred Sites).

While many of us observe a baby dedication of one form or another, I think a small separate ritual of thankfulness to the Divine is appropriate whenever you are given charge over a new life (be it human or animal). Light a candle, acknowledge your appreciation, and leave a small token on your altar as a way to recompense the gift you have been given.

25 RELATIONSHIPS

When love with unconfined wings, hovers within my gates.
♦ Richard Lovelace, *To Althea* ♦

THE PURSUIT of love, finding love, and maintaining love have occupied humanity's free hours more than any other pastime. Spells and charms for adoration have been passed down through the centuries. Somehow confusion over how to cope with the opposite sex, and the inherent contrast in those polarities, give pause to even modern minds.

In the 1400s a woman by the name of Matteuccia was famous for her work with love magic. She made everything from hand and face lotions to attract a mate to contraceptives purportedly made of the ashes of a male mule's hoof mixed with wine. History indicates she was a professional, and people traveled from miles around to visit her. Her public practice of these old ways was brave, because the Church dealt harshly with such practitioners.

Even into the late nineteenth century, many people still believed that a toad hopping across a bridal path meant a happy marriage, and that a knife should never be given to a sweetheart lest it cut the relationship.

While modern magic approaches love rituals and spells with caution, not wishing to infringe on another's free will, there are still times when these enchantments are appropriate. To illustrate, a love potion can be prepared by a couple for their handfasting. The same potion could play a part in a forgiveness ritual between married partners. Or, a romance spell can be woven (with the awareness of both spouses) to improve the zest of a suffering marriage. In all instances, the people involved are willing, conscious participants—which should make the results even more favorable.

Discord

If you meet your lover on the stairs and kiss, if love letters are written in pencil, if a knife is given as a gift by a suitor, or if a letter is posted on February 29, there will be serious discord in your relationship and possible cutting of ties.

This type of symbolism might prove useful to a couple who have decided to part. In the separation ritual, they could begin by being tied together, then share in one knife to cut this cord, thus cleanly severing their ties to each other.

Friendship

Wearing sweetpea flowers may attract people to you and promote friendships. Have some on your table any time you are entertaining an old friend, or burn them in incense to inspire kinship.

Gloves

The giving of a glove may have actually been an extension of the medieval custom of bestowing favors to protect men in battle. Swearing by the glove was a custom of conversation, much as someone might swear by all that is holy. A person's gloves were removed from him as a sign of degradation or disapproval by a superior. Also, a personal glove was sometimes sent as a sign of consent to a particular proposal.

With this in mind, gloves are an optional component for relationship magic where you wish to keep a loved one safe (wrap their image in a glove), for matters of honor, or to bind an agreement.

Honeymoon

The term *honeymoon* comes originally from the Teutons, who celebrated marriages over thirty days (a full cycle of the moon) with a honey-
mead. The bride and groom were the center of these festivities.

Love Magic

Many of the early forms of love magic recounted by various texts are
almost incomprehensible to us now. They range from placing bat's
blood on a cloth under your loved one's pillow to using herbs, worms,
and even stag testicles to help arouse sexual desires in an intended mate.

Just after the American Civil War, a series of books were produced
called *Mother Bunche's Closet*. The directions given therein for discovering the identity of one's future love were definitely creative, but
they were based on actual folk customs. They include the following:

On Midsummer's Night, take a smock and dip it in fair (very clear or
rose scented) water. Turn this inside out and place it on a chair before the
fire. Have a vessel of wine and a little salt before the hearth. Do not
speak. In a little time, the likeness of the one you will marry will come and
turn your smocks around, then drink to you.

Take some hemp seed to a private place, carried in an apron. Then
toss the seed nine times with your right hand over the left shoulder saying, "Hemp seed I sow, he that must be my true love come after me and
mow." After this, expect to see the figure of your love.

Go to a churchyard at midnight with a sword. Go around the building nine times, saying, "Here's the sword, where's the sheath?" On the
ninth time the person will meet you and steal a kiss.

Other common beliefs of the era included wearing goldenrod on the
night of a waxing moon to glimpse your future love the next day, and
twisting off the top of an apple to the alphabet to learn the first letter of
your true love's name.

A unique way to combine these instructions into your own personal
love ritual (intended to help bring the right person into your life with
divine guidance) would be to use apple peel, hemp seed or a little rope,
salt, and a dash of wine as part of your incense. In this case, present
yourself to the Goddess as a sword (for men) or sheath (for women)
which seeks the appropriate counterpart to itself. Then release the
energy of your spell to the winds with rose petals to help draw or reveal
the individual to you.

As a side note, this example is not meant to be sexually insulting to anyone. The symbolism is very old.

Marriage

It is ill luck to marry in May, a belief probably rooted in the fact that this is an important planting month and all able-bodied hands were needed in the fields. Conversely, June is the Roman month of marriage and very suitable for handfastings. For these rituals, flowers present (or given) represent wishes for the couple's further joy. Rice is thrown so the couple will never want for food; in old times families gave provisions to help the newlyweds get started properly. In Italy, wheat is substituted for rice.

A bride wears something old to retain good memories, new to celebrate new friends and life, borrowed to encourage frugality, and blue to bring serenity.

Rosemary is sometimes placed on the bride's bed for luck, or in her bouquet as the herb of remembrance. Valerian tea is said to bring love and harmony to a marriage. Any or all of these beliefs can be incorporated into a magical wedding by having valerian tea in the ritual cup, strewing rosemary to mark the sacred space, and throwing bread bits at an outdoor wedding (see Chapter 23: Plants).

Moon

If young people meet their sweethearts during the new moon, it is considered good luck, with a possible wedding in the future. With this in mind, betrothal might best be planned during the new moon. The wedding should follow on a waxing to full moon to bring flourishing love.

Reconciliation

While the original intention for this bit of folk magic, written in a medieval text called *Picatrix*, was to cause dissension, a slight variation allows it to rectify a rift between two people.

Begin by taking two stones, one named after each person involved. Hold one in each hand, then separate your arms as far as they will go. Slowly bring them together saying, "I do not reunite these stones, but _____ (insert appropriate name) to _____. Once the stones touch, they are to be wrapped together so they stay touching, either with cloth or ribbon, the color of your choosing. Finally, bury the stones in fertile soil with a flowering seed so magic blossoms.

Rendezvous

Country people tell us that it is best for lovers to meet on a hillside near running water, in the heart of the woods or near heather to help ensure no deceit will come from their lips.

This symbolism can also be used when two people wish to make amends, the rushing water moving hostility away from them and the heather to ensure honest intent. If fresh water isn't available, a kitchen sink makes a very handy substitute.

Sanding

This Persian marriage custom dates back to an incident when a king shook some sand from his shoe as a wish to a newly-wedded couple for as many children as there were grains of sand. (Please check with the couple, however, to be sure that a full house is what they desire!) Alternatively, sand can be considered as a spell component for magic involving productivity (see Chapter 24: Pregnancy and Children).

Sex

In some instances, ritual sex was used as a means to invoke divine power for dire circumstances. The kings of Babylon, for example, would go through a sacred marriage with the Goddess Ishtar to ensure fertility and prosperity for their lands. In this region, the king performed all the magic for the country and her people. Similar traditions were followed in many different cultures to help crops grow and bring humanity into closer communion with the God/dess.

Today, this ritual is known as the Great Rite. It is considered a sacred marriage, which may be performed symbolically using a wand and cup, or by two consenting adults in time of great need. It is also sometimes performed as part of handfasting, where the couple wishes to celebrate their union through a holy joining.

Shoes

In Scotland, the bride's left shoe is thrown towards the left after the wedding ceremony to be sure any malevolent magic is thwarted. For contemporary handfastings, this can be mimicked by sweeping the left half of the sacred space from the center outward, moving any ill-luck away from the couple (see Chapter 17: Luck).

Smithy

There was a long-standing English tradition which held that young eloping couples could go just over the border into Scotland and be wed by the smithy.

This dates back to the time when the smith was considered a magical part of the community, as a healer, master of fire, and attendant to the sacred metal, iron (see Chapter 7: Crystals, Gem, and Metals).

As such, a piece of iron ore severed in two and placed in two matching medicine pouches makes a unique gift for newlyweds. It is an emblem of health and a blazing hearth full of love.

Stones

Romans considered sardonyx the best stone to ensure marital bliss, and topaz secured faithfulness between the two people. These stones can be used in handfastings, either as gifts or part of the altar arrangement, to grant steadfast devotion.

Sword Dance

Today, you will sometimes see an occasional sword bearer at weddings, or a dance with swords performed. This custom comes from an ancient tradition of the sword as a symbol of strength and protection. The use of this implement in wedding rituals is to scare away any evil spirits and guard the couple against all dangers which would try to steal their joy.

Recently, I was able to incorporate this tradition in a wedding: a sword was placed on the ground behind the couple first, for safeguarding them. At the end of the ceremony, they jumped over the sword to mark the beginning of their new life together.

Threshold

Carrying the bride over the threshold marks the line between the old life and the new. In some countries, the bride carries dough or oats with her to ensure the couple will never hunger (see Chapter 15: Kitchen and Household Lore).

In the interest of equality of the sexes, the couple could hold hands and jump over the threshold together instead.

Turquoise

Turquoise is considered the lucky stone for lovers. This probably has connections with the idea that blue is the best color to wear when meeting your love (see Chapter 7: Crystals, Gems, and Metals).

Weddings

The word *wed* means "to pledge" in Anglo Saxon. Many numbers of superstitions have come into being regarding what is required for a joyful union. In the Middle Ages, ears of corn were carried by the bride into the church ensure their plenty. A little corn can be worked into flower arrangements. The church is always entered by the right foot for luck.

The tradition of having groomsmen at the wedding comes from the time of bride captures. In this instance, the groomsmen would actually help perpetrate the abduction!

Wedding Rings

Wedding rings were and are worn on the left hand's ring finger. This stems from the belief that this finger had a vein running straight to the heart. Since Apollo (a Sun God) ruled the heart, it was the next logical step to have a golden ring placed there as a token and pledge between lovers. This way the power of the symbol would be conveyed directly to the emotional center.

26 SACRED SITES

Where now hides the unicorn, or mythic Elfin Glens?
Where now are the fables born, and, Gods, where have they been?
♦ Marian ♦

THROUGHOUT THE earth there are items, objects, and stretches of land with unique, lively energy that seems to transform us. The Sacred Geometrist (see Glossary) studies these areas. Through such examinations, we discover a network of power lines that link everything on the planet together. Along these routes, energy flows and wanes to maintain the balance. Someone who is psychically sensitive can feel these areas. Where the fields are strongest, sacred sites have often been established, the best known example of which is Stonehenge.

Located on the Salisbury Plain of England, the oldest portions of Stonehenge date to 2800 B.C. In 8 B.C., Diodorus described a spherical temple to Apollo in Hyperborea (Britain). This is probably the earliest written reference to Stonehenge. In A.D. 1136, Geoffrey of Monmouth called this region the Giant's Dance and characterized it as a place of great magic. It was also a gathering place for druidical rites.

While an area as potent as Stonehenge may not be around the corner from you, there are special spots you can discover if you keep your higher senses open. As you find these areas, note them in your magical journal—what you felt there, what types of magic might be aided by working at the site, and so on. Later you can share this information with others who visit or travel your way.

Not every sacred site will be marked with an unusual physical feature. Sometimes these places are made sacred simply because of your attitude in approaching them. When you treat the natural world with reverence, it responds in kind with energy that is healthy and helpful for any magical goal.

Arches

In many civilizations, most notably Roman, arches were used to mark victory for various noble warriors, and also as meeting places for business. In the latter instance, they would be placed where four roads met, offering shelter. In both cases the symbolism is very close to that of bridges and crossroads, in that it marks not only achievement, but hopefully success for the merchant traveling there.

Small arches can be constructed for your own use out of plywood and grapevines and decorated with any number of fresh or dry flowers, or many nursery and garden shops sell them. This entryway can be used for personal magic when you need to overcome difficult circumstances. It may also be employed by groups at gatherings to mark the line between the mundane and esoteric, or for handfasting rituals to indicate the transition in lifestyle.

Babylon

Known widely for its lush, hanging gardens and the tower of Babel, Babylon was built on the wealth of the Euphrates river. Most important to this site for the contemporary magician is the fact that the Goddess Ishtar was venerated here. Ishtar was considered the creator of humanity in this culture and a Goddess of benevolence. She is depicted as pouring water from a never-empty jar to show her generosity. Ishtar is an excellent Goddess to call on in times of need.

Blarney Stone

Northwest of Cork in Ireland, the ancient remains of Blarney Castle stand along with this wonderful stone. Anyone who kisses this relic receives persuasive, but not always totally honest, speech. While the actual location of the stone is disputed, its power is not.

One story from the seventeenth century says that the lord of the castle, after being taken prisoner by the English, promised to surrender the fortress. Whenever the English demanded fulfillment, he made up plausible excuses to delay them. Thus the term *blarney* came to indicate deceitful but convincing speech.

If you can't get to the stone, carry an agate with you instead to impart eloquence and truth (see Chapter 7: Crystals, Gems and Metals).

Callanish

This is an incredible stretch of standing stones in Scotland overlooking the North Atlantic Ocean. This set of stones has not been walled off yet by local authorities, and you are still welcome to go there by day or night to enjoy a little tranquillity.

Callanish is located on the Isle of Lewis, which can only be reached via the Stornoway Ferry. The entire island is inhabited by farmers who, for the most part, speak a derivative of old Gaelic and tell the tales of dragons, ghosts, and fairies.

While visiting there some years ago, my husband and I were struck with the ancient power radiating from these stones and the people who lived among them. It was as if, for a moment, time had not moved. When you stand in the middle of these monoliths, it is easy to understand why ancient couples came here to pledge their troth, and easier still to know why Scotland is considered by many to be the most haunted country in the world: no self-respecting ghost would want to leave!

My favorite story from Callanish was recounted to us by an elderly man on the ferry ride home. He told us of a great dragon who appears periodically throughout the year to check all the standing stones of the

British Isles. The only ones who ever see him are believed to be his children and kin.

On this side of the ocean, if you have a small yard you may wish to do a little research into the forms of various standing-stone structures. Then make one on a smaller scale for use during ritual, or just as an extra blessing for your land.

Cemetery

This is the meeting-ground between the living and the dead, where careful respect must be maintained. Many superstitions have arisen pertaining to this space. One of the most popular superstitions held that, to keep a spirit from wandering, you should walk around its grave three times.

A cemetery is still a very appropriate place to commune with a deceased loved one or to seek spirits. I do issue caution, however, as the life forces you encounter can be both good and bad.

Cheesewring

The cheesewring is a pile of rocks thirty-two feet high, looking much like a child's top with the point downward. It is located near Liskeard in Cornwall and is repudiated to be where a druid would stand and give travelers a drink from his never-empty cup. Interestingly, in the early nineteenth century, a golden chalice was found nearby dating back to about 1500 B.C. There is no doubt that this particular story has some connections with Grail lore, and other horns of plenty (see Chapter 18: Magic and the Supernatural).

Keeping in mind the story of this cup, if your home has many guests, you might want to have a special cup kept aside to offer them. It should always be filled with the liquid of their choice and shared as a token of welcome and hospitality.

Church

Considered holy ground, a church has always been the safest place for mortals during any time of crisis. Many early churches were built over sacred Pagan sites, adding even more potency to the protective powers there.

It is said that, if a bird flies into a church (or magic circle) during a rite, it is considered a very positive sign that the prayers and ceremony have been blessed.

Cornwall

There is a unique megalith in Cornwall known as the holy stone. It is named so because it appears much like an erect doughnut. This stone was used throughout history as a place of healing. The patient was passed through the stone three times (head to foot) and then moved across the grass counterclockwise three times. This cure was thought most effective for back problems.

If you happen to find a small version of a holy stone (see Chapter 27: The Sea) at the beach and also have a back problem, a functional home-version of this cure can be effected by rubbing the stone in some rich, green grass counterclockwise, then carrying it during a healing meditation or ritual.

Crossroads

In England, the meeting place of two roads also marked what was considered a magical spot. People would bury charms at these crossroads, believing they would be far more effective for the effort. The location of the crossroad and the type of charm would vary depending on the need or wish. For example, if a silver coin were buried, it brought fertility, and a horseshoe conveyed luck.

The reason for this may have come from a far more archaic source—the symbolism of the four directions and winds. In some countries, it is traditional to bury those who commit suicide at crossroads with stones across their faces to keep the confused spirit from wandering. In Hungary, people of unsound mind are likewise buried there.

The Scots believe that, if you sit at a crossroad on a three-legged stool on Halloween at midnight, you can see who will die in the next year.

In magical rites, after an outdoor circle has been closed, you might consider placing wish tokens for yourself or coven members at the center of the four cardinal points to benefit from the residual magical energy.

Dumpden Hill

This hill in rural England is believed to be an ancient site for rituals. The local people claim that the stones and trees of this site defy counting while you stand on the hill; no matter how many times you try, you will get a different figure. However, it is claimed by the same people that there are ninety-nine trees on the mound. This particular conviction may have its origins in the fact that nine is three times three, three being a potent magical number (see Chapter 21: Numbers).

Gardens

No matter the historical period, the garden has held a unique fascination. There were the ancient hanging gardens of Babylon, medieval monastery gardens, kitchen gardens, and the intricate Victorian gardens.

The Zen Buddhists of Japan have a slightly different version of gardening using stones, attempting to place them in the landscape so that they appear as if water were moving naturally through. The greatest way to learn patience, the Buddhists claim, is to sit in a meditative state and watch this garden grow.

Magical gardens today are no less interesting for someone who loves the land and working with it. A wide variety of herbs can be cultivated specifically for ritual use (see Chapter 12: Gardening and Farming). To discover which you would like to grow, make a list of those you use most frequently, consult a good field guide to herbs for climactic limitations, then stop at a seed shop. Bless your land in whatever manner feels appropriate and add stones and crystals in as accents. These become standing reminders of the quality of forbearance.

Knossos

In 1500 B.C., this was the center of Minoan civilization. It was known mostly for its incredible labyrinth, the largest ever constructed. Labyrinths have long been affiliated with magic, and regarded with a certain amount of trepidation, yet are an amazing tribute to skill. Today, the image of a labyrinth might prove useful in meditations to sort out confusing situations, or when you are trying to hone specific proficiencies in your life. As you visualize the tangled path, keep one hand always on the left wall to find your way clear.

Obelisks

The most famous obelisk is Cleopatra's Needle near London Harbor. This was constructed in Egypt as a towering token of honor to the Sun God, Ra. Smaller versions of obelisks are available today in a wide variety of crystalline or metallic bases at New Age stores and are an excellent addition to any sun-related magic. Elongated versions can become an alternative wand to direct your spiritual energy.

Pyramids

The mystery of the pyramids has been explored by scientists and psychics alike. While some of these structures' stones are smooth, others are rough, and still others conceal rooms. Many  theories have been proposed about the use of these great architectural feats, from their being astronomical markers to systems of measurement. They may even have the mystical power to help plants grow and keep food fresh within.

Today many mini-pyramids are available inexpensively through fluorite crystals. Should you wish to use one of these as a component for magic, the symbolism includes precision, preservation, and evaluation.

Rivers

The Tigris and Euphrates rivers were revered by ancient Middle Eastern cultures as sources of creation. In lower Babylonian nations, they were thought to be the home of the Divine. Because of this, one cultural group known as Mandaean (or Baptists) partake in ceremonial bathing here so rushing water can renew their spirit, vitality, and virtue.

This particular religious sect regards itself as descended from John the Baptist's followers, but consider the present Christian means of baptism dreadful because it is done in still (or dead) water. To them, such an act is unthinkable, because the movement of the river symbolizes and embodies life.

If you are fortunate enough to have fresh running water near you, definitely consider all its functions for magical work, especially those rites pertaining to movement or cleansing. For modern homes, alternatives include a hose, sink, sprinkler system, shower, and even the toilet.

Sphinx

Ancient legend claims that when a sphinx is buried up to its head in the sand, you can seek wisdom from its lips by placing your ear there. Many New Age shops carry likenesses of the sphinx in jewelry or small statue form. Apply the symbolism to magic pertaining to discernment and judgment.

Taj Mahal

Mughal emperor Shan Jehan (A.D. 1628—1658) built this incredible edifice for his beloved wife Mumbaz Mahal, who was known among the people for her keen wit, charity, and wisdom. The number four, which represented completeness in this culture, was used frequently in the design of this building, which contains four lawns, four large flowerbeds, and four hundred flowers per bed (see Chapter 21: Numbers).

For magic, the image of the Taj Mahal might be used in visualizations regarding development of devotion, humor, and insight.

Valley of the Gods

In the Valley of the Gods, located in Arizona, Native American shamans believed that one should greet each day the same way as the first morning, with the Word, movement, and chanting. In this way, they believe they are literally bringing new life and beauty into the world through their rituals.

In this region sweat lodges are common. Within, elder members of the tribe teach the young the blessing-ways of songs and prayers of their people. It is here, through the process of sweating (cleansing), that the members of the tribe are purified. During this time they are reminded to respect the natural world. They are also encouraged to speak to the Holy Ones daily outside the lodge, the essence of the Great Spirit being found in all things.

For those of us who cannot travel this far to have such an experience, perhaps consider renting a sauna for a coven meeting sometime, where the elders of your group can share insights with initiates or those about to be accepted into a higher degree.

Waterfalls

Waterfalls are sites where both wonderful rituals and terrible accidents have occurred. The power of the rushing water has an almost hypnotic effect, and often draws people inward. Some cultures say the voices of their ancestors are echoed in the crashing waters, and can grant wisdom and insight as well as reverberate with warning.

Being a native western New Yorker, I know from personal experience that Niagara Falls is one such place, but smaller waterfalls can also be very empowering, especially for water-based people (see Chapter 10: The Elements). They make a beautiful place to give offerings of flowers, on which wishes may be floated. Small homemade waterfalls can be produced by a pile of stones and a hidden hose.

Wells

Wishing wells were once believed to be guarded by faeries or other spirits, who had to be appeased with a coin before the wish would be heard. These and other holy wells may have first gained their reputations because of healthful minerals present in their water. Since early people would have drunk from them unaware of this benefit, they regarded the curative powers with awe. Romans were known to bring valuable gifts to please the well spirits before they drank, thus gaining their favor.

The temple of Demeter supposedly had a divinatory well which foretold the outcome of sickness with incredible accuracy. For this, the individual querist would say prayers and burn incense to the Goddess, then lower a mirror to the surface of the well and scry therein for their answer.

In Ireland, sacred wells are connected to the Great Goddess Dana (or one of the other popular Celtic goddesses), in the belief that this divinity blessed the water within. Frequently, the person coming to this well was instructed to crawl around the base while praying, perhaps as an act of meekness and humility before such a presence. If the well had an ash or thorn tree nearby, it was all the better. In their bowers small 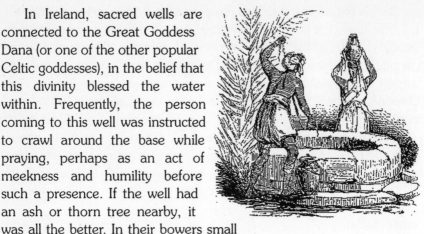 ribbons or cloth were hung to remind the Goddess of the individual's prayer. It is also considered a sign of thankfulness to the well's spirit.

With the advent of indoor plumbing, the number of active wells has greatly decreased today. However, there is no reason why you can't build and bless one of any size for yourself. For an apartment dweller, one of clay could be fashioned, kilned, ritually painted, and left near the front door for loose change. For the home-owner, larger versions are sometimes available at garden shops, or perhaps a birdbath could act as a surrogate. Such objects make a good marker for the western point of your magic circle.

Wheels

Across the North American plains and Rocky Mountains, several ground structures which look like great wheels made out of medium-sized white stones can be found. The most widely known is the Bighorn Medicine Wheel in Wyoming, possibly created as early as A.D. 1100, most probably to mark the seasons and special days.

Similar smaller creations can be made in your own yard, or smaller yet, on a wooden board which sits in the window like a sundial. You will need to first decide where your central point is. Go to this spot before sunrise. Mark where the sun first appears in your area each day using trees, houses, and other unmoving objects as reference points. Lay your first stone in the direction of that point, with several others moving inward towards the center. Continue in this manner until you have a full wheel, which can later be used for your magical circle celebrations.

27 THE SEA

Thou meanest what the sea has striven to say
so long, and yearned up the cliffs to tell.
♦ Stephen Phillips, *Marpessa* ♦

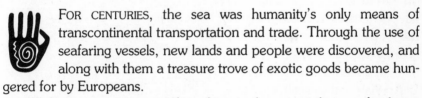 FOR CENTURIES, the sea was humanity's only means of transcontinental transportation and trade. Through the use of seafaring vessels, new lands and people were discovered, and along with them a treasure trove of exotic goods became hungered for by Europeans.

While we may not use sailing ships to the extent that our forebears did, many of the superstitions and amulets created for this mode of transportation can be applied to the modern modes of car, bus, train, plane, and even bicycle travel.

Albatross

The albatross is one of the most fortuitous sea-birds for a sailor. To kill one is a sin, as evidenced in the *Rime of the Ancient Mariner*. The sailor in this story transgressed by killing the lucky bird and in punishment had to wear it around his neck as penance and a mark of shame. From this we get the phrase "wearing an albatross around the neck" as a sign of serious error and guilt.

Among the Ainu of Japan, the albatross is also sacred, being a servant of the Sea God and a fortunate omen. Here, the head of an albatross is kept as a fetish to ward against disease.

If you happen to be performing a spell to rid yourself of guilt and bring forgiveness, burning a picture of an albatross with herbs of liberation (basil, thistle, wintergreen, and lilac) might prove a powerful symbol.

Baby's Caul

Seafarers carried a baby's caul to prevent both the child and themselves from drowning at sea. In the Middle Ages, these were sold at a high price.

Since this is considered highly unsanitary today, it is best to simply carry a picture of your child near to your heart, thus bearing their love for you at all times.

Cat

If you throw a cat overboard while sailing, a terrible tempest will soon follow. Cats were valuable crew members on the old sailing ships. These adept hunters helped keep the rat population, and consequently disease, from exploding onboard (see Chapter 2: Animals and Insects).

If you have trouble with motion sickness, consider keeping a bit of your cat's hair specifically blessed for comfortable travel in your wallet. Those allergic to cat hair may substitute valerian root or catnip.

Coal

A sailor finding a piece of coal washed up on shore considered himself quite lucky. This coal was then carried aboard ship to protect him from all dangers (see Chapter 17: Luck).

Coins (Found)

An old sailors' superstition says that tossing a coin found on deck into the winds before sailing brings favorable weather. At home, save pennies you find, and toss them towards the wind before venturing out for the day (see Chapter 15: Kitchen and Household Lore).

Ebb Tide

The water from ebbing tides is very auspicious. If a couple is wed during low tide, especially near the shore, it means great happiness. It is also thought that more births take place during this period.

This is a wonderful time to be at the seashore and collect specimens for your water-related magic. All manner of holy stones, shells, sand dollars, and marvelous driftwood are left waiting for the creative eye. In return, I often leave a little token for the sea, such as a stone from another adventure, to thank Mari, the Celtic Sea Goddess, for her treasures.

Figureheads

It was firmly believed that a ship would not sink without its figurehead, because it was a part of the life and soul of the ship. These carvings were regarded with a ritualistic respect which might be translated to an unusual hood ornament for your vehicle or even a crystal hung from the rearview mirror.

Holy Stones

A holy stone is a small stone or shell with a natural hole formed in it by water-wear. It is believed to portend safe journey and a good catch to the sailor who finds one, because they are a gift from the sea.

Besides enabling them to be easily carried or worn for safe travel, the holes make these treasures from the Sea Goddess useful for jewelry and decorating staffs.

Lady Trees

An endowment from the Sea Goddess herself, these bits of seaweed which resemble trees should be dried and hung near the hearth, or placed in a vase to keep the home safe from negative magic.

Include seaweed or kelp in any magic for protection. Once dried, use seaweed to asperge the sacred space by dipping it lightly in saltwater.

Playing Cards

Generally, playing cards have not been allowed aboard ship due to the negative influence gambling had on the men. Sometimes called the devil's cards, if a deck was allowed on board it was quickly thrown to the sea as soon as any sign of trouble was detected.

Carry a few playing cards with you when you travel. If you begin to have a lot of little mishaps, throw one over your shoulder and leave it behind to change your luck. Depending on your viewpoint, you may wish to use a black card, particularly the Ace of Spades (considered ill luck) so that you are literally throwing the negativity away. Or, conversely, throw a red card so that positive energy stands between you and your difficulties (see Chapter 6: Color).

Porpoises

Porpoises are great weather prophets. It is a positive omen to see them playing by the ship during a storm (see Chapter 2: Animals and Insects).

Many New Age leaders believe that the gap between human and animal communications might first be bridged by these creatures. In Florida it is possible to swim with these marvelous animals through the dolphin institute. For those who would like more information, their address is: Dolphin Research Center, Box 2875, Marathon Shores, FL 33052. Phone number: 305-289-0002.

Sailor's Collar

It was lucky to touch a sailor's collar, because the sight of a sailor meant a new ship in port carrying food and goods for households.

Since we cannot usually carry such an item with us today, an alternative might be a bit of rope from a sailing vessel or a fishermen's net as part of your medicine bag.

Seagulls

In Great Britain and Ireland, these birds are thought
to be the spirits of dead fishermen. If one comes
near the house, it is a warning of danger at
sea. If many of them move inland, it
portends a raging storm. This last superstition
has been proven out by time to be a fairly accurate gauge of weather.

If you happen to find a gull feather at the
shore, keep it to use for weather, protection,
and safe travel magic. Be sure to clean
the feather thoroughly.

Sea Vapor

Ancients believed (and modern science concurs) that the sea was the
source of all life. A vapor known as the Veil of Isis carried life to the
land throughout the world and even to the heavens. Part of this lore
had to do with the fact that the sun and moon appear to rise and sink
into the ocean.

For your personal Craft, dew gathered near the seaside could have
interesting applications. Since it is associated with the element of water,
any magic dealing with creativity, intuition, or health could be enhanced
by using it as a component (perhaps by way of anointing). Another
application would be to drink a little of the blessed dew to aid fertility
magic or as a libation to Isis.

Ship Names

Seamen believe it very unlucky to change a boat's name after its first
berthing. On the other hand, it is a good idea to speak its name, to
empower the symbol that the name bears. For example, in a difficult
storm if the boat is named Victoria, repeating the name will help keep
the boat aright.

I know that many magical people today have a fondness for naming
their personal computers, cars, and other objects. With this folklore in
mind, name your property according to attributes you would most like
to see in that item. My computer, for example, is named after a favorite
science fiction character who is very analytical.

Starstones and Sand Dollars

The starstone (or starfish) has a symmetrical form with five arms radiating out from the center. When it dies its crustaceous exterior hardens to appear much like stone. Sand Dollars are round in shape and thin and have markings looking like a star emanating from their central point.

These two gifts of the ocean are considered sacred because they have the natural imprint of a pentagram which makes them powerful protective amulets.

Tides (Norse)

In the northern continents, the time of day when the tide arrived had great significance, and when combined with magical goals, was unerringly potent. Here is a chart to give you some idea:

- ◆ Morning tide: awakenings, fertility, life.
- ◆ Day tide: gentility, growth, finances.
- ◆ Mid-day: sustenance, will-power, perseverance.
- ◆ Before dusk: change, perceptiveness, parenting.
- ◆ Evening tide: joy, spirituality, pregnancy and children.
- ◆ Night: creativity, deeper knowledge, enlightenment.
- ◆ Midnight: healing and recuperation.
- ◆ Before morning: rest, sleep, quiet contemplation.

28 SOUNDS

Make me thy lyre, ever as the forest is.
♦ Percy B. Shelley, *Ode to the West Wind* ♦

BEFORE COMPLEX rituals protected against the dangers of the night, early humans used the sound of their voices. As people moved through the woods, they might make a loud cry to frighten off an undesired animal, shake a crude rattle, or hit a tree in hopes of securing enough room to save themselves.

Slowly, different types of sounds and instruments became the means of either frightening away or appeasing spiritual entities. This became so commonplace in most ancient rituals that the use of musical instruments and sound in religious observances is nearly universal.

As technical abilities advanced, so did noise-making devices. In the Middle Ages, these devices were so closely guarded in Byzantium and Muslim lands that, when Westerners saw mechanical angels blowing horns, or a clock with moving horses signalling the hours, they were left in awe. Even when these objects were popular, especially among the wealthy in Elizabethan times, there were still whispers from the common folk of magic being afoot. After all, how could a mechanical object ever recreate the noises of nature if not by some powerful supernatural means?

Now, thanks to synthesizers and a myriad of unique instruments, we can listen to waves on the shore, the woods by night or any number of other soothing tones without leaving home. This music is excellent for private and guided meditations.

In magic circles, we have not lost sight of the power or impact of rhythm and sound. A beat is created to help raise the cone of power, while soft music might fill the room to prepare for rites. No matter the source of sound, however, when used for spiritual ends, it should be approached with the same reverence as any magical tool. In this way our contemporary intonations can provide an opportunity to connect with time and the harmony of the universe.

Bells

Bells were attached to the skirts of Aaron, the high priest of the Hebrews. This was done for ritual purposes to help drive evil spirits away. Later, bells were placed around the necks of horses, camels, and cattle for the same reason. It is because of this belief that so many church steeples continue to have bells (mechanical or otherwise). Bells were also rung during labor pains or harvest festivals to ensure the safety of the child or crops. The grease from a bell was considered a curative for skin disorders, because it absorbed the sound, and transferred the power of the bell to the patient.

In the magical home, small silver bells can be blessed for whatever purpose you desire and hung in a window. Each time the wind blows, it sends the magical energy in tinkling waves throughout your house to reinforce your working.

A larger bell, a Tibetan prayer bowl, or a gong, can be used to help center oneself during meditation. This exercise is most effective if aided by a visualization of concentric circles moving inward toward your center of gravity or toward the third eye for psychic awareness.

Drums

In Celtic realms, the drumhead of wolf skin would always drown out the sound of one made of sheep hide because the sheep is afraid of its natural enemy. In Mesopotamia, priests sounded drums of copper and bull-hide to aid in curing sickness.

The preparation and appearance of the drum is considered just as important to its effectiveness as its sound and rhythm. Some drum makers searched for wood struck by lightning, others gathered trees never touched by sunlight. Once prepared, the undersides of drums were decorated with brass and bone, then painted with spirit animals and other mystical representations.

Many Lapp homes owned a drum, feeling it was good luck, and kept it in a special part of the dwelling restricted to men. Sometimes, as a form of divination they placed a brass ring or frog on top of the skin and watched it for movement.

Certain tribal cultures strongly believe that, if a malevolent spirit cannot be displaced by the village's largest drum, it cannot be defeated at all.

A very famous drum is presently kept at Buckland Abbey in England. Formerly owned by Sir Francis Drake in the sixteenth century, legend claims that he returns to aid his country whenever the drum is sounded. Many claim it has been known to reverberate without aid just before the advent of war.

Drums are known to help induce a trance-like state, making them a preferred instrument for magical workings. A drum is an excellent accompaniment for sacred dances, especially those associated with celebrating the rhythm of seasons or the Great Rite. Like bells, the low sounding of drums in sync with your heartbeat or breath can be an effective meditation aid.

Echo

There are many areas of the world where the mountains meet the valley in such a way as to allow sound to reverberate in a wonderful circuit. One such place is the Eagle's Nest in Ireland, where the power of sound moves out from the individual or animal, then returns to them manyfold.

Early humans must have at first thought these sounds to be some type of natural spirits answering them. Depending on how many times an answer came, or other variations of the echo, it was interpreted as a positive or negative omen. And while the contemporary mind under-stands the explanation for echoes, it certainly hasn't decreased our love of listening to them move through the countryside.

If you have access to such a place, consider using it when there won't be a lot of people around to hear you. Go to a favorite spot and begin to chant, sing, or voice an invocation. Allow the echo to carry your prayer to the land and sky, then bring it back to you with blessings.

Eisteddfod (August 18, Wales)

This ancient festival reveals the significance of music and storytelling in the Welsh druidic tradition. This festival is important enough to be announced a year and a day in advance. The beginning of the celebration is a parade of bards wearing blue and green robes, blue for those wishing office and green for candidates. The druids don white to show purity.

Once everyone is in position around the standing stones, prayers, literary recitals, and music follow. Prizes for the most talented attendees include recognition as a bard, for those who seek the title. This position is acknowledged by the new bard's reading from a rune book, being touched by a sword, and the presentation of blue knotted rib-bons. From that point forward the bard joins the ranks of those so hon-ored in Wales.

Music of the Spheres

This type of music comes from the Pythagorean belief that heavenly bodies join in a cosmic chant as they move through the sky, as if the heavens were a giant chord waiting to be plucked. Then all things of the sky, especially those that moved, would cause this chord to sound. This produces a melody indicative of life itself. Some of these sounds were likened to the sacred vowels now used in toning.

Each element in nature is said to have a key note in this celestial waltz. In the Old Testament, Job describes a time when the "stars of morning sang together."

This concept is what I refer to as the music in people, but this description is inadequate for the realm that Pythagoreans were pondering. Their idea was of the symphony of all things, created when we are working in accord with the rhythms of nature and the universe.

It is not always a music which can necessarily be heard by the physical ear, but one that is appreciated on a sublime, spiritual level. When we meditate, chant, sing, or dance, we set up a resonance which is trying to mimic this heavenly timbre and eventually move into symmetry with it. On the more common level it is the simplicity of songbirds, children laughing, and a brook moving gently over the stones.

Magic also calls to us to listen closely to our inner and outer worlds so that we can begin to hear the divine voice in all things. The power of that rich sound is what will eventually allow us to develop an awareness of ourselves as important spiritual creations.

Rain Sticks

A rain stick is a specially-crafted piece of bamboo which, when filled with small stones and tipped over, makes a sound similar to rain. Known throughout Africa, South America, and Mexico for its use in rain ceremonies and percussion, the Rainstick has recently made a reappearance in the Western world. In a ritual atmosphere, the rain stick functions as a sympathetic bond, reproducing the experience of gentle showers in the hopes that a beneficent spirit will hear the tenor and respond.

Should you like one of these to adorn the western point of your altar or for use in your own weather-related magic, some really beautiful ones are available through Charley Barley, 232 Brook Rd. Warren, VT 05674, (802) 496-7665. The sound is also very relaxing if you get a small version and hold it in your hands during meditation.

Rough Music

This was a type of communal punishment practiced in Cambodian villages for an individual's offense of incest, wife beating, and other violence. Here the sin is thought to affect the whole community via crop failure or plague. To signify their disapproval of the perpetrator, and hopefully frighten off the negative spirits, all the men of the village gather together with pots, pans, kettles, whistles, and any other noisemakers they can find and walk the entire perimeter of the land. This was repeated over three nights, sometimes with the additional measure of leaving a token at the door of the person to mark him or her for public shame.

We find evidence of similar activities in other remote regions. In Alaska, medicine men beat loud drums and yelled to overcome sickness, sometimes to the point of breaking their instruments. If a disease spirit could not be sent away by using the largest ceremonial drum and best criers, then the patient was doomed and put out of his or her misery. In China, children wear bells to conciliate the bell demon who, when angered, steals the lives of infants.

The use of noise to try to disrupt harmful energies is a long-standing tradition. Something similar can be done any time you feel your home or sacred space has been tainted by ill-intentioned or random forces. By making a circuit of the area with joyous music (perhaps some good old rock n' roll), you are in effect creating a protective magic circle.

Song

Certain Renaissance mages wrote about a special type of singing called the Orphic Hymn. Marsilio Ficino, an Italian philosopher of the 1400s translated the *Orphica*, songs to Pagan deities, then played them on a lyre to work toward self-improvement. This music was a combination of harmony, words, and spells, which created a magical effect on the audience.

Ficino felt that, by singing to a specific deity on the correct day and hour, he could connect with the power of auspicious planetary aspects. For example, if singing of Apollo, he would wait for the sun to reach Leo or Aries and perform on Sunday, wearing a crown of laurel while surrounded by sunflowers to set himself into harmony with the heavens and thus God.

The later users of such music were Neoplatonists and saw it as a natural mysticism and way of bringing joy and peace to the people. I think we are beginning to see the rebirth of such powers in New Age music today. As more people are seeking to be attuned to celestial spheres, those songs come forward to help deepen our spiritual insight.

Sound Dynamics

Many cultures, particularly those of the East, have great respect for the spoken word and its potential power. Singular terms, or a combination, when employed properly, can create force in the invisible world, and eventually gain visible results. Examples of this include the Sacred Word of Creation (the power-word God used to manifest the world in John 1:1), the Lost Word that Masonry seeks, and the creative tones of the Hindus (the three-old divine name). In each of these cases, sound is venerated as a vital force in the universe.

For contemporary magic this represents a confirmation of age-old verbalized affirmations, spells, chants, and incantations. By sounding our desires to the winds, we allow them to carry power to their destinations. By moving our words on waves, we have the ability to create and heal. The tongues of fire give power to our magic, and the earth gives these sounds a place to grow and disburse to heal the land. Consider the potency and significance of your words.

Tambourine

The earliest form of this instrument was probably the sistrum, associated with Isis. Similar devices, such as cymbals, are often used as part of ecstatic dance and worship. Through the early 1900s the tambourine was considered a valuable instrument for divination because it was sensitive to the touch of a spirit.

While it is not always considered a popular instrument today, the tambourine should not be overlooked for ritual music. It is easy to play as long as you have a sense of rhythm, and it is an inexpensive substitute for other forms of percussion.

Trumpet

Mentioned frequently in the Bible as heralding many events, and used in the Middle Ages in the royal court (among other occasions), the trumpet is sometimes used in European countries today as part of the New Year's celebrations. Four people stand facing each of the directions. The first person sounds a single note of a song. Once this note is totally silent the next is played, in clockwise succession, until the complete piece is finished. This is believed to be a way to salute the powers of each direction and call for protection from both heaven and earth.

In this respect the sounding of a trumpet (perhaps on tape) or kazoo would be an appropriate beginning for any magical circle, to mark the division between the mundane and esoteric.

29 TREES, BUSHES, AND WOODS

Before the first of the druids was a child
long didst thou sit amid our regions wild.
♦ John Keats, *Book IV* ♦

TREES HAVE played a unique role in human history. Not only were they a part of our habitat, but they offered living space and shelter in times of need. To early minds, the tree must have seemed very magical. It was rarely harmed by weather but for a few broken branches, returned to life yearly after appearing to die, and in some instances remained green even in the harshest of winters.

The Celtic Tree Calendar symbolizes the reverence this culture had for trees. This calendar is comprised of thirteen months, each having twenty-eight days, with one day left over at year's-end. There is a good chance the magical training period of a "year and a day" may have derived from this ancient tradition.

Trees offer us hundreds of uses for creative magic. Leaves, flowers, and bark can all be part of incense preparations, many having medicinal qualities; branches make good magical wands, staffs, and dousing rods; and all types of wood can be used to create inexpensive rune sets or symbolic carvings for the sacred space. In visualization they are excellent for healing and grounding work.

To choose which tree you want to use for any of these applications, first consider the goals of your magic and your own personality. For example, while the flowers of an almond tree are appropriate in incense before a job interview, you would probably not use this tree for health-related matters. For the latter, meditating under an elder is a better choice because of its applications in folk medicine.

Alder

Alder branches were used to make the musical pan pipes. It is considered to be aligned with the element of fire, its leaves being water-repellent. The leaves, bark, and twigs may all be employed to make natural dyes.

For magic, use alder wood for creativity, rites honoring Pan, and any fire-related festival.

Almond

The seed of this tree prevents drunkenness if eaten and guards against the evil eye. There was also a time when individuals might have climbed a flowering almond tree to ensure the attainment of a business arrangement.

While you may not wish to go so far as climbing a tree, the almond flower is an excellent choice to carry or use as a spell component in work-related magic. Almond leaves and/or nuts should be kept in the home for protection.

Apple

The Norse gods ate magical apples every day in Asgard to bring strength and youthfulness. The saying of "an apple a day keeps the doctor away" may have its roots in this story.

Until a few hundred years ago, it was not uncommon for an apple farmer to go to his orchard on Twelfth Night and sing to the trees. It was also considered very important to leave the last apple on the tree for the Apple Tree Man (a faerie), who would insure good harvests the following year.

The fruit of an apple tree is associated with profound knowledge and insight, which may or may not prove beneficial to those who seek it (note specifically Adam and Eve). However, it is also a traditional fruit in love divination (by peeling or counting as the stem is twisted off), and when cut in half, its seeds exhibit a perfect pentagram, which can be part of any sacred space.

Ash

If you find an ash leaf with an even number of points, make a wish or place it
under your pillow to dream of your future
mate. Ash is one of the trees believed
by the Norse to have been Yggdrasil,
whose roots form the earth and whose
branches blossomed into the heavens.
Odin had a special spear of ash, and in
some cultures a bit of ash wood is
thought to protect one from drowning.
With this in mind, carry a bit of ash
when going to sea or, for wish magic, or
use an ash wand when performing any
rituals to honor Odin.

Despite its fiery name, ash is usually asso-
ciated with the water element. The druids often used ash branches for
wands, and it was considered a wood of healing and insight. As such, it
is an excellent ingredient for anointing oils or incense.

To make your own magical wand, look for a piece of ash (or other
preferred wood) during the spring when the bark will be easily released
from the core. Once this is peeled and sanded, use a sharp knife to
carve out any knots and then set stones of your choosing within the hollow. It is also nice to add a handle and a crystal point for directing
energy. Please note the process for making a staff is essentially the
same, except you may wish to add a foot of some sort (such as a rubber
cane end) to protect it from wear.

Aspen

A leaf of aspen placed under your tongue ensures persuasive speech.
Alternatively, wax an aspen leaf and keep it in your wallet to help
improve general communication skills.

Aspen was used in folk medicine as a cure for shaking diseases
because its leaves were so easily moved by the winds. This symbolism

might be employed the next time you are very nervous about a presentation or other pending matter. Simply take a little swatch of personal fabric and attach it to the tree, thereby affixing your fears. Then turn away, leaving them neatly behind you.

Bay

A bay bush in any garden near the home is considered a strong prevention against lightning. The bay was sacred to both Apollo and Aesculepius, God of Medicine. Because of this, it is a good leaf to use in healing incense (see Chapter 23: Plants) or to bring attributes commonly associated with Apollo into your life (i.e., strength, courage, etc).

Beech

Used for hundreds of years to make writing tablets, the beech tree represents learning and wisdom. It also has the unique ability of melding its branches. If branches of this tree lay against each other, they will grow together. In this way, beech wood might be burned for introspection, flexibility, unity, and tolerance, or when you need to feed the well of self.

Birch

A popular Yule decoration, the birch is considered the Lady of the Woods. Its timber is part of the traditional witch's broom, and in some countries the blossoming of its branches marks the beginning of the planting season. It is the tree of abundance and new inception. As such, its flowers are appropriate for both initiations and handfastings.

Bramble

The Norse believed that when this bush grew in the shape of an arch, it was a potent cure for skin disease to crawl under it from east to west. For modern magic, bramble may be used for health matters or protection.

Cedar

Certain ancient Babylonian texts indicate that magical cedars can grow gems. This may have given rise to the use of cedar for spells or rituals pertaining to prosperity, or for developing personal gems of virtue. It is also a favored wood base for incense that cleanses and purifies the sacred space.

Elder

In France, apples are packed in elder flowers to enhance the flavor and longevity of the fruit. In this manner, elder may be a symbol of consistency and freshness.

Elder flowers are also popular in many types of washes and creams (see Chapter 22: Personal Care). To make an elder flower cream, pick the flowers in early morning and soak them in a half-cup of warm almond oil until they turn clear. To this add four inches of a white taper candle, a quarter slice of cocoa butter, and two capfuls of aloe (the cocoa butter and aloe are optional if you have an allergy to either). Melt these in the warm oil, then beat into the consistency of cold cream. Seal in an airtight container and apply as desired to moisturize your skin.

Fig

Eastern legend tells us that the Buddha found enlightenment while sitting at the base of a giant fig tree. In Rome, figs were gilded for prosperity and given as gifts on New Year's Day. As such, the fruit of a fig tree might be blessed and eaten before you meditate, or any time when finances are stretched to their limit. If you don't happen to like the taste of figs, dry a few fig leaves and burn them instead.

Harvesting Trees

For greatest durability, cut chestnut, oak, and other hardwoods in August before noon, just after the full moon. Pine, maple, and other white woods are treated similarly, only between the new and full moon, and when the sun is in Virgo. Consider these guidelines if you plan to harvest any woods for making magical tools. Please, however, ask permission of the tree before cutting away a branch, and take care to cover the wound with a sealant so the tree will not become infested with insects.

Hawthorn

Joseph of Arimathea's staff was said to produce a hawthorn bush. Tradition also claims that the hawthorn never blossoms until spring has arrived to stay. So, when you feel you need a change in mood toward the freshness of spring, use hawthorn as part of your ritual.

Hawthorn is called the wishing bush. It was common to make a wish while holding a small bit of appropriately-colored cloth (see Chapter 6: Color). This scrap is pierced on a thorn of the tree, then left to represent your desire.

Hawthorn is considered sacred to the Fey, the maiden aspect of the Goddess and is most fitting on the Beltane altar (white flowers).

Hazel

The traditional divining rod is made out of a hazel branch, and is thought to have been first used by the Chaldeans. It is quite possible that the Rod of Moses, used to get water from a rock, was also made of hazel. Early Celtic bishops carried a staff of hazel. Thus it might be said that hazel wood is one of spiritual leadership and insight, and would make a wonderful wand for any priest or priestess.

Amulets made from hazelnuts impart wisdom to the wearer, especially with regard to magic and the Crone. The fruit is one of patience.

Hazel was long a popular magical name because the ninth month of the Celtic tree calendar was named after the hazel. Hazel also makes an excellent herbal pendulum. Make this by suspending a bit of the wood from of a still string. Then, concentrate on a question. If the pendulum swings forward and back, the answer is yes; from side to side, no.

I have yet to discover the reason why, but the Victorians had a love for hazelnut divination. To discover if a lover was faithful, the querist would place two hazelnuts side by side on the bars of a roasting grate. If they burned as one, true love was assured. To find the name of the person you would marry, you would write the names of all the young men/women you knew on hazelnuts, one name per nut, and roast them on an open fire. The first to jump or pop represented the expected lover. An interesting variation of this today, would be to use similar methods for deciding a particularly difficult question.

Other predominant magical associations for the hazel are fertility, knowledge, and the muse. The nuts are similarly identified with love and childbirth. In Wales, leaves and branches from the hazel are woven together into a cap shape and worn to bring luck and fulfillment of wishes.

Holly Bush

The holly bush is a standing emblem of life and longevity, and a sacred plant of the druids. During the Middle Ages, an infusion of holly leaves was sprinkled on infants during baptism. As a poultice, the bark and leaves of this bush were applied to heal broken bones, and the wood, was carved into tool handles to engender endurance for the owner. Magical symbolism includes healing, energy, protection, and durability.

Knocking on Wood

Today, people knock on wood to affirm a good turn of fortune or in hopes that luck will continue. A hundred years ago, people knocked on wood to draw good luck into their lives. This tradition dates back to days when the druids venerated tree gods, and even perhaps to the stories of how Olympians turned humans into trees when called to protect them. You can continue this tradition for luck, or carry a piece of wood to remind you not to "knock" a good turn of fate.

Laurel

Laurel falls under the protection of the Greek god Apollo. A crown of laurel was used for victory and to signify courage in ancient Greece. The most commonly used form today is bay laurel for success. It is used in an unique form of divination known as *daphnomancy*, where the sound made by burning laurel leaves is interpreted. If they pop loudly it is a positive sign. Flames smoldering or dying are negative.

Linden

Known also as the gallows tree, linden is often found at crossroads and places of public gathering. Linden is a good to carry, burn, or carve for any matter pertaining to law.

Maple

The maple tree, with its five-pointed leaves, might well be interpreted as nature's pentagram and a symbol of our senses or dexterity. Also the bearer of wonderful syrup, the maple is the emblem of sweet, simple joys. In fall, these colorful leaves make a wonderful altar decoration and can be waxed for a special addition to your Book of Shadows.

Myrtle

In some areas of the world, planting a myrtle bush on either side of your doorway ensures harmony and peace for all who dwell within. To be most efficacious, have the bushes planted by a woman. If the woman is pregnant, it also promises plenty (see Chapter 12: Gardening and Farming).

Oak

The oak was sacred to Jupiter, Thor, and Zeus. Many people in northern Europe carved pieces of oak wood to honor their dead. The tree of strength and endurance, the oak's roots reach as deep in the ground as its branches do toward heaven. King Arthur's wizard friend Merlin was captured in the base of a powerful oak tree, according to Arthurian legend. Oak is a very effective tree to use in visualizations for unwavering convictions.

The Druids, whose name dreives from the Gaelic word

for oak *deru,* especially appreciated the oak because it was there that the sacred mistletoe could be found.

The seed of the oak, an acorn, is a symbol of fertility. Because of its size and associations, the acorn also makes a workable medium for runes, especially for men, since it was thought to improve male virility. The Greeks and Romans used the sound of wind through oak leaves as an oracle. A dried oak leaf is an effective addition to incense for vision

Olive

As the Goddess of Peace, Athena is credited with the creation of this tree. Use olive branches in any ritual for forgiveness or rite to honor Athenic qualities such as strength, honor, artistic adeptness, and creativity.

Pine

The Roman cult of Cybele used this tree in rituals which bore some resemblance to Maypole celebrations. Cybele was a goddess of nature and the consort of Attis, a god of fertility. This association, combined with the fact that the pine stays green year around, gave it magical associations with longevity and fruitfulness. Pine needles and oil figure heavily in cleansing, purification, and health lore, and are a wonderful natural additive to homemade incense. Small quantities of pine oil in a hot bath improve circulation.

Rowan

An emblem of shelter or security, and favored by the faerie folk, this tree was regarded as magical because of the thirteen sections of its leaves (corresponding to the thirteen lunar months). It was employed to dowse for metals in Celtic lands.

Wearing a necklace of rowan berries affords great safety from any trouble. Should you wish to make yourself such an accouterment, allow the berries to dry a bit before trying to pierce them. Once they take on a raisin-like texture, you can string them on a strong bit of thread to wear in protection rituals or use as decorative beads in your belt.

Tree Divination

The Germans of old cast lots by marking strips of wood and dropping them onto a white cloth. Eventually this developed into the *raunen* (runes) which means "to whisper." Runes made from wood can continue this tradition.

Wittan wands are another Celtic form of divination using twigs. The "wands" are allowed to fall to the ground, and the earth's energy sorts out the answer for the querist.

Willow

Another favored wood for witches' brooms, the willow represents the Crone aspect of the Goddess. It is associated with rebirth and magic because of its flexible nature, reminding us that true magic is a bending of energy.

A special fever charm can be made from willow branches. When chills first come on, note the hour of the day, and then pick an equal number of willow branches. These branches are then burned as the inflicted person watches. Usually some form of chant is added to this folk medicine, such as "as these rods burn, let the fever also burn away." Interestingly, white willow bark is a natural aspirin, helping to reduce pain and fever.

Yew

Yew is a magical substitute for the ash, some-times considered the World Tree, or Yggdrasil, a giant tree in Norse myth which holds the earth and heavens together by its roots and branches. It was used in Celtic regions to make wine barrels and bows, and is considered one of the five magical trees of Ireland.

Yew wood is valued for being both flexible and durable, showing us how to withstand the winds of change.

30 WEATHER LORE

*The skies in their magnificence, the lovely lively air,
oh, how divine, how soft, how sweet, how fair!*
♦Thomas Traherne, *Wonder*♦

EARLY PEOPLE'S dependence on the land subjected them to nature's whims. Floods or drought could leave families or entire communities without proper food stores and protection against the harsh environment. Every sign of change was noted with great care, like a jot and tittle in the manuscript of creation itself. Busy spiders portended warm weather, while hungry birds were a sign of rain. Ants were welcomed when they brought their eggs out to hatch in the sun, indicating a fair day ahead.

In almost all types of weather lore, the critical times of observation were sunrise and sunset, the general forecast for the day being established no later than 11 A.M. Omens of weather become muddled during long periods of drought or flood, Mother Nature herself being somewhat grumpy for having been disrupted in Her cycles.

For contemporary magic, a sense for the seasons and understanding of natural sequence is important to the overall connection with the earth. The skills of observations and interpretation are useful in almost any of life's circumstances, not the least of which is spiritual discernment. From the subtle movements of the breeze to the weaving of the universe itself,

many clues are hidden in natural activities that lead to a deeper awareness of self and the divine.

On a less lofty level, there is also a great deal of pure enjoyment to
be gained from looking at the world around yourself a little more closely.

Blackberry Winter

This term was used by farmers to describe a period of cold weather and
snow that shows up about three weeks after the first bad case of "spring
fever," usually in the month of May. Most accomplished gardeners
advise that, especially in northern climates, it is not really safe to plant
your magical gardens (or anything else) until after Memorial Day, or
after Blackberry Winter's cold edge has been broken.

Symbolically, this momentary chill could be a good time to work any
magic pertaining to bindings, restriction of movement, or freezing negativity. Take an item outside that represents the problem you wish to put
on ice and bury it in the snow. When the warm weather comes, the
snow will melt, taking the opposing energy deep into the earth away
from you.

Clouds

High, fluffy clouds dispersed over the sky with winds coming from the
west mean fair weather. Gray-yellow clouds, or murky, vaporous ones
that thicken, portend a storm, especially if the wind is coming from the
east or if they are accompanied by a hazy sun. Clouds with harsh,
defined edges mean gusty days, and high clouds crossing in a different
direction from low ones indicates a change in bearing for the wind.

One interesting bit of cloud lore comes from
the Navajo, who use special tobacco
pouches in rain ceremonies. They believe
the Great Spirit places a special ray of sunlight in each pouch specifically for lighting
His pipe. When He smokes, it is seen by
humans as clouds.

Clouds in China were thought to follow specific universal patterns. These
patterns could be interpreted to give
answers to questions, or to determine

what was happening elsewhere, because they reflected a network of all things. This particular approach is part of what later became the detailed art of geomancy around A.D. 220. Cloud-watching is also fun for children, especially picking out shapes. If you wish to divine a meaning from that shape, you may. Clouds also make good material for visualizations. For example, when they are moving away from you, envision your tensions tied to the clouds like a kite so they, too, fly away. For protection, envision yourself inside a white-silver cloud of energy. When you feel everything is going badly, imagine a dark cloud being turned inside out, and discover the silver lining within!

Dew

Heavy dew indicates dry weather to come and possibly the need for irrigation. If there is a heavy dew at the end of a spring day, the next day will be clear. If mist rises off the dew early in the morning, it is the sign of a fine day to come.

Dew collected on specific dates or at certain times is thought to be beneficial for magical beauty techniques. For example, dew collected on May Day will help get rid of freckles. However, this symbolism need not be confined to one date. Collecting a little dew right after it is touched by the first rays of sun would make an appropriate filling for the ritual cup, or for asperging your sacred space. This will bring increased, flowing power to your rites.

I have always loved the idea that the dew was actually the work of the faerie folk, who took jugs of nectar by the light of the moon to nourish the land. Thus, drinking this moisture brings sustenance to humans and a special connection with the unseen world.

Fog

If there is fog in the morning, the afternoon will be warm and clear. Another sign of the same thing is the smoke from a nearby chimney rising straight in the air.

Holding a circle in a natural setting during fog is rather like adding scenery to a bare stage; it enhances the effect for the participants. An alternative is to use a little dry ice for similar ambiance.

Another fun thing about fog is that it improves visualizations that employ deep breathing techniques. Here, by shining a white or pale green light into the fog, you can create the image of literally breathing in positive energy.

Hail

A manuscript dated 1486 from Lucerne, Switzerland, recounts a tale of a woman standing with a neighbor at a well. One of the two reached behind three times to scoop water out, bringing it over their head and then pouring it. Hail followed shortly thereafter. Whether or not this was actually the desired effect of the well-work is indeterminable, but the superstition that this action would bring hail developed.

Similar types of sympathetic magic using water to bring rain or other outpourings have been recounted in numerous lands. Because of this, the symbolism is very applicable for any contemporary weather magic. If a well is not available, an earthenware bowl or cauldron would make an appropriate substitute.

Moon Changes

The four quarters of the moon were very significant to early farming and breeding efforts. Most people who followed moon-gardening techniques also believed that the time when phases changed had a direct impact on the weather to come. If the moon quarter changed near midnight, it was said the next seven days would be fair.

To know the following day's prediction, check what time the phase changes. If it is between midnight and 2 A.M., the day should be clear.; between 2 and 4 A.M., the weather should be chilly and stormy; four to 8 A.M. is said to bring humidity and wetness; and 8 A.M. to 12 P.M. is variable.

For afternoon hours, if the transformation occurs between 12 and 2 P.M., dampness and winds should follow; between 2 and 4 P.M. portends rain, but mild temperatures; between 4 and 8 P.M. is a sign of a clear but cool day; and finally, from 10 P.M. to midnight is once again thought to precede pleasant weather. If the full moon rises with clouds, this also portends rain; if it is red, winds are called for. Most Pagans today do not look to the moon so much for its weather signs unless trying to see if an alternative site should be chosen for a ritual. Usually instead the four quarters are employed for their symbolism: waxing to full to bring things into our lives and fruitfulness, and waning to dark is used for banishing and change (see Chapter 12: Gardening and Farming).

Rain Signs

You can tell rain is coming if salt becomes damp, and likewise with a piece of seaweed left hanging on the wall.

If the horns of a crescent moon point upward, it will be fair for the next month; downward means an outpouring of rain. In Britain, however, the upturned moon is considered a sign of rain, like a cup running over. Halos around the moon and earthshine also indicate drizzly weather to come.

Hissing geese, loud hens, and birds weaving "baskets" in the air are omens of a shower, as is the turning-up of leaves or pine needles bent to the west.

Other signs of rain from the turn of the century included sheep bleating or skipping about, doves cooing late in the evening, swallows flying low on the water, fleas biting, toadstools suddenly appearing, numerous shooting stars, and toads hieing home.

If water happens to be a powerful element in your magic, you might do well to watch for these signs, and then dance or sing your spells into the rain. It is a very refreshing activity, not unlike jumping in mud puddles with childlike glee. As the water moves into the earth, it carries your power with it to whatever destination you need.

Green jade, placed in a bowl of water outside or thrown in the air with water helps to bring rain. Knots are also frequently used in rain magic to bind or loose as needed (see Chapter 16: Knots).

An early version of the well-known childhood rhyme goes, "rain, rain, go away, come again tomorrow day; when I brew and when I bake, I will give to you some cake." The cake was an offering to appease the wind spirits and hopefully get them to change direction.

Rainbow

Since the Old Testament story of Noah and the great Flood and God's covenant with humanity, the rainbow has been a beneficent sign. In Scandinavia, it is a symbol of the bridge of souls opening a gateway to the next life, as are beams of light shining through clouds after a storm. If you place a Celtic cross made of wood or stone on the ground after sighting a rainbow, it aids a restless soul's journey. And every child knows a pot of gold waits at the end of the rainbow.

If a rainbow appears around the moon, it is a sign of very harsh weather soon to come, such as a tornado.

For modern magic, the symbol of the rainbow can be applied in visualizations for luck, promises, and prosperity. It would make a good decorating scheme for Summerland rituals, too. The next time you see a rainbow, try to see yourself beneath its center with your arms reaching skyward. As you touch the rainbow, send a message to a loved one and let it slide to them on beams of light.

Rain Ceremonies

Performed over a five-day period in early to mid-May by local priests in Guatemala, the exact date of this observance/ritual is determined through divination. Once started, the priests implore their gods (both Pagan and Christian) for weather aid. Villagers say prayers at the local church while, over the next four days, the prominent men of the village climb mountain paths stopping at shrines. On the last day, everyone gathers again at the village church with as many icons as possible, hoping their supplications were acceptable and that rain will soon follow.

Sailor's Breeches

A bright patch of blue sky appearing within a quilt of heavy rain clouds is often called "sailor's breeches." The belief is that when a large enough section materializes (vast enough to make breeches out of, as if it were fabric) then fair weather is soon to follow.

This particular cloud formation offers us the visual impact of a break in the storm. As such, if you are having a particularly trying time of things when these breeches appear, allow them create a magical gulf between you and your problems, shedding light on the darkness which has plagued you.

Sun

According to Ozark lore, a hazy sun in the morning is the forerunner of a damp afternoon. Roosters, when atop a weathervane, symbolize the sun in the midst of all creation, or the four elements or directions (see Chapter 2: Animals and Insects). Many ancient civilizations, including those of Greece and Rome, regarded the sun as a potent harbinger. If it shone on special occasions the omen was very positive (see Chapter 5: Celestial Objects).

For sailors, a red sun first thing in the morning indicates a storm in the making, while one at night means fair weather ahead.

Magically, the sun is an emblem of potence, fire, logic, protection, and the masculine aspect of the divine.

Thunderstorms

Old wives' tales say that thunder is caused by clouds bumping, and that it can cause milk to turn sour and unborn chicks to die. The folklore of native peoples such as the Bantu of South Africa is filled with thunder magic. The Egyptians, Greeks, and Romans all believed that thunder and lightning were the wrath of the gods.

For the Greeks, lightning was the weapon of Zeus, the father of all Gods. Thunder was the creation of Minerva, the Goddess of Wisdom. Battle could be turned by thunderbolts thrown at the enemy of the people of Zeus. Romans revered any spot where lightning hit and often built temples to Jupiter at these sites. Perhaps this is why wood brought down by lightning is considered a good base from which to make magical wands and staffs.

The Muslims attribute the activities of thunder and lightning to Allah, the Hindus to Indra, and the Norse to Thor.

In the days of thatched roofs and wooden homes, thunderstorms were feared for their destruction by lightning. Ancient Roman customs to protect the house was to grow a leek on the roof; people also stayed under the covers, and bay leaves were carried in the belief that such measures would keep lightning away. Since bay was the most sacred tree in Rome, one could see how the last superstition came into being. The Romans thought that even Zeus would not strike such a holy plant.

It was long accepted by country people that placing an iron bar over beer would keep it from spoiling during thunderstorms (which often happened due to high heat and humidity). Because iron is sacred in honoring Thor and beer is his favored beverage, this was a way to mark the keg so that his wrath would pass it by. With this in mind, it wouldn't hurt to use iron or beer in rituals to Thor, especially if he is your patron deity.

If any one in your family is restless during thunderstorms, a fun hobby for fidgety children is guessing how far away lightning has struck. Since sound travels one mile in five seconds, counting in progressions of 1001, 1002, 1003 provides a fair estimation of how far away lightning has struck (counting from time seen to time heard).

The extent to which thunderstorms fascinated our ancestors is evidenced in an early fourteenth-century chart of divination by thunder. Direction and time of year were the two most important considerations for this type of forecast. If thunder moved in from the east in January, it meant great bloodshed, war, strong winds, and abundant fruit in the growing season. Thunder in February portended death to the rich, and in December it was a sign of an excellent crop year and peace among peoples.

The best type of magic to work during a thunderstorm is that which is intended to shake things up, bring motion or information, or to increase power. If it is safe enough, these are probably best attempted outdoors for closer connection to that reverberating energy.

Warring Elements

Paracelesus believed the elemental kingdoms could not fight among each other. Not all his contemporaries shared this opinion. Some felt that they could attack each other, resulting in physical storms experienced by humankind. For example, a lightning bolt hitting a rock indicate a conflict between the salamanders and gnomes.

Wind

Much wind lore has comes from the days when sailing was the best means of transportation over long stretches of water. It was believed that a witch could raise or calm the winds by throwing a rock over one shoulder, tossing sand in the air, burying sage leaves, whistling, or speaking appropriate incantations.

The north wind brings cool, dry weather; the south wind, warm and damp. The best time for fishing is believed to be when the wind is coming from the west or south. In Scotland, the north wind bears hail, and tradition tells us that a gusty May is good for hay and corn crops.

For the purposes of magical rites today, wind is added depending on its directional association. West winds are connected with water and the intuitive faculty; north winds, with Earth and blessing or support; south winds, fire and energy; east winds, most powerful for wind magic, being of the air element and symbolic of creativity (see Chapter 10: The Elements).

The only caution in working with the winds for magic is the fact that they can change direction with a whim. Since your energy moves with the wind, the result of your magic can be quite a surprise indeed (see Chapter 16: Knots)

Winter

Many very logical superstitions, based on observation, have grown regarding how to know when winter will be long and harsh. Heavy coats appearing on animals (even your pets) equal a long winter, as do bulky corn husks, late falling autumn leaves, fruit trees bearing early, root crops growing deeper than usual, nut shells being thicker, and a tree's north side bark being denser than normal. When collected for a sachet or amulet, such items would be well used for protection, because the reason for this change is to harbor the plant or animal from harsh environments.

To illustrate, cut a slice of wood out of the north side of your favorite tree when the bark there seems heavier. Thank the tree for its gift, and carve a hole in the top portion of the slice large enough to get a jewelry loop through. Next, carve the rune of protection on the sanded surface. Wear this regularly to help increase your personal protective energy.

CONCLUSION

We shall spin long yarns out of nothing.
♦Ezra Pound, *Elegy V.2*♦

IN PRESENTING folklore and superstitions, it would be unfair of me not to point out that folk beliefs have often been used to prey upon frightened minds in order to secure a profit. Dubious artifacts sold in gift shops around the world illustrate this dramatically. For example: a jar of Egyptian darkness caused by Moses; a feather claimed to be from Gabriel's wing; a container filled with beams from the Star of Bethlehem; a sliver from the table from used for the Last Supper; a piece of the cross of Christ. The last item saw so much abuse that one could build several housed with the remains from this one cross!

I point these artifacts out not to scoff at these beliefs, but as a gentle reminder that things are not always what they seem. The only magic most of these items contained came from the power of human belief, which should not be underestimated.

The New Age movement, for all its wonders, has also attracted its share of profit-seekers. Because of this I issue caution about accepting credentials or claims without verification of some sort. Frequently, the best guide to honest business people is through word of mouth, not television.

History has given us many marvelous lessons, not the least of which is perhaps learning not repeat past mistakes. Humanity's knowledge and spirituality has advanced and continues to advance beyond that of those who developed many of the folkways in this book, yet when it comes to the mystical we are still in awe. Everyone wants to experience *real* magic, yet some of the most genuine spiritual experiences are not full of flash and theatrics, but those shared from a loving heart and giving hands.

Blessed Be.

WHO'S WHO

AESOP: Greek writer of fables who lived during the sixth century B.C.

ALBERTUS MAGNUS: German theologian and alchemist (A.D. 1206-1280), canonized in 1931. Originally named Albert, Count von Bollstadt.

AUGUSTINE: Early Christian author and monk who lived from A.D. 354-430. Those who promoted Augustine's ideals believed that the Catholic Church and its dogma is infallible and that man was the crowning achievement of Divine creation.

APHRODITE: Greek Goddess of love and beauty; also called Cytherea.

APOLLO: Greek God of the sun, prophesy, music, medicine and poetry.

ARACHNE: A maiden of Greek mythology who was transformed into a spider after she challenged Athena to a spinning contest.

ARES: Greek God of war, equivalent to the Roman God of War, Mars.

ARISTOTLE: Greek philosopher, pupil of Plato and tutor of Alexander the Great. Authored works on logic, natural science, ethics, and politics.

ARTEMIS: Greek Goddess of the moon and hunting. Sister to Apollo.

Astarte: Phoenician Goddess of love and fertility.

ATHENA: Greek Goddess of wisdom and the arts.

BACON, FRANCIS: English philosopher and statesman who lived from 1561-1626. His writings constitute elements of transcendentalism and stoic philosophies.

BUDDHA: Title of Gautama Siddhartha, the founder of Buddhism. Lived in 500 B.C.

CAESAR: Roman statesman and historian who lived from 100-44 B.C.

CAGLIOSTRO: Originally named Giuseppe Balsam, Cagliostro lived in Italy between 1743-1795. He was both a magician and an adventurer.

CRONUS: A Greek Titan who ruled the universe until dethroned by Zeus. The lord of time.

CULPEPPER, NICHOLAS: Physician, herbalist and astrologer who lived in fifteenth-century England and cataloged hundreds of medicinal herbs.

CYBELE: Phrygian Goddess of nature and consort to Attis.

DIANA: Roman Goddess of chastity, hunting and the moon.

DIODORUS (c. 44 B.C.): A Sicilian historian who wrote a forty-volume history covering creation to 60 B.C.

FATHER CHRISTMAS: British version of Santa Claus.

FREYJA: Norse Goddess of love and beauty.

GALEN: A Greek anatomist, physiologist, and physician who lived around A.D. 130.

GEOFFREY OF MONMOUTH: Welsh bishop and historian who collected Arthurian tales. Lived around A.D. 1100.

HECATE: Greek Goddess of Fertility, protector of witches and Goddess of the Underworld.

HERMES: Greek God of communication, invention and cunning. Messenger of the Gods and patron to travelers.

HERODOTUS: Greek historian from 5 B.C. called the "Father of History."

HORUS: Greek solar deity shown as having a hawk's head.

INDRA: Hindu Vedic Goddess of rain and thunder.

ISHMAEL: Son of Abraham by Sarah's handmaiden. His name means "god hears" (Genesis 16:1-16).

ISHTAR: Assyrian/Babylonian Goddess of love, fertility, and war.

ISIS: Egyptian Goddess of fertility. Wife of Osiris.

JEROME, SAINT: Latin scholar, doctor of the Church, preparer of the Vulgate Bible, who lived from A.D. 340-420.

JOSEPHUS: Jewish historian and general from who lived from A.D. 37-100.

JUNO: Principle Goddess of the Roman pantheon. Wife of Jupiter. Protectress of marriage and women.

JUPITER: The supreme Roman God, also called Jove.

KRISHNA: Eighth avatar of Vishnu; also depicted as a handsome man with a flute.

MAHOMET: Also known as Mohammed, prophet and founder of Islam; lived around A.D. 570.

MERCURY: Roman equivalent to the Greek Hermes.

MILTON, JOHN: Fifteenth-century English poet who wrote extensively on the afterlife.

OANNES: A Chaldean fish god who provided the people with insight into writing, science, and the arts.

ODIN: Norse creator God whose domains included wisdom, art, culture, and the dead.

ORION: In Greek mythology, the giant hunter, and lover of Eos, who was killed by Artemis and made into a constellation.

OSIRIS: Egyptian self-renewing God of fertility and nature.

Ovid: Roman poet who lived from approximately 43 B.C.—A.D. 17.

PAN: Greek God of the woods, fields, and flocks. Depicted as having the body of a man but legs, horns, and ears of a goat.

PLEIADES: From Greek mythology, the seven daughters of Atlas who were made into a constellation.

PLINY (THE ELDER): Lived from A.D. 23-79. Wrote *Historia Naturalis*; noted source of herbal information. Pliny lived in the Italian province of Rome.

PLOTINUS: Egyptian born neo-platonist philosopher living in Rome who lived from A.D. 205-270. Neo-platonists concerned most of their studies with higher metaphysics, especially those with secret rituals, symbols, and allegories.

PLUTARCH: Greek biographer and philosopher who lived from A.D. 46-120. He followed the teachings of Pythagoras, believing that geometrical figures had significance and could express Divine natures. For example, he associated the triangle with Pluto, Bacchus, and Mars.

PROCLUS: Philosopher of Neo-platonist school at Lycia. He wrote avidly against Christianity, defending the Old Ways. He lived from A.D. 410-485.

PTOLEMY: Egyptian-born astronomer, mathematician, and geographer who lived during the second century A.D. near Alexandria. He diagramed the universe as a network of relationships between the divine and every living creature.

RA: Egyptian sun God with a hawk's head and crown shaped like the solar disk.

MICHAEL, SAINT: The name means "he who is like god." Michael was the guardian angel of the Jews in the Old Testament (Daniel 10:13). He is honored on November 29 at Michaelmas.

SATURN: A Roman God who is identified with the Greek God Cronus.

STRABO: Greek philosopher and geographer who lived from 63 B.C.— A.D. 24. He traveled throughout Egypt, Syria, and Palestine writing about geography.

TELEMACHUS: Son of Odysseus and Penelope of Greek mythology.

THOR: Norse God of thunder.

THOTH: Egyptian God of the moon, wisdom, and learning.

ULYSSES: Latin name for Odysseus, the clever King of Ithaca who lead during the Trojan War.

VALKYRIES: Odin's handmaidens who choose the human heroes to be taken to Valhalla (paradise). The name in Norse means "chooser of the slain."

VENUS: Roman Goddess of love and beauty.

VIRGIL: A Roman poet, who lived from 70-19 B.C.; thought to be a magician and diviner. His greatest work is the *Aeneid*.

VISHNU: Chief Hindu God and second member of the trinity which includes Brahma and Shiva.

ZEUS: Greek ruler of the heavens; Father of many gods and heroes.

ZOLAR: Writer and philosopher on the topic of magic and occult practices.

ZOROASTER: Persian prophet living during the sixth century B.C. His name means "owner of old camels." The Magi who came to Christ's birth were reputed to be of the Zoroastrian priesthood.

GLOSSARY

AMULET: Something worn on the body as a charm against evil.

ANIMISM: A prevalent belief among primitive peoples that natural phenomena and objects possess an innate soul.

ASPERGE: A ritual sprinkling of water to provide purification and disperse negative energy.

ASTROLOGY: The study of the positions of heavenly bodies and their believed influences on the course of human affairs, personality, etc. This word comes from the Greek term *astrologos*, literally meaning "speech of stars."

ASTROLOGY, NATAL: The study of planets, stars and their position at the time of one's birth to determine personality traits and portend ones fate.

ASTRONOMY: The scientific study of the universe. This study includes, but is not limited to, theoretical interpretations of movements, measurements, motion, and evolution.

AUGURY: The art, ability, or practice of divination by signs and omens. An augur was a group of religious officials in ancient Rome who forecasted events in this manner.

AURA: A term meaning "invisible breath or emanation." In Greek, the word *aer* means "breath or vapor." In New Age beliefs, this is sphere of energy surrounding an individual or object. It is most directly experienced through body heat, but certain people with psychic vision actually see colors and shapes. These images have specific meanings with regard to the character and health of the viewed object/person.

AURORA: Multi-colored, high altitude luminosity visible in the polar regions probably caused by charged solar particles in the atmosphere.

AUSPICE: A favorable omen.

BESTIARY: Medieval collection of allegorical fables about animals, both real and mythical.

BLESSING WAY: A dedication ritual for young children.

BOOK OF SHADOWS: A collection of spells, herbal recipes, rituals, and other magical knowledge.

BUDDHISM: A reflective discipline and philosophy developed by Gautama Siddhartha Buddha that developed into a widely-followed religion in Eastern and Central Asia.

CABBALA: An occult theosophy with rabbinical origins. Most popular in medieval Europe, it is an esoteric interpretation of Hebrew scriptures.

CADUCEUS: In Greek mythology this is the winged staff entwined by two serpents carried by Hermes. The word comes from a Greek term *karukeion* which means herald.

CAULDRON: A large, three-legged kettle or pot used in boiling. The term comes from the Latin *caldara*, meaning "warm bath."

CAULDRON OF DAGDA: A great pot for the Irish Good God, Dagda.

CHARM: An object, action, or word, believed to have magical powers.

CONSCIOUS MIND: The intellectual, materialistic, logical half of the human mind which attends to daily activities.

CONSTELLATION: Any of 88 stellar groups which resembles and was named after a mythological character, animal, or object.

CRONE: The third and eldest aspect of the triple Goddess, depicted as elderly and wise.

CUNNING FOLK: An old name for people who practice magic because they lived by their cunning, insightful abilities.

CURSE: An appeal to supernatural powers for injury or harm to another.

DELPHIC: Of or pertaining to Apollo's Oracle at Delphi, located in an ancient town of central Greece on the southern slope of Mt. Parnassus.

DIVINATION: The practice of trying to discover the future or other unknown things through a specific medium, such as crystal-gazing.

DOLMEN: Any prehistoric, megalithic structure with two or more upright stones and a capstone. Sometimes called a *cromlech.*

ECLIPSE: The partial or complete obscuring of the moon or sun, because another object passes between earth and that celestial sphere.

ENVOUTEMENT: The wax predecessor of the poppet.

FAMILIAR: Usually an animal that acts in the capacity of a magical partner, guide, or teacher. Common familiars include cats, dogs, and birds.

FETISH: Any object believed to have magical power.

FLOUROMANCY: Divining by flowers. Popular during the Victorian era.

FOLKLORE: A body of creative ideas about the supernatural, health, etc. developed and orally maintained by a group of people sharing common factors.

FOLK MAGIC: The practice of using the emblems within natural objects and the world around to cause change. These emblems are combined with the personal will of the magician for manifestation.

GHOST: The spirit of a dead person which is bound to the mortal realms for some reason. Explanations include untimely or sudden death, unfinished business, or concern for loved ones.

GNOSTIC: The doctrines of early Christian sects that valued inquiry into spiritual truths, even if those truths disproved one's faith.

GORGON: From Greek mythology, a beast with a human face but hair formed from snakes. Looking upon this creature turned one to stone.

GRAIL: In Medieval tradition, this is the cup used by Christ at the Last Supper. Many people believe it has much older origins, probably with druidical rituals, based on the story of King Arthur.

GRAPHOLOGY: The study of personality traits as exhibited in handwriting.

GREAT RITE: A celebration of the God and Goddess in either literal or symbolic terms so the two can be united, bringing tremendous potency to magic.

GRIMOIRE: Taken from the Latin term for grammar, the medieval grimoires were collections of spells predominantly for High Magic. Today, however, the term can be applied to any collection of metaphysical knowledge.

GROUNDING: A shutting down of psychic awareness and returning to conscious thought patterns.

HERALDRY: A branch of knowledge pertaining to family lines, specifically familial arms and symbols.

HORN OF PLENTY: Also called a *cornucopia*, this is a goat's horn overflowing with fruits, flowers, and corn. It is an image of prosperity and providence.

IMITATIVE MAGIC: Used frequently in the hunting, imitative magic invloves mimicry to attract like energy from the Universe for success. One example is cave paintings where animals are drawn already slain before a hunt begins.

INCUBATION: The practice of going into temples or other sacred places alone for a period of time to receive divine visions or dreams.

JINN: In Moslem legend, a creature of supernatural powers able to take the form of humans, and usually bound to servitude to one master for a period of time.

LAPIDARY: Someone who cuts and polishes precious stones. May also refer to a collection of data on crystals and gems.

LEFT HAND PATH: Black magic. The practice of using magic to harm, manipulate, etc.

LUNAR GARDENING: The art of timing the sowing, trimming, and reaping of crops according to the moon phase and lunar sign.

MAGIC: Controlling the outcome of natural events or forces through supernatural means. This includes the use of spells, charms, and rituals.

MAGIC CIRCLE: A specially-prepared protective sphere of energy within which rituals and spells are performed.

MEDITATION: Equated with deep thought or prayer, this is a method of stilling one's mind to become more aware of psychic impressions/information.

MEGALITH: Any large stone used in prehistoric architecture or monuments.

NECROMANCY: Conjuring the spirits of the dead to commune with them for the purpose of divining the future.

NUMEROLOGY: Divination by numbers.

OBELISK: A large, four-sided shaft of stone that usually tapers to a point; usually monolithic.

ORACLE: A shrine built for and dedicated to a prophetic god or goddess, or anyone who transmits prophesies is an oracle

ORAL TRADITION: The art of passing on information, specifically genealogy, through memorization and recital.

PALMISTRY: Divining one's personality and future through the lines on the palms of the hands.

PHRENOLOGY: Divination of personality traits as determined by the configuration of the head.

PHYLACTERY: In Judaism, a small leather box containing parchment inscribed with quotations from the Hebrew scriptures.

POPPET: A figurine made in the image of a person or animal which acts as a focus for magic.

PSYCHIC MIND: The subconscious, intuitive side of human mental activity, known most commonly through dreaming and meditation.

RITUAL: Specific movements, words, and/or actions designed to produce specific results and often repeated for those results.

SACRED GEOMETRY: The study of measurements, angles, and relationships of energy lines upon, within, and above, the Earth to discern greater spiritual mysteries.

SACRED MARRIAGE: see the Great Rite.

SCRYING: Closely studying an object or surface while in a trance state to obtain information.

SHAMAN: Usually the spiritual leader, also known as a medicine man, among tirbal cultures around the world.

SHAMANISM: The religious practices of certain peoples who believe spirits may be summoned and heard through an inspired priest.

SINISTER: Another name for the left hand side of the body dating back to the time when this was regarded as the side of evil.

SOMA: Wine made from a mountain plant in central Asia, believed to be so magical that it gave power to the Gods.

SUNWISE: Clockwise, the natural direction of the sun. Considered the best direction to move when working growing, positive magic.

SUPERNATURAL: That which goes beyond experience or existence in the natural world; something inexplicable through natural forces. A miracle.

SUPERSTITION: The belief that actions or objects effect or influence events/outcomes through magic, chance, or dogma.

SYMPATHETIC MAGIC: Relies heavily on the power of symbolism to augment magic. For example, to ensure the water from a well was pure, one might wash their hands, then place them in the water before drinking from it.

TALISMAN: A ring, stone, or other object engraved with figures to bring luck, health, and protection.

TALMUD: Collection of ancient rabbinical writings which form the body of Jewish civil and religious law.

THREE-FOLD NATURE: Found in both people and the divine. Each person has a body, mind, and soul or spirit. The divine persona of Christianity consists of the Father, Son, and Holy Spirit.

TOTEM: An animal or natural object which is taken as the symbol for a person or group.

VALHALLA: In Norse mythology, the great hall of immortality where slain warriors are honored.

VISUALIZATION: Directed imagination and/or energy. Forming mental images of a goal during meditation or ritual.

WANING MOON: After a full moon, the period when the lunar sphere shrinks in visible size.

WAXING MOON: After a new moon (no visible moon), the period when a small crescent appears and grows larger until it becomes full.

WIDDERSHINS: Counterclockwise.

WITCH BOTTLE: A container filled with reflective or sharp objects, that is enchanted and buried near the home to turn negative energy away.

BIBLIOGRAPHY

Ainsworth, C.H. *Superstitions*. New York: University Press, 1973.

Andrews, Ted. *Animal Speak*. St. Paul, Minn.: Llewellyn Publications, 1993.

Barber, Richard and Anne Riches. *Dictionary of Fabulous Beasts*. Baydell Press, 1971.

Black, W. G. *Folk Medicine*. New York: Burt Franklin, 1883.

Bradley, Sculley. Editor. *American Tradition in Literature*, Vols. 1 and 2. New York: Random House Publishing, 1981.

Budapest, Z. *Grandmother of Time*. Los Angeles: Harper and Row, 1979.

Budge, E.A. Wallis. *Amulets and Superstitions*. New York: Dover Publications, 1930.

Bullfinch's Age of Fable. Revised by Rev. J. Scott. Philadelphia: David McKay Publishing, 1898.

Campanelli, Pauline. *Ancient Ways*. St. Paul, Minn.: Llewellyn Publications, 1991.

Campbell, Joseph. *Power of Myth*. New York: Doubleday Books,1988.

—————— *Way of the Animal*. Vols. 1 and 2. New York: Harper and Row, 1988.

Cavendish, Richard. ed. *Man, Myth and Magic*. New York: Marshall Cavendish Publishing, 1985.

—————— *History of Magic*. New York: Taplinger Company, 1979.

—————— *Illustrated Guide to the Supernatural*. Massachusetts: GK Hall and Co, 1986.

Chaundler, C. *Book of Superstition*. New Jersey: Citadel Press, 1970.

Cochrane, Peggy. *The Witch Doctor's Manual*. California: Woodbridge Press, 1984.

Coleman, Elliott. ed. *Poems of Byron, Keats and Shelley*. New York: International Collectors Library, 1967.

Complete Book of Fortune. New York: Crescent Books, 1936.

Cooper, Gordon. *Festivals of Europe*. London: Percival Marshall, 1961.

Cooper, J.C. *Aquarian Dictionary of Festivals*. Northamptonshire, England: Aquarian Press, 1990.

——————— *Symbolic and Mythological Animals*. Northamptonshire, England: Aquarian Press, 1992.

——————— *Symbolism, The Universal Language*. England: Aquarian Press, 1982.

Cunningham, Scott. *Magic in Food*. St. Paul, Minn.: Llewellyn, 1983.

——————— *Magickal Herbalism*. St. Paul, Minn: Llewellyn, 1983.

Day, Cyrus L. *Quipus and Witches' Knots*. Lawrence, Kansas: University of Kansas Press, 1967.

DeGivry, Grillot. *Magic, Witchcraft and Alchemy*. New York: Bonanza Books.

——————— *Witchcraft, Magic and Alchemy*. England, Spottiswood, Ballantyne and Co., 1931.

Drury, Nevill. *Dictionary of Mysticism and the Occult*. New York: Harper and Row Publishing, 1985.

Dundes, A. *Study of Folklore*. Englewood Cliffs NJ: Prentice Hall, (1965).

Encyclopedia of Ancient and Forbidden Knowledge. Los Angeles: Zolar, Nash Publishing, 1970.

Encyclopedia of Occultism and Parapsychology. 3d. ed. New York: Gale Research Inc., 1991.

Farrar, Janet and Stewart Farrar. *The Witches' God*. Washington: Phoenix Publishing, 1989.

——————— *The Witches' Goddess*. Washington: Phoenix Publishing, 1987.

"Folklore and Anthropology": Vol. 66 *Journal of American Folklore*, (1953)

Fox, William. M.D. *Model Botanic Guide to Health*. Bradford: White and Son Publishing, 1907.

Froud, Brian, and Alan Lee. *Faeries*. New York: Souvenir Press, 1978.

Gaer, Joseph. *Holidays Around the World*. Boston, Mass.: Little, Brown and Co., 1953.

Gayre, R. *Brewing Mead*. Brewers Publishing, Co., 1986.

Godwin, Joselyn. *Mystery Religions in the Ancient World*. San Francisco: Harper & Row, 1981.

Gordon, L. *Green Magic*. New York: Viking Press, 1977.

Hall, Manley P. *Secret Teachings of All Ages*. California: The Philosophical Research Society, 1977.

Harper Atlas of World History. New York: Harper and Row Company, 1986.

Hurley, J. Finley. *Sorcery*. Boston: Routledge and Kegan, 1985.

Hutchison, Ruth and Ruth Adams. *Every Day's a Holiday*. New York: Harper and Brothers, 1951.

Ickis, Marguerite. *Book of Festival Holidays*. New York: Dodd, Mead and Co., 1964.

Ingpen, Robert and P. Wilkinson. *Mysterious Places*. New York: Viking Studio Books, 1990.

Johnson, Jerry M. *Country Wisdom*. New York: Doubleday Co., 1974

Kieckhefer, Richard. *Magic in the Middle Ages*. New York: Cambridge University Press, 1989

Kowalchick, Claire and William Hyloon. eds. *Rhodale's Illustrated Encyclopedia of Herbs*. Pennsylvania. Rhodale Publishing, 1987.

Kunz, George F. *Curious Lore of Precious Stones*. New York: Dover, 1913.

Lasne, Sophie. *Dictionary of Superstition*. New Jersey: Prentice Hall, 1984.

Long, William. *English Literature*. London: Ginn and Company, 1909.

MacNicol, A. *The Art of Flower Cooking*. New York: Fleet Press, 1967.

Mercatante, A.S. *Magic Garden*. Los Angeles: Harper & Row, 1976.

——————— *Zoo of the Gods*. New York: Harper & Row, 1974.

Michell, John. *The Earth Spirit*. New York: Crossroads Publishing,1975.

Muller. *Selected Essays on Language, Mythology and Religion*. Volume 1, London England (1881).

Mystic Places. Time-Life Books - Mysteries of the Unknown, Virginia, 1987.

Newall, Venetia. *Encyclopedia of Witchcraft and Magic*. Great Britian: Hamlyn Publishing, 1974.

Nicolson, Iain. *Astronomy*. New York: Grosset and Dunlap, 1971.

Norton Anthology of English Literature. 4th ed. Vols. 1 and 2, London: W.W. Norton Company, 1979.

Oesterley, W.O.E. *Sacred Dance*. New York: Dance Horizons, 1923.

Palaiseul, Jean. *Grandmother's Secrets*. New York: GP Putnam's Sons, 1973.

Pennick, Nigel. *Magic in the Northern Tradition*. London: Aquarian Press, 1946.

Radford, M.A. *Encyclopedia of Superstition*. Pennsylvania: Dufour Editing, Inc., 1945.

Riotte, Louise. *Sleeping with a Sunflower*. Vermont: Garden Way Publishing, 1987.

Ryall, Rhiannon. *West Country Wicca*. Washington: Phoenix, 1989.

Sanecki, Kay N. *Complete Book of Herbs*. New York: MacMillan Publishing, 1974.

Showers, Paul. *Fortune Telling*. Pennsylvania: Blakiston Company, 1942.

Singer, C. *From Magic to Science*. New York: Dover Publishing, 1958.

Starhawk. *The Spiral Dance*. Los Angeles: Harper and Row, 1989.

Steele, P. *Ozark Tales and Superstitions*. Vermont: Pelican Publishing, 1983.

SummerRain, Mary. *Earthway*. New York: Pocket Books, 1990.

Telesco, P. *Victorian Grimoire*. St. Paul, Minn.: Llewellyn Publications, 1992.

"The Art of Living", "Touching the Timeless" Millenium. Buffalo, New York: PBS Television Series, Ch. 17.

"The Materials of Folklore" Vol. 66 *Journal of American Folklore* 1953.

Thoms, William John. "Folklore." Vol. 5 *California Folklore Quarterly*, 1946.

Tuleja,Tad. *Curious Customs*. New York: Harmony Books, 1987.

Tyson, Donald. *How to Make and Use a Magic Mirror*. St. Paul, Minn.: Llewellyn, 1990.

Walker, Barbara. *Woman's Dictionary of Symbols and Sacred Objects, San Francisco:* Harper and Row, 1988.

Wheeler, William. *Familiar Allusions*. Massachusetts: James R. Osgood and Co., 1882.

Wootton, A. *Animal Folklore, Myth and Legend*. New York: Blandford Press, 1986.

Zink, David. *Ancient Stones Speak*. New York: EP Dutton Co., 1979.

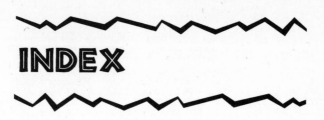

INDEX

On the following pages you will find listed, with their current prices, some of the books now available on related subjects. Your book dealer stocks most of these and will stock new titles in the Llewellyn series as they become available. We urge your patronage.

TO GET A FREE CATALOG

You are invited to write for our bi-monthly news magazine/catalog, *Llewellyn's New Worlds of Mind and Spirit*. A sample copy is free, and it will continue coming to you at no cost as long as you are an active mail customer. Or you may subscribe for just $10 in the United States and Canada ($20 overseas, first class mail). Many bookstores also have *New Worlds* available to their customers. Ask for it.

In *New Worlds* you will find news and features about new books, tapes and services; announcements of meetings and seminars; helpful articles; author interviews and much more. Write to:

Llewellyn's New Worlds of Mind and Spirit
P.O. Box 64383-787, St. Paul, MN 55164-0383, U.S.A.

TO ORDER BOOKS AND TAPES

If your book store does not carry the titles described on the following pages, you may order them directly from Llewellyn by sending the full price in U.S. funds, plus postage and handling (see below).

Credit card orders: VISA, MasterCard, American Express are accepted. Call us toll-free within the United States and Canada at 1-800-THE-MOON.

Special Group Discount: Because there is a great deal of interest in group discussion and study of the subject matter of this book, we offer a 20% quantity discount to group leaders or agents. Our Special Quantity Price for a minimum order of five copies of *Folkways* is $71.80 cash-with-order. Include postage and handling charges noted below.

Postage and Handling: Include $4 postage and handling for orders $15 and under; $5 for orders *over* $15. There are no postage and handling charges for orders over $100. Postage and handling rates are subject to change. We ship UPS whenever possible within the continental United States; delivery is guaranteed. Please provide your street address as UPS does not deliver to P.O. boxes. Orders shipped to Alaska, Hawaii, Canada, Mexico and Puerto Rico will be sent via first class mail. Allow 4-6 weeks for delivery. **International orders:** Airmail – add retail price of each book and $5 for each non-book item (audiotapes, etc.); Surface mail – add $1 per item.

Minnesota residents add 7% sales tax.

Mail orders to:
Llewellyn Worldwide, P.O. Box 64383-791, St. Paul, MN 55164-0383, U.S.A.

For customer service, call (612) 291-1970.

A KITCHEN WITCH'S COOKBOOK
Patricia Telesco
Appetizers • Breads • Brews • Canning & Pre-serving • Cheese & Eggs• Desserts • Meats • Pasta & Sauces• Quarter Quickies • Salads, Dressings & Soups • Tofu, Rice & Side Dishes • Vegetables• Witches' Dishes

Discover the joys of creative kitchen magic! *A Kitchen Witch's Cookbook* is a unique blend of tasty recipes, humor, history and practical magical techniques that will show you how cooking can reflect your spiritual beliefs as well as delightfully appease your hunger!

The first part of this book gives you techniques for preparing and presenting food enriched by magic. The second section is brimming with 346 recipes from around the world—appetizers, salads, beverages, meats, soups, desserts, even "Witches' Dishes"—with ingredients, directions, magical associations, history/lore and suggested celebrations where you can serve the food. (Blank pages at the end of each section encourage you to record your own treasured recipes.)

A Kitchen Witch's Cookbook makes it clear how ingredients found in any pantry can be transformed into delicious and magical meals for your home and cir-cle, no matter what your path. Let Patricia Telesco show you how kitchen magic can blend your spiritual beliefs into delectable sustenance for both body and soul!
ISBN: 1-56718-707-2, 7 x 10 • 320 pp., illus., softbound $16.95

A WITCH'S BREW
The Art of Making Magical Beverages
Patricia Telesco

This is the first book to unite creative brewing with magic. Find out how beverage-making can be a fun and unique way to enrich your life from a magical perspective!

In magic, the cup is a symbol of the Goddess, that ever-fruitful fountain from which the nectars of wisdom and blessings flow. *A Witch's Brew* keeps the symbolic her-itage of beverages in mind, offering options for a wide vari-ety of enchanted drinkables—alcoholic and otherwise—that can be imbibed for health or simple pleasure, or to celebrate the Wheel of the Year or encourage specific positive attributes.

Here you will find 275 recipes for magically symbolic brews that will delight your tongue, give your creativity a new outlet and enrich your ceremonies and other special occasions. Each recipe lists ingredients, directions, magical associa-tions, history/lore and alternative ingredients. In addition to the recipes them-selves, you'll get background on everything from the history of brewing and brewing as a magical activity to serving vessels and creative toasts.

Find out how magical brewing can be with this practical handbook!
ISBN: 1-56718-708-0, 7 x 10, 256 pp., illus., softcover$16.95